SEMITISM

Rabbi Ben Ezra, the night he died
Called sons and sons' sons to his side
And spoke: 'This world has been harsh and strange:
Something is wrong: there needeth a change
But what or where . . . ?

Holy-Cross Day
Robert Browning

SEMITISM
The Whence and Whither
'How Dear Are your Counsels'

KENNETH CRAGG

sussex
ACADEMIC
PRESS

BRIGHTON • PORTLAND

2 4 6 8 10 9 7 5 3 1

First published 2005 in Great Britain by
SUSSEX ACADEMIC PRESS
PO Box 2950
Brighton BN2 5SP

and in the United States of America by
SUSSEX ACADEMIC PRESS
920 NE 58th Ave   Suite 300
Portland, Oregon 97213-3786

British Library Cataloguing in Publication Data
A CIP catalogue record for this book is available from the British Library.

Library of Congress Cataloging-in-Publication Data
Cragg, Kenneth.
   Semitism : the whence and whither, "how dear
are your counsels" / Kenneth Cragg.
   p. cm.
   Includes bibliographical references and index.
   ISBN 1-84519-071-8 (pbk. : alk. paper)
   1. Bible. O.T.—Theology. 2. Zionism. 3. Jew—
Social conditions. 4. Judaism—Relations—
Christianity. 5. Christianity and other religions—
Judaism. I. Title.
BS1192.5.C73 2005
261.2′6—dc22
                                           2004022660
                                                 CIP

Typeset and designed by G&G Editorial, Brighton
Printed by MPG Books Ltd, Bodmin, Cornwall
This book is printed on acid-free paper.

CONTENTS

Preface   vi

Introduction   1

one   'The Place of the Name'   7

two   Our Human 'Corn and Wine and Oil'   24

three   Interrogation from Within   36

four   'Gentiles'   49

five   Through Jesus to a Human Inclusion   62

six   'This World Harsh and Strange'   79

seven   Zionism – The Realized Quest?   96

eight   Zionism – The Great Forfeiture?   118

nine   Inter-Testamental Relations Now   141

ten   Marc Chagall's Prayer Shawl   160

Notes   171

Index of Persons, Places and Names   198
Index of Themes and Terms   204
Index of Biblical and New Testament Passages   212

PREFACE

Cyclone and anti-cyclone are comprehensible contrasts. Semitism and anti-Semitism are of a different order. The former is hardly current at all and is liable to take the dictionary to skill with Semitic languages. The latter is all too grimly familiar as a virulent plague. How and why should it so darkly attach to the other? Both terms seem only to have come into use in the late 19th century. The reality is harsh centuries long.

Semitism is a human story of distinctive intimacy with God, believed to belong with birth, sealed in history and homed in given territory. 'How dear are Your counsels to me, O God', the psalmist cried – how precious, yet how costly this privilege between us, whereby we are Yours and You are ours, in this indissoluble unison. 'Thou' is uniquely ours to use as uncommonly 'Thy people'.

Yet these three denominators of tribe, territory and storied time belong alike to all human identities, understood as one creation in a single cosmos alike in the Bible and the Qur'an.

Anti-Semitism is a strange and tragic 'misprision' of this long conviction of the Judaic mind, bringing endless suffering to the one, shame and guilt to the other. Its effect has been to make 'those counsels dearer' still, whether in Zionist will to recover and rule territory or in a diaspora struggling to know and be itself aright. The former has been drawn into the barbarity of a dividing 'Wall', a scar across a land allegedly 'beloved above all', alike to God and people. It resembles Solomon's judgement on a disputed child.

Semitism: The Whence and Whither attempts to understand, to find the true perspectives, then and now. But what and where? Rabbi Ben Ezra asked.

Semitism, as political Zionism, bravely sought the answer in being once again among the nations. It still defeats itself as the militarized shape of a 'people dwelling apart'. The goal of geographical compatibility still eludes it in the homeland of its spiritual meaning.

The cover has two images in statuary from the portal of Strasbourg Cathedral. They are symbols of superiority and inferiority, sensed on either side in pride and pain, enmity and isolation. Zion forlorn, with its broken staff, a figure of distress and humiliation; and a version of the Church in pride, with straight staff, as a figure of resolve and dignity – these capture the long guilt and suffering entailed in anti-Semitism. The two demand that we learn why Semitism endured so long a travail. How well does its contemporary Zionism avail to rescue and fulfil it?

SEMITISM
The Whence and Whither
'How Dear Are your Counsels'

INTRODUCTION

'Semitism' is a word of little currency, whereas 'anti-Semitism' comes with great frequency. The pro and the con with such terms are usually in better balance. A 'Semitist' – for the dictionaries – is more likely to be a linguistic expert (Arabic, Aramaic, Hebrew, Ugaritic) than defined as 'Jewish'. Thus, all too often, 'Semitism' exists only to be dominated or distorted by that which rejects it. What, precisely, can it be that anti-Semitism exists to resent or vilify?

The puzzle deepens when we realize that the 'anti' term only came into use around 1873 as first coined in the German by a certain Wilhelm Marr, a precursor of the Nazis, who insisted that Jewishness was wholly a biological identity which a racist German culture must decry. His cast of mind needed the new term as something more venomous and hostile than mere 'anti-Jewish'. Few things being more potentially vicious than the racial factor, the – then – new term gave a tragic vehemence to attitudes outside Jewry towards all things Judaic, Yiddish and again Zionist.

The invention of the new term brought an intensified antipathy to the age-long Jew/'Gentile' situation for those who willed to shape it on those racial terms. They were the very terms which it was most urgent to disavow in the vital quest for inter-human community. For they distorted and bedevilled crucial areas of meaning which could only be sanely undertaken when racialism, with all its emotive thrust, was emphatically disowned.

There were, to be sure, those in Jewry as well as non-Jewry in need of that sanity. The philosopher Franz Rosenzweig argued in *The Star of Redemption* that the covenant

> preserves itself in the eternal self-preservation of the pro-creative blood through shutting the pure spring of blood off from foreign admixture.[1]

Comparably in 'The Christian Blasphemy: A Non-Jewish Jesus', a writer declared:

I

The Holy One of Israel is wholly other . . . because, and as, God has been Jewish and therein 'holy', then God has been not Aryan, not even American and not simply and universally human (were there such).[2]

Such sense of hereditary, blood-stream, identity – perpetuating 'holy seed' – while certainly a dimension of the inter-human theme, runs counter to strong accents of the Jewish mind in yearning for the discovery and acceptance of the human neighbourhood. While, for all cultures, the hereditary factor is inescapable, and duly elemental as a theme of conscience, its status, as contributory and not inherently definitive, is no less present for the Judaic than for the non-Judaic. There is point for all identities in the 'non-factor' – what consciously we are not. To make it paramount, as in the gall of 'anti-Semite', is to traduce humanity itself. Such traducing has brought grievous anguish into Jewish experience. A resolute 'anti- anti-Semitism' is, on every count, the only true humanism, one which can then soundly undertake all that remains at issue – for scrutiny, eulogy or contention – in respect of the Hebraic, the Judaic, the Zionist in all their diversity.

Semitism, freed of the age-long tribulation of reciprocal discrimination, might then belong in mutual integrity with an inter-human scene. Then the only obstacle will be the perception any hold as to the status of what makes them distinctive. It seems clear that, in this regard, Semitism, or Jewry, or Judaism, have a uniquely difficult task, given the theological mystique of 'covenant' and 'election' inherent in their self-awareness. Is it not these which have led to the world's most tellingly differentiated people being also historically the most persecuted?

A study of Semitism with that task might aptly take a sub-title from the charming story of 'The Well and the Oath' in Genesis 26. Abraham, the great founding 'Semite', is gone from the scene but his son Isaac, that most gentle of 'the fathers', is in the neighbourhood of Philistines around Gerar, at the southern end of what is now the anguished Gaza strip. The narrative – which would now be about 'settlements' and a ravaged air-strip – has an Isaac 'feel' to its conciliatory temper. The Philistines said:

Leave us, for you have become much more powerful than we are. So Isaac left: he pitched camp in the valley of Gerar and there he stayed. Isaac dug again the wells made by the servants of his father Abraham and sealed by the Philistines after Abraham's death, and he gave them the same names as his father has given them. Isaacs' servants digged in the valley and found there a well.

Strife, however, persisted over wells old and new, even after one at Rehoboth ('ample room') seemed to promise co-habitation. However, Abimelech, the Philistine 'king', came again with signs of belligerence, saying enigmatically, 'It became clear to us that YAHWEH was with you.' So Isaac proposed to him and his a 'sworn treaty' of mutual non-molestation in line with Isaac's earlier 'unfailing kindness'. There was a late night meal and

> 'Rising early in the morning, they exchanged oaths. Then Isaac bade them farewell and they went away in peace. Now it was on the same day that Isaac's servants brought him news of the well they had dug. "We have found water!" they said to him. So he called the well Sheba and hence the town is called Beersheba to this day.'[3]

All was still semi-nomadic and a far cry from how Zionism might have negotiated its 'Palestine'.

That 'well of the oath' always marked the southern limit of landed Jewishness, stretching from 'Dan to Beersheba'. Wells were the ancient celebration of psalm and folklore: 'running waters out of thine own well' the proverbial confidence (Proverbs 5.15). In the sterner weightier days of Moses another *beer* in Moabite country had elicited the great 'Spring, O well: sing ye to it', of Numbers 21.17.

'Wells and oaths', however, on the blessed Isaac model could hardly stay 'Rehoboths' ('ample room') where striving elements could 'move over' and 'make space'. There was that other 'oath' to 'our father Abraham', sanctioned by the Exodus into entire territory donation, where other elements would be incompatible. For, by it, according to Psalm 105.8–11, it made the whole 'land of Canaan, the lot of (their) inheritance'. A wistful Hebraic Isaac would have to give way to an invasive Hebraic Joshua, 'delivering out of the hand of them that hate us', where 'them that hate us' would be 'those with whom we may not share'.

Thus, the abiding, haunted problem of Semitism has been to find the viable 'oath of Isaac' by inter-humanity, inside the divine 'oath' conferring an ever inalienable status with YAHWEH. Where is the 'ample room' perceived by the one in the 'dwelling alone' advertised by the other? Must there be in Semitism an implicit frustration in its explicit destiny of 'benediction to all nations'? Or can the inward sense of unique identity be so interiorized that, beyond all ghettoes, it can joyfully realize 'the promise of its given promise'? What does the State of Israel signify as the sharp politicization of that question in the here and now?

Semitism: The Whence and Whither means to try to emulate an Isaac on behalf of the answers. Its first chapter must perforce examine the basic human theme of people and territory and their joint story – the who and where and whence of all humanity, 'the place and the name' theme of tenure in the earth. This trilogy of people, place and past is the common scene of our mortality, the shared text of all cultures, the inclusive constituent alike of economy and polity.

The Judaic had its own perception of these three dimensions of the physical, psychic and spiritual world-in-one via a 'divine we', fusing the reality of YAHWEH with the 'being of His people'. Deep problems turn –

historically – on the birth and the perpetuity of this reading of 'covenant' and 'election'. However these might be resolved, facts of belief became facts of the situation.[4] They are in the story as being in the heart. Identity thereby is both told and felt. Vital here is full exploration of the defining experience of the Exodus – as enshrining Hebrew memory and ritual.

Yet, as ventured in Chapter 2, it is important for all hope of Semitism to appreciate how 'landedness' and its yield to tenancy – the 'corn and wine and oil' of a Palestine/Israel – belong *mutatis mutandis* to all human experience. Chapter 3, therefore, has to take up – with the guidance of the gentle prophet Hosea – the urgent 'interrogation' from within that had to engage the Judaic mind living in close contiguity with the ba'al-worship of their 'pagan' neighbours. That salutary capacity, Hosea so well exemplified for interior self-question, leads congenially into the vexing notion of the 'Gentiles'. This prompts the mind to query whether Jewry and Judaism have ever really sensed the problematic of being in the category of 'a Gentile', where Jewishness is prone to suspect 'patronage' if it is honestly saluted for its satisfaction as 'distinctive', or of willful denigration if it is not. A genuine inter-human-ness is hard to attain if the assumption of one is conditioned to be negative about the other. In what does 'the necessity of the Gentiles' consist? Why should it be, as so often, the breeding ground of anti-Semitism?

The most difficult aspects of these questions lead inevitably to the Christian relation, where massively the questions multiply and work emotional havoc. Was the faith concerning 'God in Christ' a Jesus-generated thing? Was there legitimately a new incorporation, Church-wise, of a 'people of God'? The issues were further sharpened by the fidelity of the 'new peoplehood' to their Hebraic sources, leaving the old possessors to register an unwarranted invasion of their 'divine right'. There seemed no escaping the antipathy once Jewry at large stood committed to non-recognition of the alleged fulfillment. The legatee was no heir at all. Yet there was no dispassionate denying that deeply Jewish dimensions had fashioned the 'new covenant'. 'The Word made flesh' certainly stood squarely inside the old tradition of Messianic 'servanthood' as being integral to the very nature of God as 'compassionate Lord'.

There were two 'dispersions' just prior or long subsequent to the Fall of Jerusalem – that of the Jewish diaspora and that of the expanding church. The distant consequences of either issued at length into 'the world harsh and strange' (as Robert Browning had it) – the world of the ghetto and 'the Pale' of expulsion, wandering and persecution, the world of 'chronic Christian anti-Semitism', of forced *Conversos* still maligned, of callous making ignominious of the Jewish self, and – at dire length – the Shoah, the apex of all pogroms.

This tragic theme of Chapter 6 made the ultimate case for political Zionism from the incurable disease of anti-Semitism of which, it was argued, the 'Gentile' world could and would never rid itself or ever concede a viable, secure, honest, decent existence for the Jewish soul. There were no Rehoboth-style Isaacs in that ever-hating world and never could be. The only saving Jewish logic was a Jewish nationhood in the long-promised, ever loved, never heart-abandoned, 'land of Israel'.

Chapters 7 and 8 examine the promise – and the prejudice – of this conclusion and the success attending its courageous translation into a *de facto* statehood more than half a century old. Its *de jure* borders still await vital definition. It would seem that Israel has reached a juncture where it can neither actualize a just peace nor fulfill itself in the ongoing lack of one. Hence the contrasted 'Realized Quest' and 'Great Forfeiture' as the dire issue dogging the tormented dream of Zion.

Only realistically in its light can Chapter 9 resume Judeo/Christian relations now, in their spiritual and theological tensions. These aside, many have been emotionally involved in their responses, to the point of alienating themselves from their own Jewish or Christian fidelities in the very stress of their self-perception. 'Hurts', then, are only 'healed slightly' or quite the more embittered.[5]

Important here is the need to think more carefully about the now popular notion by which all issues between Jew and Christian can be resolved in the theory of 'two covenants' – the one perennially with Jewry for ever unextended into universal reach, the other exclusively designed for 'Gentiles'. It is a thesis only reached in total betrayal of the New Testament text. It also postulates a realm where Jews are unwanted and unwelcome – a place where they may not properly be. This makes it unwittingly a very 'anti-Semitic' idea. It pays dubious tribute to the vitality of an enduring Judaism – Judaism in its authentic, time-proven status. That is surely a status that deserves better from the Christian mind than to be exempted from the deeply human issues, both secular and religious, which belong with the Christian Jewishness of those New Testament Scriptures.

Much is forfeit for all when we are satisfied to be no longer fully mutual. Dialogue does not elicit convictions but it must maintain a climate in which they can be discerned. It is part of the burden of Semitism that its dimensions should be neither minimized nor ignored.

Robert Browning proved a deeply kindred mentor, with his affection for the 'potter's wheel' metaphor of Jeremiah (18.2–6) and his enthusiasm for his Rabbi Ben Ezra. With his ever questing Christianity,[6] he brings us, in frontispiece lines, back to the travail of Chapter 6 and, with a layman's candour, to the theologians' tangle of Chapter 9.

If poets in these realms are truer mentors than pundits, so also are artists with their colours on canvas or figures in glass. The hope in *Semitism: The Whence and Whither* can find its surest kinship of spirit in the superb 20th century Jewish painter Marc Chagall, with his favorite imagery of Jesus in the *tallit*, or 'prayer shawl', of Judaic synagogue tradition.[7] As the *tallit* proclaims, it was the genius of Semitism that God was to be loved in 'minute particulars'. For these were a 'placing before the Name', the seeking and the finding of the divine presence. In its genesis and its abiding fidelity, Christian faith knew itself in love for Jesus as the Christ, who, wearing our humanity 'in the form of a servant', made that divine Name present to us in the 'minute particulars' of 'the Word made flesh'. Marc Chagall, a genius of Jewry's diaspora and reckoning as only his medium could with the horror of the Shoah, drew into one – with sustained imagery – the 'prayer shawl' of Jewish devotion, the ladder reaching to and from the Cross and Jesus – present in a silence he would leave only his interpreters to break.

There was, there is, a Semitism that unites us.

Chapter One

'THE PLACE OF THE NAME'

I

'There is where' is often the cry of the human heart in glad or bitter recollection of crucial event. The mind returns to a locality as bound for ever into memory, not merely in the familiar sense of 'poets in their landscapes', but as the anchorage of fact. Even forgetfulness will often say: 'I cannot place it.' Like Rashkalnikov in Dostoevsky's *Crime and Punishment*, criminals will revisit where their deed was done, captive to its fascination. With equal instinct religions engender pilgrimage to repossess the territory of their origins or to tread the soil they think to be 'homeland'. If 'en-homed' there has come to be explicit – as with Jewry – in the very substance of their faith, then 'here is where' is the very language of allegiance. 'There is nowhere else,' the believer sings, 'where I would rather be.' Faiths' meanings, situate in ritual and doctrine, are by these situate where place holds the aura of their origin or can minister to imaginative renewal the mystique of a founding story.

'Then was when' will quickly follow in habits of recall. For time as well as place, fraught with oblivion as well as preservation, offers points and occasions to defeat the one and ensure the other. Calendars, via festival and season, will serve the vigilance of memory.

Nowhere is the double agency of place and time more effectively religious than in the 'household of Israel'. 'Place and Name' are familiar in *Yad va Shem* of the Jerusalem Memorial to the victims of the Shoah, whereby they should no longer lack 'a place and a name', in corporate re-assertion of their personhood against a brutality that sought, even in death, to desecrate all human dignity. That shrine both of lament and defiance echoed a steady refrain from Hebrew history reverberating from the Exodus as the great 'where' of their making as a people in emancipation and the sacred 'where' of their entering on to territory in 'the land'.

Their .YAHWEH 'brought them out that He might bring them in'. Nowhere was the clay metaphor on the wheel or in the kiln of history more apt than of the slave-people whom Moses was bidden to deliver from the tyranny of Pharaoh. The Exodus became 'the place of the Name', central to memory and liturgy through succeeding centuries to this present day. It was 'there and then' that they had come to be the identity they for ever cherished. 'All our fathers passed through the sea' and 'this was their memorial from generation to generation'. The ethnic denominator, there always stressed, corroborated the historical. Isaiah later, and the psalmist, could even merge the passage of that 'Sea of reeds' into the imagery of creation itself when, according to ancient mythology, all things came into birth through the towering entrails of the slain dragon.[1]

That reading might be discerned also in how quickly the Book of Genesis moves, in a bare eleven chapters, from the shaping of the earth to the call of Abraham, as if to say that humankind would be subsumed in Jewry as 'his seed'. History is dimmer for the patriarchs than with the Moses of the Exodus and, in sum, the early cycle of nomadic patriarchs, treading the holy ground in proleptic claim, was tradition's prelude to what the Exodus alone would consummate. The twin elements of tribe and story, of ancestry and oral archive, thanks to exodus and land, moved into the triple dimension of liberation, transit and terrain – that equilateral triangle, set in duplicate on the Israeli flag today, to make the six-pointed 'Star of David'.

Thus the first Hebraic sense of *Ha Maqam*, 'the place', which comes to be a descriptive of YAHWEH himself, lay in the event of the Exodus as the great defining 'where' of people-formation. All is there in what must surely be the meaning of the resounding phrase (Exodus 3.14) from which the very 'Name' YAHWEH derives – 'I will be there as whom there I will be.'

Moses, prince of an Egyptian nurture – as tradition has it – steeled and weathered in the wilderness where he married Zipporah, encounters vocation in a theophany via 'a burning bush'. However reflection wishes to interpret the event, the imagery is compelling. Something inexplicably inextinguishable possesses Moses' Hebrew soul. In his desert exile a destiny awaits. It has to do with the Egypt of his rearing and the captivity of his people, the people he had once rashly sought to succour only to become himself the fugitive he had so long remained. The summons at 'the burning bush' broke that long hiatus, calling to a wiser resumption of his zeal for 'the affliction of his people'.

Mysterious narratives must be read in their sequels. Dramatically arrested as to why a fire still burns, Moses is in himself reluctantly kindled: 'Come now therefore, I will send thee' to 'bring forth my people . . . '. The seer knows they are a down-broken folk, that Egypt is a river-clinging society only the well-equipped will sanely leave. His own demur apart, he is instinctively alert to foreboding about them. 'When I come and say: "The God of your fathers has sent me to you," they will say to me: "What is his Name?" What shall I say to them?'

8

To ask after 'the Name' is to puzzle about credibility. It is to want assurance, to require guarantee. The situation is one of excited and near incredulous trepidation – his and theirs – and no fit occasion for philosophic subtlety such as 'I am that I am'. That present tense could only have living meaning for the there-and-then in a future way. Only in exodus would the God of Exodus be known. In the very nature of the real it could be in no other way. The enterprise would prove itself only in the going; meanwhile there must be trust. 'I will be there as whom there I will be.' Then 'there was where' – but only in sequel – will be the abiding truth of the YAHWEH so known. Such knowing, in turn, will for ever identify the knowers, saying, as only now they will know to say: 'This God is our God' . . . 'We are his people.' The narrative captures the tense sense of drama because it is written out of the long aftermath of ripening realization of its meaning. The deep crisis of exit from Egypt by erstwhile slaves passes through a strange panorama of events – those famous 'plagues' – and even creation itself is invoked to characterize Judaic liberation with 'waters' for its yielding and its conveying arena.[2]

Guardian deities, presiding over migratory peoples, were familiar enough. Moab had her Chemosh, the Philistines properly as 'sea-people' had Dagon, the fish-god. The patronship stayed when their people became sedentary and began a no longer nomadic relation to a given territory now in labelled possession. Possession in dispute, itself a legacy of nomadic habit, meant deity-in-dispute. What was unique about the Hebrew version of this pattern was the intensity of the conviction and the storied drama of its Mosaic incidence, and both thanks to the passion in retrospect with which the very narrative was cherished. Centuries later we have to add to the exceptionality the ethical nobility of mind the Hebraic reached in the likes of Hosea and Isaiah, when the sheer belligerence of Joshua and his time could be overtaken by a universal yearning. Meanwhile the exceptional Exodus, made exceptional by the very fervour with which the generations hailed it, became the very prescript of an exceptional people, their collective self-awareness only 'given' because it was so mysteriously 'taken', the conclusion of a unique concluding, the first Biblical shape of self-referring history as itself marvellously self-referred.[3]

II

The story has it that a long period of nomadism ensued. Yet the Exodus was not a destiny into patriarchal wandering but en route to territorial finality, to what is well defined as 'enlandisement'.[4] Whether or not there were agricultural elements in the Passover ritual, it came to be effectively the perennial celebration of land-destiny as the future tense of a wider 'I will be there' by which YAHWEH would have 'dwelling-place' among a holy people warranted to be exclusively territorialized in the same mutual 'place of his Name'.

The narratives leave us in no doubt that the entry into Canaan was a ruthless conquest, preceded by the very modern device of spies-to-inform. YAHWEH was vitally their 'Lord of hosts' – not, as Isaiah would later have it, of the starry host of heaven above, but the battle-line hosts of Joshua's forces, or in David's later parlance, 'the God of the armies of Israel'. Joshua's success was not so complete, and perhaps not so sanguinary, as his chronicler supposed.[5] 'The whole land' certainly did not then include Jerusalem, whose acquisition would be the supreme achievement of David. But since history told is so much history lived and believed, the conquest of Canaan was possessively emphatic. It was read as divine destiny, inaugurating the triple bond of Lord, land and living human lineage.

Something of that defining situation was wistfully caught far away on another continent by the 20th century American poet Robert Frost. For one of its puzzling legacies – to which we must return – has been an impulse to its emulation. Frost wrote of 'land and its pilgrims' as a destined inter-possession, either set to be the making of the other. 'The land was ours before we were the land's . . . our land before we were her people . . . we were England's, still colonials . . . ' When they willed away that old nexus they 'found themselves' and they 'found salvation in surrender' in one and the same inter-acquisition.

Moses' people, similarly, by subjugation were 'Egypt's' but when 'they gave themselves outright to the land' they too, in Joshua, 'realized' themselves 'westward' over Jordan into her 'such as she would become' both to herself and them by virtue of their conquest. The model is uncanny though it does not wholly tally. Neither America nor Canaan were 'unstoried, artless, unenhanced', only so in respect of what the arrivees would bring. But there is the same instinct to neglect the givens in their taking.[6]

Is it not out of this Hebrew scenario that the theme of 'covenant' and 'election' have their origin? Sinai was at one and the same time a wilderness and a drama. The transaction of the people with their Lord took place symbolically outside the land as the clue to it, the spiritual goal of their journey. The event underlies the narrative but the narrative brings the perspective that reads it. The 'I have been what by exodus I am' becomes the imperative of a Hebrew theism: 'I am the Lord they God: thou shalt have no other God save me.' The historic translates into the credal because a history has inaugurated a faith to which distinctive believers are for ever distinctively bound. 'I will have no other people but you' in and by the terms in which 'You have no other God but I.' A theology is born of a story because the story has been read for a theology. The land ahead will be the seal of either.

Before we can usefully take further this intense Hebraic particularism, it is well to remember how it belongs, for all its exceptionality, with two great determinants of human history and experience and, so belonging, is to that extent not unique, if for ever distinctive in the reach of its impact on culture at large. The two are shared human viability on the one earth and the other a given human tribalism. Canaan, Palestine, Judea, Gilead, Samaria – the whole territory however named – participated in elements of space, time, climate and all else comprising habitability in universal human condition on the sustaining earth.

This single denominator of creaturehood viable on earth calculated to be, however diversely, benignly or malignly, its arena, is endlessly diversified in circumstance but constitutes the inclusifying factor making land tenancy and earth occupancy the creaturely fact of all. If perceived within the concept of creation it must preclude any conviction of exceptionality. If 'the place of divine Name' was to be 'land defined' then from this angle it could only well be on inclusive human terms. This urgent point about 'place-theology' must be taken up in Chapter 2 under the rubric, so loved in Hebrew Scripture, of 'corn and wine and oil'.

Thanks, however, to the fact of tribalisms on every hand, territories of that common denominator of habitation were possessed in traditionally exclusive terms, for which creaturehood was 'us' and 'ours', dimly conscious of a cosmos but sharply alert to neighbourhoods in suspicious or envious mood. Their sanction was local presence and tribal memory, as heirs to ancestors and guardians of their tombs. Jewry under Moses, in retrospect to wandering patriarchs and led forward by their Joshua were, from the strictly tribal angle, no exception, unless in the tenacity of their historians.[7]

For 'historians' in this Biblical context were shapers of memory in which 'a tale told was a reality lived'.[8] Given that, in both these senses, it was theirs alone as a singular people, its instinct was to be separatist and confrontational. Centuries later, in the time of the great prophets, its yearning was for 'every man under his vine and his fig tree, none making them afraid'.[9] Though aliens might be had to dress and tend these, aliens too could well displace the residents and occupy their couches in their stead. Fear could always attend on possession, the acquired become the forfeited. On its own terms 'the place of the Name' could be physically precarious. What then of the indubitable 'naming of YAHWEH'? The ultimate burden of the exilic condition was latent in the whole theology of covenant and election. Only slowly was it realized that 'the Name' which had been 'eventuated', 'told in a history', might be 'eventually' annulled or rescinded by happenings to its 'land and story'.

That 'the born part of man is decisive' is a dictum of psychology with which the Hebrew genius agreed as a truth for theology.[10] 'All our fathers' was its constant sense of time past, 'from generation to generation' the refrain alike in narrative and psalm. It seems to have made for a long dominance of the weight of community over the sense of private personality. It would be late before Biblical tradition reached the intense 'me-awareness' of Psalm 139. Only with Moses did YAHWEH 'speak face to face' in 'the tent of meeting' lonely situated in the centre of the camp. Only in centuries ahead would the loneliness of a prophet amid the apostasy of the nation kindle the perception of a personal covenant summoning the private soul.

Or when, as with Job, a private anguish drew the impassioned question about God: 'O that I knew where I might find Him' the instinct to ask 'where', not 'whether' seemed almost to be in despair about the confident 'where' of Exodus memory and communal confidence. Through the long story of pre-exilic monarchy, from David as the fulfiller of Moses to the last sorrowing kings, the assurance of national, ethnic covenant seems to have immunized the Semitic mind from the intellectual searchings so characteristic of the Greeks. Only exilic experience among the Persians would make alive to them the 'weight of all this weary world', and arouse a strategy of wisdom by which to cope when 'vanity is all and all is vanity'.

'Land-possessing, covenanted Jewry' seems to have been relatively uninterested in the wideness of the world as well as in the depth of universal human enigma hovering round all. It tended to register other nations when their depredations threatened Jewish heritage or their power waxed in menace to them. This relative seclusion of mind from humanness at large was doubtless a consequence of the necessary avoidance of 'pagan' contact, irresistible to the likes of Ahab as the fascinations of Jezebel proved. 'Avoidance', to be sure, could never be entire, whether of material and crafts for Temple erection, or the blandishments of heathen shrines, rituals and 'high places'.

Always incomplete as effort in self-seclusion had humanly to be, the duty that imposed it, i.e. devotion to covenant-land and holy seed, faced deep self-interrogation when compromise accused it or external foes menaced its fulfilment. Was 'the place of the Name' in memorialized Exodus in mind when the psalmist heard either himself or his deriders use that laden 'where' in lament or ridicule? 'Wherefore should the heathen say, "Where is *now* their God?"'[11] Perhaps neither he nor they were deliberately challenging the Exodus 'guarantee', but perhaps they were. Land and covenant could hardly be supreme tokens without also being the theme of acute anxiety. It was proving no serene security to be 'the people of God' despite the 'whereabouts' of YAHWEH in their very identity. In Psalms 42.2, 79.10 and 115.2 that heavy 'where, now?' query, in sorrow, sarcasm or surprise had concerned the Temple at Jerusalem. The psalmist himself was far off amid the streams flowing down from the slopes of Hermon; pagans were scorning a Temple burned; idolaters intrigued at the idea of a shrine that had no idols. The aspects of Semitism we are studying all had their focus, their iconography, there where, in the achieved Temple where YAHWEH had 'placed His Name'.

III

If the land was for the sake of the city, the city was for the sake of the Temple, whence, at its high peak, sanctity flowed down reciprocally to hallow its urban entourage and the whole 'promise' of the land ikoned in itself. There is no doubt that sage politics lay behind the physical centrality of Jerusalem after its ultimate conquest under David. For on its high ridge it joined into one kingdom the northern territory to Dan via Shechem and the southern area down to Hebron and beyond. The association of Moriah with Abraham translated into his 'rock of testing' becoming 'the altar of burnt sacrifice'. For all its Jebusite origins, it was fitted to be the symbol of the triple rendezvous of 'Lord, land and people'. Jerusalem's Temple crowned the memory of the Exodus as being its anticipated future, the climax in the end of the meaning of the beginning. Hence the haunting recurrence in Solomon's dedicatory prayer of the 'place' language. The 'I will be there where . . .' of people-liberation moved out of the feared precariousness of travel into the grounded solidity of holy precincts, transferring the assurance of nomads into the ritual purification of a nation of citizens. 'When we pray towards this place, of which Thou hast said: "My Name shall be there," then hearken and hear . . . ' (1 Kings 8.29).

That crucial shift from the mobile 'Name' divine symbolized by the ongoing Tabernacle, to the 'mountain of the Lord's house', meant that YAHWEH had, in the Temple, a 'dwelling place' but – as it were – only in the co-residence of 'his people'.

> The Jewish people, in their flesh, are God's possession . . . God chose the holy land, resides in it . . . It belongs to God and to God's people . . . of course God has preferences . . . The Jews are God's bloodline. There is no escape either for God or for the Jewish people.[12]

Thus YAHWEH was Himself 'the place', pledged and symbolized in the double placing of the Jews in the land and of the Temple as His 'palace', as by the analogy of 'kingship' YAHWEH being Israel's King. Thus again, Jerusalem, via the Temple, becomes allegory of 'the heavenlies', for (Psalm 11.4 and often elsewhere) 'The Lord is in His holy temple: The Lord's throne is in heaven' – whence the long Christian hymnology of 'Truly Jerusalem name we that shore' and of the visionary on Patmos.

The political centrality of David's Jerusalem was followed by the mandatory nature of sacred rituals at Solomon's Temple, in a decreed exclusivity. Apart from the ubiquity of the Tabernacle, there is ample evidence of several local worship points at Shiloh, Shechem, Samaria, and Bethel, deriving from theophanies of old. Exodus 20.24 had ordained 'altars and offerings . . . in all places where I record my Name . . . ' but

Deuteronomy 12.5–7 laid down they should be 'in the place the Lord shall choose . . . there shall ye seek and thither shall ye come'. The new succeeded the old without eliding it from the code, to represent the passing of the years. By 170 BC it was possible for exiled Jews in Egypt to build a 'temple' at Leontopolis, citing their warrant in Isaiah 19.19: 'There shall be an altar to the Lord in the land of Egypt.'[13]

The exigencies of exile – as read in Egypt – explaining that aberration, could in no way disqualify the abiding 'place and Name' of YAHWEH at Jerusalem. For 'this Presence cannot play games with itself'. All is part of the Jewish conviction of 'sole power' acting in its own freedom and insisting on being moved only by inner 'elective counsels' of decree.[14] There is no human scrutiny of YAHWEH's mind and will. 'The place' chosen is as inviolable as the divine 'Name' is inviolate. There is somehow in Semitism the mysterious location of divine action in the joined recruitment of people-identity and a given land-locale.

In a paradox to which we must return, Solomon's dedicatory prayer acknowledged that 'heaven and the heaven of heavens' could not 'contain' God: 'how much less this house?' Yet YAHWEH's 'eyes would be open toward' it 'night and day' (1 Kings 8.27–29). When at length, in the tragic reign of Zedekiah, the house where Solomon prayed had fallen prey to heathen power and bitter exile ensued, that paradox became the harsh education of diaspora. 'The songs of Zion' could not be sung 'by the waters of Babylon', yet the loyalty in that very silence was proof of 'the Lord's indwelling'. Since they were still 'His people' they might seek the good of the immediate land of their exile – as Jeremiah advised – without forfeiting land and worship-in-land. 'The other pole of their orbit' was intact in themselves. Its being so ensured a resumption of the Temple, once a physical reunion transpired. The Book of Daniel could picture its hero with 'window open toward Jerusalem' – prayer thitherwards as Solomon had said.

The so-called Second Temple in the days of Haggai gave modest renewal to this 'shrine and people' bond. For both parties were to remain in low estate, far from the assurance of the splendid Solomon. Despite the ardour of the Maccabees, it would need the half-Jewish Idumean, Herod the Great, to renew and embellish the ancient majesty of Temple Mount. Was he bidding for acceptance as a vassal of Rome and otherwise *persona* little *grata* among those who most cared for the sanctities he might, with such Roman solidity and grandeur, bestow upon his national fiefdom? If so, he and his grateful subjects gave a new turn of irony to 'place and Name'. It was an irony set to deepen into dark tragedy in the context of Jesus of Nazareth.

The long perplexity of exile and the less than Davidic yield of hopes in the centuries between Nehemiah and Herod served to interrogate the whole tradition of 'Lord and land and people' nexus and these abiding 'wheres' of divine presence. Zealots, in their anger at the vicissitudes of Roman power after the demise of Herod, might respond by intensifying their conviction and calling it to arms. That way, at length, they would forfeit all that ritual enshrined and, against the grain of everything they prized, be retrieved from despair only by allowing into their tradition the thought that they might have been mistaken as to its true ambivalence.[15] For ambivalent even in its surest moments it had always been through the irony always present in any location of the universal, any timing of the eternal.

IV

There cannot but be such irony in any and every religious pattern of interpretation, any shrining shape in liturgy and doctrine. The question will always be how intrinsic to the realities of human experience, pattern and shape 'the where of the Name' is found to be. It would seem that having these (i.e. pattern and shape) in separate peoplehood and local place cannot avail as sufficient bearers of the universal. For they are so far diversely multiplied. Inasmuch as any might arguably serve, why should one plead or argue its indispensability? The question belongs in the very core of Semitism.

The Christian would say – as we must explore in Chapter 5 – that Semitism must will to co-exist if it is agreed that we cannot isolate grace.[16] Yet co-exist, with 'place and Name' land and people-based, it may not do, in fulfilling its given role. It 'contains' divine action within its own 'election' and in the benediction that election houses. Thus inevitably it withholds itself from those who do not belong.

The fascinating fact is that this quandary is fully sensed inside the Hebrew Scriptures and in Judaism – sensed but readily absorbed in terms of paradox.[17] Solomon, as we noted, realized at the Temple's dedication that no 'house' could 'contain' YAHWEH. The prophets told of 'a house of prayer for all nations' – a pledge that Jesus asserted in his own ministry. In his inaugural vision in the Temple, Isaiah heard the seraphim cry: 'The whole earth is full of His glory.' Significantly, 'between them' was 'the empty place', where – as Pompey discovered to his surprise when he forced his way into 'the Holy of holies' – there was neither idol nor image. The very 'dwelling place of YAHWEH' had at its heart this significant emptiness.

Large in that significance was the truth that found its most daring and eloquent expression in the Temple sermon of Jeremiah when he stood at the gate of the Temple and gave voice to its perpetual contradiction, namely that the very haunts of worship could be the source of their own futility, the spur to their own delusion. All those entering were warned not to 'trust in lying words saying: "The Temple of the Lord, the Temple of the Lord (thrice repeated to match the triple *Sanctus*) is here."' By social injustice and disloyal reliance on their holy selves steeped in unholiness, they had only been deceived by the notion of an inviolate Temple. Its very credential as indeed God's 'dwelling' could only tell against their violating selves. The charge against a 'den of robbers' would echo and reverberate down the centuries against all pseudo-shrining of 'vain oblations'. There must be an Amos, an Isaiah, in vigilance around all haunts of prayer.

In their view, it followed that there was always a moral factor crucial to divine 'dwelling', a necessary scruple about its incidence as never to be unconditionally assumed. If 'oblations' were 'vain', then in moral terms there was a divine abhorrence of what we might call 'the sanction of the sanctuary'. 'I despise your sacrifices and I hate your solemn assembly' (Isaiah 1.13f). There had been no Temple in the Wilderness, when the divine and tribal had been nomadic. Given that 'righteousness' was the paramount criterion about divinely 'right' worshippers, could there be an inviolate designation of any in the assumed tribal terms? Would it not argue some universal accessibility into the calling? Or did the Temple's 'court of the Gentiles', marked off with rigour from the Temple proper, symbolize that its being a 'house for all nations' needed a visible sign of the ambivalence?

Alertness to this hidden problematic in its ethnic 'election' was not only lively in the Hebrew mind over the Temple and its worshippers. It was also present in self-query about the covenant of the land. The Deuteronomist saw Israel as 'this great nation, a wise and understanding people' (4.6) yet knew (7.7) that

> The Lord did not set His love upon you, nor choose you because ye were more in number than any other people: for ye were the fewest of all people but because . . . He would keep the oath He had sworn . . .

On that highway ground of much more pretentious powers, it was a logic of necessity, yet the more assuring for that very reason. A fact of life could be a shape of destiny. What is clear is that, at least by the time of Deuteronomy, Israel's 'election' had a deeper introspection than at first. It was one that deepened more and more through prophethood and exile and the abortive fortunes in the Hasmonean period. 'The blessing of Moses' (Deut. 33.29) had saluted the happiness of Israel, with YAHWEH as 'the sword of her triumph', as 'treading on her presumptuous foes'. Time sobered the exuberance.

By the late pre-Christian centuries, prophethood had mysteriously ceased and Judaic obedience to the Torah exposed to the mercies of foreign power, whereas Torah had always been assumed to belong with political independence. When with exile after AD 70 the future turned on the synagogue and law-fidelity and, as in Psalm 74.9 'there was no longer any prophet', the 'oath YAHWEH had sworn' partnered 'the fewest' in the most complete form of that condition. What seemed to deprive could still be understood to designate a loyalty to its own fidelity. Even adversity could corroborate 'election'. The covenant had a perennial resilience. The more its heirs might be moved to interrogate its mystery, the more confident of its reality they might become.

Yet in one sense the more assurance persisted against seeming counter evidence, the more two aspects of the 'place and Name' faith came into view. The one was a more thorough grappling with a theology alive to its own ambivalence, the ambivalence we have studied. The other was the burden of the future.

During the long and dark centuries of diaspora among the 'Gentiles', to be studied in Chapter 6, the accentuated 'place and Name' faith – now absent from 'place' as 'land' – was minded to ponder its being uniquely related to God in terms of the intensity of inner conviction reciprocal to the decisive purpose of YAHWEH discerned as the corollary of that intensity. Judaic particularity lay within the divine prerogative exercised by the divine will. YAHWEH had every – indeed inscrutable – right to be selective. Divine 'election' indicated how 'concrete' (as opposed to abstract or conceptual) theology needed to be. Indeed, there could be no abstractions for theological faith. All is, and must be, 'down to earth', where alone 'signs of the universal' can duly be. YAHWEH's deeds have 'a home in time and space'. All is inside a 'volition' constituted by the divine nature and kindling on the human side an answering sense of being so purposed under God – a kindling which is the essence of Jewish awareness as 'the people of God'. Outsiders may wonder whether the formula reads like a sort of 'insider dealing' but there is no doubt of its sincerity, even if it seems to do no more than re-state the mystery.

One exponent writes that Israel's idea of God was

> the product of the immediacy of the religious consciousness . . . not grounded in an abstract idea of God but in an intensely powerful will which rules history . . . As God imposes his will upon that of man, so man becomes aware of the nature of his relationship to God.[18]

Perhaps one should read 'ordains His will' here rather than 'imposes', or at least have the one as meaning the other. For then it tallies with the theme of *Halakhah*, or 'Torah-obedience' in Jewish thought, in what some have called 'a legal spirituality'. As a Torah/text oriented world, Jewry assumed an adequacy reciprocal to the divine will – by divine aid, to be sure, but not by further divine engagement via redemptive forms of grace that must imply we are inadequate for law alone. True learning, expended on the Torah both written and oral, ensures faithful human counterpart to what YAHWEH has entrusted and this 'concreteness' is how 'You remain our God and we remain your people.' This theme of Jewish intensity of inter divine–human awareness was notably stressed in the 20th century by the Jerusalem thinker, Martin Buber. He insisted that Hebraic monotheism was not any propositional formulation but an affirmatory summons to existence in peoplehood. Thus,

> It is not so decisive whether the existence of a Unity exalted over all is assumed in one's consideration, but the way in which this Unity is viewed and experienced, and whether one stands to it in an exclusive relationship which shapes all other relations and thereby the whole order of life.[19]

The divine Name did not mean merely that God could be spoken about, but spoken to. 'I have no doctrine,' he wrote, 'I conduct a conversation.'[20] Jewish life was existence in the Presence. The only possible theology had to do with relationship to God, and the truth of God and the salvation of Israel were somehow reciprocal. Even those sacred words of Exodus 3.14, *ehyeh asher ehyeh*, were not a 'self-naming' on YAHWEH's part or a 'self-defining' in conceptual terms but strictly in the eventfulness – 'I am there such as I am there', or 'that which is, is there'. For 'that which reveals is that which reveals.[21] God – we might say – is 'man's everlasting *vis-à-vis*', so that Moses at the burning bush represents what it means to encounter the eternal Thou. In such encounter the soul of the Decalogue is found. It is precisely in this direct experience, confessed as being such, which constitutes Israel's being 'the people of God', confessing the ultimate monotheism in their very identity.

The 'Gentile' may well wonder whether a theology of encounter could be thus transacted and known in a particular history without that history being exceptionalized in the Judaic form, requiring that other eventuations in other human 'nomadism' of soul and story be not comparably interpreted. For there would always be multiple denominators of the natural order, of habitat, agriculture and cultures thereby. It is perhaps significant that Buber's theme of 'encounter' issued into his *I and Thou* treatise, where it remains an open question whether or not the Jew/'Gentile' distinction is overcome.[22]

The point will recur in Chapters 2, 3 and 4. Meanwhile it requires a careful note of how Abraham Heschel expounded this 'personalism in the place of the Name' in clear difference from Martin Buber. He too saw dogma as 'the diminutive of faith'. Doctrine may preserve and inform faith but faith has depths for which it can have no dogma. All is encounter and encounter is all. Heschel loved to cite Rabbi Shimon Ben Yochai: 'If you are my witnesses I am God: If you are not my witnesses, I am not God,' transferring the 'I am' – as it were – from 'the bush as burning' to the human 'sandals shed', and these, bye and bye, treading the waters.

Even nature and a theology of the natural order are not finally a matter of argument but of heightened awareness. More deeply still prophethood, as measured in its supreme examples, stands in, and speaks from, 'a fellow feeling with God', or *unio sympathetica*, which is the only form of the divine word.[23] An Amos, an Isaiah, a Jeremiah, 'enter into God', into His pained engagement with the human world, so that His employment of them in their 'sending' transmutes them into partners in His mind. The divine 'most moved mover' has 'most moved humans' to move the unheeding world towards the divine seriousness concerning it. In these terms prophethood becomes the symbol of our human destiny, 'the name of the place' we humanly occupy in the world and time. 'Prophetic sympathy' is thus the analogue of 'divine pathos'.

Heschel's sense of 'the place of the Name' has incurred sharp criticisms from many Jewish writers who see it as too close to the Christian doctrine of 'the Word made flesh' – to which indeed it approximates remarkably. He is reproached as departing from the Judaic truths of divine 'otherness' and supreme transcendence in which God has 'no need' of humankind. Paradox, to be sure, is present but is no less present if we want to say that the Creator is in 'no need' of His creation. For indifference to an art is no part of the artistry nor consistent with the Biblical truth of 'upholding all things by the word of His power' (Hebrews 1.3) in a perpetual sustaining of creation. To suppose an indifferent Lordship is to affirm an obsolescent one. A spectator sovereignty is a contradiction in terms. In Heschel's idiom we might well say: 'If there is no place of the Name there is no name to the place we inhabit,' and that would be a far cry from the Biblical world where under God 'we live and move and have our being'. Buber and Heschel alike agree that only in relation to others do we exist ourselves and that we are invested with significance by the fact of others who have need of us. If Torah itself can be understood in such 'we–Thou' sense, need it be a Judaic privacy? Were some 'Gentiles' mistaken in also making it their own? When Heschel wrote his *Who is Man?* his Jewish perspective was unmistakable yet his answer seems all-embracing.[24]

Two recent mentors from inside Jewry must suffice here, with the large readership and esteem they have enjoyed outside Jewry. The underlying problem of where the Jewish privilege inheres and what it implies for the rest of humans remains.

V

Could part of the solution about 'place and Name' as somehow both a unique prerogative *and* a universal relevance be sought in concepts of the Temple which developed notably after exilic contact with non-Jewish cultures and patterns of mind, whether in Ben Sira or Philo or Josephus or other less known figures like the author of The Book of Jubilees? For these read in the restored Temple a mystical incorporation of all humanity. Noah's sacrifice (Genesis 8.20) sealed the Noahid covenant with all humankind, as to seedtime and harvest and answered to the 'rainbow' confirming a sustained fertility after retreat of the waters. The Temple rites repeated this all-human acknowledgement to God and sealed it daily on behalf of all. Similarly the priesthood of the 'chosen' in Abraham renewed the sacrificing pattern of that founding father. The high priest in the Temple represented all humanity in the offering both of praise and penitence. The Temple per se was a model of the universe, its triple areas symbolizing the seas, the dry lands and the heavens whence came the fructifying rains. The names on the high priest's breastplate of the twelve tribes stood for all peoples. He himself was seen as an inclusive 'Adam' offering the ritual beasts in token of human nexus with the world and God. The 'blood' which was ever central to the significance of sacrifice ran in all veins so that Temple ritual was evidently undertaken on behalf of all. The seven candlesticks figured sun, moon and stars and the five planets. All the minutiae – given this post-exilic perception of the duty to relate externally – could be recruited to be emblematic of how far, on behalf of the wide world, Jerusalem's one and only Temple could contrive to be.[25]

There was also the ever available David, king and founder-dreamer of the First Temple. In his royalty he had been the partner in the renewed covenant of the political land, achieving that of a prospective Sinai. It stood, through all generations, in 'the house of David'. By 'anointing', king and priest had shared in Biblical terms a dignity in which either could be analogy of the other.[26] Thus while the Temple lasted its 'priesthood' celebrated the Davidic heritage as passing over into the dignity, for example, of the Zadokite high priest, Simon whose ritual acts 'sum up' the whole human race and celebrate before YAHWEH the pledged stability of the earth.

Inasmuch as 'the house' promised to David was to be his royal descendants, this linkage may seem a dubious incorporation of all humanity. Moreover, the whole Temple sacrificial system was meant also to recall the patriarchs Abraham, Isaac, Jacob via the calendar of festivals, of Weeks, Tabernacles and Unleavened Bread, which intended them and the theophanies they had known. Nevertheless, the association that could be made between priesthoods and 'Wisdom', especially in the repute of Solomon, arguably extended the Temple's aegis into realms of non-Jewish culture, even though 'the court of the Gentiles' remained sharply demarcated against their intrusion. At least, the Temple, the intricate symbolism of its vestments and furnishings, all witnessed to the divine ordering of the universe precisely in its being fashioned for the sake of Israel. Its worship could hardly solemnize their role without the natural theatre, the global scene, in which they did so. The Temple told both, in its style of inclusive exclusivity. Psalm 148 has the whole story: 'Praise ye the Lord from the heavens . . . kings of the earth and all people . . . above the heavens and the earth in majesty . . . of Israel, a people dear to Him.'

That sublime aura of the Temple as *Ha Maqam*, 'the place' of 'the Name', alone explains the strange story of one, Heliodoros, in 2 Maccabees 3, who conspired to gain a malign hold on its Treasury, serving apparently as a kind of national bank. 'They praised the Lord who had miraculously honoured His own place' (v. 30) in frustrating nefarious designs against it. The narrator links the incandescant figure of the high priest in a holiness overawing the conspirator, as if numinous in its own defence.[27]

Of that menacing incident in threat to the Temple's safety the writer had been sure that

> It was altogether impossible that such wrongs should be done unto them that had committed it (i.e. the money) to the holiness of the place and to the majesty and inviolable sanctity of the temple, honoured over all the world ... For He that dwelleth in heaven hath His eye on that place and defendeth it. (v. 13 and 39)

But what power in 'the place of the Name' would avail to ensure its abidingness in the far more inclusive dangers on the world stage, of times to come? These would be more than a mere plotting Heliodoras. How, in their shared vulnerability, were land and city and holy place to be secured from evil?

The logic of 'place/Name' faith would have to extend unfailingly into its own future. So it was 'that the 'I am where I am' of Exodus memory and of Temple actuality had its future tense in what Jewry knew as Messianic hope. It had been future anyway for Moses until he returned to Egypt from the burning bush scene and for himself and his people up to the actual Passover. 'I will be there' was the form of the pledge. Thus, through repeated crises of exile and tragedy, that YAHWEH pledging had to be both the heart and hope of faith. Even in abandonment or destruction the Temple symbolized its own logic of assurance, if the durability of 'the place' was vested in the eternity of 'the Name'.

It was implicit in the faith itself that this future tense would turn on a means of fulfilment akin to what the past had known, namely an 'agency' to fit the eventuality as a Moses and a David had once done. As we have seen, priest and king shared the ritual of 'anointing' to their office. 'Messiah', likewise, as the instrument of divine 'bringing about' of what a future would require, would be the 'anointed one', whose task, it was instinctively assumed, would centre round those two 'poles' of all divine 'presence-in-action', namely 'the land and the people'. Messiah would for Israel the folk, for Israel the stretch of holy earth, be the instrument of their joint perpetuation and of the bond that wedded them. Translated as *Ho Christos*, the Hebrew Messiah would give name to Christianity as its most widespread impress on human history.

Judaically, however, the Messianic meaning stayed contained inside its

Jewish realm of covenant and election as the looked-for retrieval under adversity of their essential logic as the 'place', or role, or means, or consummation of 'people-things' in pledge.[28] It fell to the New Testament Church to comprehend a Jewry-led universal realization of the Messianic meaning – to be traced in Chapter 5, and, so doing, to fulfil the grand inclusivism of such visionaries as the Isaiah of 40–60 of the Book that bears that name and as the poet of Psalm 72. The ultimate majority Jewish exemption from that inclusive Messiah-realization was sadly crucial in 'the shaping of the pitcher' to be followed in Chapter 6.

The long story of the Messiah-theme in Jewish history had the one consistent note through all its bewildering diversity,[29] namely its constant correlation with Jewish community and with the changing concepts the community gave to its aspirations. The political one was long and recurrently dominant. The yearning for independence from foreign rule required a Messiah achieving dominion, one whose triumph demanded dedicated mass loyalty. By contrast, a 'priestly' Messiah could renew the cultic system in purging the people to establish the final purity. Or, in intellectual terms, more akin to Wisdom literature, Messiah would encompass the victory of rationality. All of these, out of radical despair, might attain to transforming the broken present age into one of righteous vindication and secured truth.

The 'capax' of Messiah – to borrow a Latin term – would 'measure up to' what the measure of hope had 'in the dream' or the vision. All belonged inside the distinctively Judaic sense of monotheism, of the divine as having willed to be thus uniquely identified with a human particularity and proven within it by satisfactory action on its behalf, with themselves the monitors of what should and could finally satisfy.

The centuries have proved too long for this intimate nexus between YAHWEH and Messiah, between hope and history, to have concrete realization. There is the 19th–20th century paradox of land-and-people Zionism of broadly 'secular' origin, one with which religious Jews have contrived a very ambivalent relation. For it has radically interrogated the mind and genius of Judaism in ways that belong here in Chapters 7 and 8.

For the rest, Messianic hope has almost renounced its yearning for concreteness in history and has come to be read as the necessarily perpetual quality of all loyal hope. Thus any Messiah identified becomes a Messiah betrayed. For to salute an actual is to forego a prospective. To claim a fulfilment is to forfeit a real. Any alleged identity will always be premature. Messiah must never 'come', in order that he may always be 'awaited'. For evil in history is manifestly perennial. To think it anywhere resolved in Messianic victory will always be falsified by ongoing wrong proving to be defiantly entrenched. Hope must 'spring eternal' or be disloyal to itself. To have been loyal, and not now to fail to stay so, is the distinguishing mark of Jewishness and the only discernible or valid meaning of the covenant as one which neither YAHWEH or His people will renounce. To want somehow to actualize the Messianic is to betray what Messiah always meant, namely 'the future as the Lord's'.

It would seem that there are two abiding issues aroused by this conclusion. If 'Messianism' is left to 'perpetual futurism'[30] is it not also left to perpetual futility? For hope, even if never realizable in fact, must surely be conceivable in content. For, if not, it is vacuous, and – as such – never a hope cognizable at all because it is destitute of meaning. Even to be deferred endlessly, hope must have conceptually a datum of some sort. Did not Messianic hope always have contours even if only for ultimate dismay? Futurism is, therefore, no haven in which hope can survive. Time becomes its morgue.

Further, when actual claimants to hope's substance are being pioneered and saluted as, for some, in Zionism, how are they to be evaluated as worthy or worthless if only a perpetual future conceals the criteria? The concept of 'loyalty' can hardly suffice as somehow 'self-employed', engaged in its own engagement, all objective apart as 'to' or 'for' its party. Does this bring us to the ultimate measure of how far Messiah and YAHWEH's people stay in mutually constituted relation?

Yad va Shem, 'the place of the Name', was a uniquely Jewish theme, evoked in history and tied into 'land and people'. Told here in its broadest terms, it opens out into perplexities both for mind and conscience, in relation to the wider world of place and history. Mind has to ask: How well does it belong with the inclusiveness of humanity inside its own doctrine of a single order of human creaturehood entrusted to all? There is surely a common custody of the good earth. Conscience, too, is concerned morally with the same question, made the more acute for it by the injustices of contemporary Zionism in its chosen locale.

The following chapter turns to these issues, with a third to explore one notable Biblical, Judaic example of how sincere inward misgiving might wait on Jewish confidence itself concerning its self-perception. We may then be ready for some study of the 'Gentiles' and the perspectives in which they have been understood.

Chapter Two

OUR HUMAN 'CORN AND WINE AND OIL'

I

One external order and varying fertilities is where we all are. If, as has been vaguely said, 'God is the reason why there is anything at all', then the natural world undergirding the social scene must be the first rendezvous for a wise theology, the initial clue to 'the where-abouts of God'. In that order and that scene as Biblically told the trinity of 'corn and wine and oil' runs like a refrain, whether in psalm or story and – for reasons to which we come in Chapter 3 – most pointedly in the prophet Hosea. Staple crops and products doubtless vary from land to land and climate to climate but these of Mediterranean 'vintage' – isolating three of them – serve eloquently to symbolize all human habitats and their extractable, exchangeable yields in human hands.

There are, to be sure, theologies which exclude such reference to the discernible world and any empirical impulses to faith in God that dignify the clues of sense experience. The argument here will be that only by beginning there, are any other, fuller reliances to be reached or trusted. This must pre-suppose a careful formulation of what we can mean by a doctrine of creation, of the 'letting be' that is so plainly the starting place of faith concerning the 'here-we-are-ness' that has us asking to under-stand, irrespective of whether we ever shall. Something of that paradox we have already traced in the previous chapter. Here our first positive has to be the inescapable interrogative itself. For there cannot be a question that is not about a situation. We are examined because we exist and of the query we are the common theme. Our being is to be received. Its recep-tion takes us to this benign planet and engages us with a mother earth, situated in the flux of time and tied into the web of co-society. To rumi-nate on 'corn and oil and wine' is to explore where all rationality must go, where all human-ness revolves.

They derive from what there is, and become occasions of it. They come via nature but are not from it in the manner of winds or rains. They tell of a fertility that must be tended, a domain that must be possessed. They have demanded skill and a sort of caring 'piety' that discovered their implicit discipline, their education of mind and will. They tell at once of a dependence and an exploitation, that is, quite factually, a 'turning to good account' via the techniques to which they are amenable by dint of enabling farmers, vine-dressers, vintners and other artificers, apprenticed to their laws. So they issue with their benison material into their relevance societal, the commodities of communities in all the reaches of these in inter-change and the traffic of the world. Whence flow, in turn, the rituals of religion, the metaphors of philosophy and the feasibility of the arts. Through them and their counterparts in any and every ecology humans become artisans and artists, poets and priests, merchants and merry-makers, guests and hosts, dramatists all, in a lively theatre from youth to age.

'With corn and wine have I sustained him' (Genesis 27.38) was a form of patriarchal blessing. 'Corn in Egypt' drew Jacob and his kindred down to Egypt and shaped the destiny of the dreamer Joseph. 'Reaping corn and gathering vintage' came sharply into Job's indictment of the indifference of violent wealth-hoarders (24.6). His anger finds an echo in the strange command to the rider of 'the black horse in the Apocalypse: 'See that ye hurt not the oil and the wine' (6.6).[1] Whatever its point in context, its relevance tells itself on the Jericho road where those commodities are the Samaritan's remedy for wounds and emergency does not find him wanting, with 'bread at the inn'.

Threshing floors belong in the saga of Abraham and of David and have place in the mystique of Jerusalem. Gethsemane was long an oil and wine-press in a garden of olives. Psalms exult in these delightful fruits and the prophet Joel identifies in 'corn and wine and oil' the satisfying seal upon a restored people (2.19). Even among the dour brethren of Qumran, Hymn xvii echoes the same trio,[2] while all their scruples about 'anointing', whether their own or those misguided in the Jerusalem Temple, turned on the auspices, vocal and venal, that had breathed on it.

The Books of the Pentateuch are for ever busy with the business of oil – in tithings and spicings and blending and pourings on altars and the shaping of meal offerings. These are the *materia liturgica* of the sanctuary. Even the vessels that contain must have their hallowing covers of heavenly blue (Numbers 4.9). Whether coursing down Aaron's beard as the psalmist sings (133.2) or proclaiming royal kings, or inaugurating prophethoods or sacrilizing oaths and bargains, oil is everywhere the holy lubricant of things divine. 'Fill thy horn with oil' is a summons to make usurpers quell and Davids come to destiny.

And what of oil as the bearer of fragrance, the necessary vehicle for the ministries to beauty, pleasure, ritual or comfort, of cinnamon, myrrh, aloes and cassia, in rites, nuptials, coronations and ordainings? The Song of Songs knew how to celebrate the virtues of oil in exalting the delights of love. What, further, of the friendly lamp and the benison of light to live by in the hours of darkness? as Job had it in recalling his halcyon days.

> When God watched over me, when His lamp shone above my head and by His light I walked through darkness, as I was in my autumn days when the friendship of God was upon my tent. (29.2–3)

His theme is the sun above but his analogy for it is the lowly lamplight a candle might supply.

The oil that caused the lamps of the old tabernacle to burn continually was 'crushed from the olive' (Leviticus 24.2) whence the ultimate Temple would inherit its perpetuity. As A. Deissmann remarks:

> In the eye of history an enormous amount of humanising civilization stands crowned with the olive branch. The tree of Homer, the tree of Sophocles, the olive is the living symbol of the unity of the Mediterranean world.[3]

As he further observes, the olive was also 'the tree of St. Paul' in that a map of his journeys would coincide with the distribution of the culture of its oil, and when he finally arrived in Rome a noteworthy synagogue in the city was 'the Synagogue of the Olive'. The olive's repute as the symbol of peace surely stems, in part, from how its oil illuminates and heals as well as feeds. The Mount eastward of Jerusalem which bears its name has within its aura the whole meaning of the Messiahship of Jesus.

> Then comes Gethsemane, Deep night of agony – Soldiers with torches through its darkness threading, Till with a kiss betrayed, Thou art a captive made, As in Thy Christhood through a winepress treading.

The very Temple at Jerusalem, which Christian tradition came to think fulfilled, as 'the place of the Name', in the person of 'Christ-Jesus', was in part financed by the copious supplies of olive-oil that Solomon was able to sell or barter to the King of Tyre for his cedar wood and skilled artificers (1 Kings 5.11). The reach of its involvement in religious symbolism drawn from living history is clear token of its range and ironies. In humbler terms the friendly olive was also a staple item of diet, exported far and wide in the fairs and markets of the Mediterranean world, where Ezekiel noted it in the wares of Tyre.

There is no quenching the celebration of the middle member of the noble trinity, the 'wine that makes glad the heart of man'. The men of Qumran and Rechabites may have banned it from their disciplines but no Samson among such devotees could always resist its charms. Prophets and proverb-minters might warn against its snares but Nehemiah, arch-guardian of due probity, could only deplore the Sabbath trade in 'wine and grapes and figs' in and out of Jerusalem (13.15). Were not the returning spies, bearing loads of grapes, the evidence that the land was not impregnable (Numbers 13.32)? – those 'grapes of Eshcol' as they did so, affording a legend for Israeli marketing today.

The very refrain around the security of 'the promised land' sang of 'every man under his vine and under his fig-tree' unmolested. Were not the Israelites themselves 'the vineyard of the Lord of hosts', found 'like grapes in the wilderness' and so 'His pleasant plant' in their migration into Canaan? The fruit of the vine might have its menace for the wayward but there could be no mistaking its role in crucial imagery throughout the Biblical tradition. The 'cup of blessing' in the Jewish Sabbath and the Passover family ritual would pass into the Eucharist of the New Testament. 'Drinking wine in the kingdom' had been for Jesus' disciples the first shape of their dream of the Messianic banquet, when they were asked if they could, indeed, 'drink of his cup', only at length to discover how costly his meaning.

II

'Wine and oil and corn', then, a triple sequence none asking for priority, with the land and soil and water they each demand and fructify, serve in Biblical terms readily made universal, to epitomize how creation may be read as 'a place of the Name', and the human scenario as authentic index to the divine nature. For creation is divine *kenosis*. It is right to take the crucial Christian term from its chief context in the faith about the Incarnation and find its anticipation in the 'let there be' of creative *fiat* coming from One named *ehyeh* – 'the One who lets be'.[4] In that 'letting be' there was a sublime generosity, a relinquishing into other – and crea- turely – hands an enterprise, a viable *mise-en-scène* for action, a situation for entrepreneurs.

It seems eminently intelligible to read our human scene this way, whether or not we have Biblical economies of 'bread and wine and oil', or whether our staples are rice and dates or maize and prairies instead of orchards, paddy fields instead of meadow pastures. Diversity will condi- tion how imagination works or cults and cultures shape and tell emotions. One essential 'dominion' is their ground and truth. The quest of 'the Name', or nature, of the Lord must study where our human perception of entrustedness takes us in the realm of things. The logic we must heed leads us through creation, to creaturehood, to creativity and, by all these, to history as a cumulative drama of humanity, of what there is as the arena of what we do with it.

Too often faith in creation burdens and distracts itself in registering immensities, speculating over unimaginable spaces and inconceivable aeons of time, while often ignoring that it is our very puniness that attains to tell these vast insensitivities how remote, how immeasurable they are in their ignorance of their own significance. The place from which faith must begin is with a 'here-we-are-ness' and proceed therefrom into the business of first acknowledging and then possessing the role we play and the powers we exercise. Human sentience, being the ground of all that may gratuitously be held to cancel it, is where such suspicion of irrelevance (in us) has to be itself cancelled. To think otherwise is merely to be vulgarized by unheeding vastnesses. Our 'dominion' includes them in very honesty. An infinite surprise about ourselves is their only proper ministry to our humility. The doctrine of creation is about 'possessing our possessions' and knowing them a given trust, a task and a hospitality. As Homer has it:

> the immeasurable heavens
> Open to their highest, and all the stars
> Shine, and the shepherd gladdens in his heart.[5]

Turning again to his sheep, the shepherd has the meaning, is the meaning, achieving where the stars look down.

For he is where significance registers and, with him, any alert doctrine of creation has to do, not with how and why 'the stars look down', but why we humans are – as the old phrase has it – 'under heaven' sub-creating the while by dint of an intention that (so faith holds) willed, and wills, we should. It must understand the stage, for all its stunning age and reach, by reference to the drama. Cosmology celestial has its point in ecology terrestrial. Nor can seeing it so be accused of arrogance. For it is that alleged arrogance which has contrived to appreciate its patent finitude and to inform those frightening spaces of their sheer dimensions.

How perfectly the old psalmist told that double theme. 'When I consider the heavens,' he cries 'What is man?' but he means no dismissive disparagement. On the contrary, the incongruity is precisely his glad surprise. 'You, Lord, esteem him so highly!' and then in exclamation – 'You have set him over the works of your hands!' (Psalm 8). He knows that if we are questing after our human meaning, it will be through and beyond the 'how' questions of cosmology and astrophysics into the 'why' answers of history, society and the environed cultures of the human scene.

These, however, must be inclusively assessed. For creation – in these terms – is no 'respector of persons', however diversely their benefactor and their bestower. There has been an unhappy tendency in some quarters to suggest that Genesis really begins at Chapter 12 with the call of Abraham for whom all else was merely setting the stage. This would be to set Semitic tribalism above humanitas at large and be unforgivably exclusive. Every particularity, tribal or topical, has its distinctive identity inside a single creaturehood commissioned into creativity so that diversity itself witnesses to common human privilege. This vital point is elusively made in a reading of Joel 2.23. The feel is highly exclusive but the logic inclusive.

> Be glad then ye children of Zion and rejoice in the Lord your God. For he has given you a teacher of righteousness. (Vulgate: quia debit vobis doctorem justitiae)[6]

In the world of nature and 'the wealth of nations' 'the school of God has its teacher'! What privatizes in 'Zion', or where-ever, belongs with what unifies all in a single ethical liability. One cannot well say: 'The world was made that Jerusalem might have its Temple', unless one concedes the same sanction everywhere subject to the same parameters of the creation of human-ness.[7] For such, in its practical outworking was the creating of a cosmos. A human mandate to creativity, a liberty of discovery and participation, were discernibly and credibly its inherent intention.[8] So the alert doctrine of creation holds and undertakes, turning the conviction into the task. The created order, in its legibility, its amenability to human cares and needs, the viability of its sundry ' . . . ologies' in their cumulative accessibility, will – to that extent and in that shape – be 'place of the divine Name'. All these characteristics, in their intelligent demands and givens, are 'its school of teachings', its *doctor justitiae*. Where science and the scientists pursue their 'obedience' to its disciplines they meet a theological territory which is simply the corollary of the meaning of creation. To its being such they owe their customary confidence concerning its being a realm of order and discernible law, 'thanks to one long training of the intellect . . . to the sense of order'. That

> habit of definite exact thought was implanted in the European mind by the long dominance of scholastic logic and scholastic divinity.[9]

When, with Descartes and Galileo, we reach the mathematization of physical reality and the increasing efficiency of lenses, instruments and capacities, the way is open for burgeoning sub-creativities all the way to computers and the cybernet. Nothing affirms creation as a realm for humanitas more evidently that the sciences, ignoring as they do all frontiers in their techniques and all ethnicities in their range.[10] We must see Adam as a royal figure in a given creaturehood that could only be ethnicized in Abraham or Jacob or Moses in the multilateral terms of a universally human 'dominion status'. So much is explicit in the mandate: 'Be fruitful and multiply' in the given talent of sexuality which, in the Genesis vision of things, had not yet been tribalized.

Creaturehood, then, by these lights, is a relation to all that is, as both a private, personal privilege and a publicly inclusive identity incorporating all diversity. The reflective consciousness that takes it all in, and can even quarrel about how fortuitous, indeed godlessly 'accidental', we may think it, has it in purposive reckoning and discovers the onus it carries for both admiration and humility. The royalty of our human creaturehood was lyrically told, albeit in deep scorn about the wealth of Tyre, by the prophet Ezekiel – none more adamantly Judaic than he.

> Thou has been in Eden, the garden of God: every precious stone was thy covering . . . the workmanship of thy tabrets and thy pipes was prepared in thee in the day thou wast created . . . I have set thee so as upon the holy mountain of God: thou hast walked up and down in the midst of stones of fire. Thou wast perfect in thy ways from the day that thou wast created . . . (28.13–15)

It was well for Ezekiel, in seeking the utmost of endowment, the largesse of human potential, to go back to the garden at creation. He could not have envisaged molecular biology or the breaking of genetic codes but his spirit could register the inherent autonomy that was the human birthright, and recognize its elements in his people's most hated cynosure.

III

There are two vital corollaries of this Biblical – and indeed Quranic – theme of creation and creaturehood. They are its witness to the nature of God and the moral quality if infuses into human experience. This 'letting be' YAHWEH is no Zeus, no Brahma, no Ra. This Adam is no Prometheus denied his liberties while tormented by their frustrating. The divine creating is giving being to another as a sphere of reciprocal love. Primordial chaos, the formless void, 'the deep', is summoned into order whereby the nothingness is taken away.[11] Those ungraspable things primordial are willed into a world destined to be intelligibly received and possessed by *Homo sapiens*, this cosmos and this creature being alike sapiental. He will be able to go behind the narrated inauguration and come to comprehend the processes by which it transpired to be the literary narrative thing his self-awareness receives as both meaning and venture.

That narrative starts from a 'not yet' (the meonic) by an act of willing and framing and then delegating. The creature not being the Creator, it follows that 'an other' is brought into being and entrusting, if not *for* itself, certainly *in* itself. This has to mean a radical revision of a too long, and too obsequious, concept of omnipotence. An 'almightiness' that so crucially 'gives away' is, in measure, giving away something 'othered' in the human – if not an 'incarnation', then a dynamism in which a partnership, not a tyranny, is brought to pass. God is Self-invested in a delegacy, is no longer invulnerable, is engaged in a wager, a venture, a theme of trust. Transcendence by creation is relational, by its own will, so that 'omnipotence' is experimentally known in being such. It is no longer a bare and blank assertion of theology.

> True, God is transcendent and eternal but He is so to the extent that His love, care and commitment transcend and overcome human godlessness.[12]

This is true for and through humanity at large before it was, or could be, fused into the relative history of Israel – as it would come to be by the telling of the Exodus via the analogy of the creation.[13]

From this central meaning of creation for theology flows the human liability under God in the trust of the creaturehood in which creation has involved its Creator. For, seen this way, creation inaugurating humanity is a perpetual continuity. 'Genesis', 'beginning', is not a passed past, but an unceasingly renewed abiding in being as 'already already there'. The taking away of 'nothingness' persists in the shape of ever 'original' liability in the human creaturehood.[14] For the mandate is never withdrawn, the situation never yet abrogated. So far is that true, that many in times ancient or recent have bewailed the sheer persistence of evil as a cycle either of absurdity or futility, making human history a massive miscarriage, a spectacle of divine folly.

For it has this moral seriousness intrinsic to its very nature as the realm of human trust. Being made a volitional scheme of things, the cosmic passes into the ethical/juridical. The same conditioning order that makes *Homo sapiens* peasant or technician, comprehending a universe has him also arbiter of ethical rights and wrongs. In presiding over feasible skills we belong with issues of justice engaging mind and will, cultures and conscience. What is materially feasible belongs with what is morally critical. The 'keeper' word in Cain's question (Genesis 4.9) about his shepherd brother (a play on words) applies to sheep or crops or laboratories because it also belongs to conscience and truth.

Hence the way in which, in the Genesis narrative, the human autonomy in the natural order engenders a 'conspiracy' notion about its being genuine. 'Has God said?' Is there some limit, some hidden veto, on the presidency we have over the place where our writ is supposed to run? A dark suspicion breaks into the scene of destiny in that the Creator's magnanimity becomes victim to calumny and scepticism.[15] The human dignity is seen as compromised by its debtedness. The Lord who wills a partnering custody is queried despite having made fellowship with His image in us the object of our liberty to be and to govern.

It is thus that the creation is still more a 'place of the Name' than in its mandating of the powers of our creaturehood. It also necessitates the judgement of our wills, the open question of our integrity. Hence, in the Biblical tradition the crucial ministry of prophethood to creaturehood. It was expressed there in the concept of 'covenant' whereby the territory and all it yielded was read in terms of 'divine glory' contingent on the rightness of human tenancy. That reading, in its historic narrative form in the Hebrew ethos, was prior to all particularist adoption there, because it was explicit already in the essential relation with God all cultures had as comparably creatures in a created order which, naturally if not historically, is non-discriminatory. If we are so minded to believe, it is the Lord of history, not of nature, who may be perceived to particularize.

If, in this way, all lands are sacred and all peoples endowed in the good earth, then the created order tells a universal ethics. Humans at large are 'servants of the soil' custodians in their habitations, in the *adam/adamah*, the 'man and soil' bond of the Genesis text. As John Milton sang:

> . . . all things that breathe
> From earth's great altar send up silent praise
> To the Creator . . . [16]

Thus creation constitutes a universal ground of ethics in an elemental way that revelatory histories may intensify but not monopolize, even as the Jewish Prayer Book tells of the goodness of God renewing the act of creation continually each and every day.

It is interesting to note how the New Testament scholar C. H. Dodd handles any tension between 'the place of the divine Name' in Israel's 'sacred history' and in the order of creation. He sees the Pentateuch, as we now have it, in debt to

> the prophetic understanding of God (applied) to the universe in Genesis 1. The writer has projected upon the universe that which he has learned from God's dealings with Israel. He saw the chaos of his people as a chaos of darkness, turbulent and ungoverned . . . It was the same in the beginning. God spoke to primeval chaos as He did to command the deliverance of Israel in Egypt.[17]

Saying 'Let there be . . . ' and saying: 'Let my people go . . . ' are plainly quite different scenarios. The first is absolute and universal, the second historical and particularist. To accept the inter-association – already noted and to be further studied in Chapter 3 – can only also mean that any theme of 'covenant' deriving from the second must obtain also for the first. Cosmos out of chaos is no less 'elective' than liberation out of Egypt, only infinitely larger so, if we have understood our creaturehood truly, 'the face of the earth', YAHWEH's earth, being as wide as us all.

It follows from a full understanding of creation that our 'letting be' relates each and every human creature to the Creator as the very principle of their experience as alive, and does so indifferently. Whatever the incidence of factors historical or ethnic, no localisms of physical land or racial breed can annul that single human dignity. In that meaning, 'every place is hallowed ground' and every tribe a 'chosen'.

It is in this perception that the 'gift of being' and the 'grudge of suspicion' come together. The intelligible and responding world – in which either way we are – makes us party to a call to be reciprocal to our Creator, made possible by the autonomy He has bestowed. That autonomy has been, from the divine side, a forfeiture of prerogative power, a quest – we may say – for our self-affirming responsive to His Self-willing. The mutuality is at once His 'grace' and our privilege. God creates in our interest and has it thereby for His own. The created order as devised for our human sake is ordered that way for its Deviser's sake in those endowing terms. Such is the meaning of 'the Name' as nature, willed for human tenancy and tenure, has it legibly written there.

Set thus within it we are ever negotiating our own identity but always in a societal relation of love or suspicion to Him who creates, and in love or subversion towards fellow mortals, thanks – on both counts – to our willed capacity as autonomous. The Creator 'lets be' but without dominating. Creaturehood discovers selfhood not as submission to an alien, malign or inscrutable will, but as the acceptance of life and the limit of death. 'God is then the desire by which all live.'[18]

Understanding the Creator in creation in these terms excludes all particularizing of 'here or there', of 'these and those'. This reading of 'covenant' can only be an everywhere. It is also the only valid monotheism. For to hold to Creator and creation this way means that nothing in creation can usurp His sovereignty or enslave us by becoming an idol of whatever origin or subtlety. We have the warrant never to be arrogant since all is 'given-gift' and never to be craven since we are 'given to ourselves' to be with God and for God because of God.

IV

Back, then, to 'corn and wine and oil'. They particularize, not being rice, or ale, or yams, or palm-wine, but they do so only representatively and it is their ethical import in the Biblical context which is their inclusive relevance. How vital *not* being particularist in letting the doctrine of creation 'rule in our hearts' is evident enough in the very stance that western anthropology – and Christian mission – too often brought to African study.

> Such was the abasement of the black man's soul that we were resigned to being thought of as a tabula rasa, a race, almost a whole continent, which for 30,000 years had not thought anything, felt anything, written anything, painted or sculpted anything, sung or danced anything.[19]

This one-culture myopia happened ironically, if not uncritically, in a Christian will to mission as well as in a secular scholarship of research. Yet perhaps it was inherent as well as ironic. For much of Christian self-awareness stemmed from the Biblical roots of a hallowed peoplehood which caused it to forget or forego the universal vision of its own 'new' testament.[20] All too readily English, Russians, Americans, misread their power equations in terms of 'chosen peoplehood' and divine destinies.

In interior terms, if rarely in external relations, the Biblical benedictions of 'corn and wine and oil' came to be told by the great prophets in demanding dimensions of justice and righteousness, in which perceptions of history were more explicit than the inclusive doctrine of creation as we have studied it. The first of them in the 8th century was Amos. Whatever his initiation into prophethood as psychic factors might have shaped it, there is no doubt of its immediate impulse in a passion against social exploitation and political chicanery.

He indicts their callous oppression of the poor, their pursuit of luxury indifferent to its human cost in the exploitation of village peasants, far removed from their urban palaces. Wine figures largely in his portrayal of their conscience-less indulgence.

> They lay down on clothes laid to pledge by every altar, and drink the wine of the condemned in the house of their god . . . whose say to their 'husbands': "Bring, let us drink" . . . (2.8 and 4.1)

> They drink wine in bowls and anoint themselves with the finest oil, but they are not grieved for the affliction of Joseph. (6.6)

These sprawling beds of sensuality ingraved with ivory stretch out in the vicinity of temple ritual, the women-folk laden with jewellery, ear-rings, necklaces and anklets.

The 'corn and wine and oil' thus mindlessly degraded in their social patterns have ceased thereby to be 'the place of the Name of the Lord', extorted from the labouring peasants by the overburdening of their debts and their reduction to serfdom.

> They (the wealthy) sold the righteous for silver and the poor for a pair of shoes. They pant after the dust of the earth on the head of the poor . . . they buy the poor for silver . . . and get a price even for the sweepings of the wheat. (2.6–7 and 8.6)

The pitch of Amos' indignation matches the vigour of his language. Over all is his awe about 'the land' so prostituted from what Hosea would call its true 'husbandry', its weddedness to YAHWEH. Those who are snugly 'at ease in Zion' are taunted in their complacence (6.1–2) and the land itself, in its desolation to come, will mourn for the crimes of its lords. Amos is moved to call into radical question the whole levitical system of ritual and sacrifice and to return in imagination to the wilderness sojourn that knew it not. At the denial of justice, Amos draws his indictment from imagery of an arable land, 'polluted' by the guilt of the economic order, 'sifted as corn in a sieve' (9.9). It is little wonder that Amos seemed a traitor like Jeremiah after him to those 'mighty' whom he accused so roundly. Certainly he did not observe his own hint: 'The prudent will keep silence . . . for it is an evil time' (5.13). Throughout the prophetic tradition in which he was pioneer, it is 'the land' which undergoes the defilement of its overlings, 'the land' that sustains the indignation of its moral guardians and gives fervour to their spirits. When, in 9.11–15, the Book of Amos turns from ruination to hope it is of 'vineyards replanted', 'the treader of the winepress overtaking the grape-tender' and 'the hills flowing with sweet wine' that he tells.

These together speak of land-love, of tillage and harvest, of joy and hospitality, of commodity into community. They epitomize the 'letting be' once and ever of the natural order and its social, human entrustment. 'Corn and wine and oil' serve well as the Bible's symbol of the meaning and the discipline of the world as fitted to and for our creaturehood. That giving and given creation as – on every count of onus and occasion – 'placing' the Name of the Lord for our human cognizance, and doing so in a magnanimity from which none can be exempt, was understood and interpreted in the Hebrew tradition in terms they read as distinctive to themselves alone. Their reasons stemmed from their reading of their history – a reading which ironically turned on land and tenancy as making exceptionally theirs what creation had left universal. Those reasons, their source and their burdened consequence, we have earlier traced. Was not the human inclusiveness implicit in the concept of creation memorably told in *Sanhedrin* 4.5? 'He who destroys one soul is as if he destroyed the entire world and he who saves a single soul as if he saved the whole world' – a 'saving' logic which finds its way into the Qur'an.

Accordingly, does a lively doctrine of creation not have to conclude that 'God has only chosen peoples', fulfilling in their several measures of given 'corn and wine and oil' a single human destiny? The prophet Hosea was minded, in part, to come to such a view.

Chapter Three

INTERROGATION FROM WITHIN

I

From one of the most loved figures in Hebrew prophethood comes a most dramatic echo of the great Exodus formula but only eloquently to dispute it. Nowhere else does the whole Biblical tradition so radically disavow itself. We may think that the prophet is only using powerful irony to startle his hearers into heeding his message but the irony is unmistakable and stands as the most forthright interrogation of the whole Hebraic self-assurance about covenant and election.

'You are not My people and I am not your "I am".' Hosea 1.9 cites Exodus 3.14 where – as studied in Chapter 1 – the 'I am' of the divine Name found its historic definition in the 'Who I will be' as only the Exodus in a lived experience would give Moses' people to know it. Via that experience and their living through it, they would 'know' YAHWEH as the Lord of their adoption and 'find' themselves as 'the people of His making', ultimately sealed, either way, in their entry upon 'the land of promise' with the fertile geography, the 'corn and wine and oil' of which we took stock in Chapter 2. Now Hosea, the vivid exegete of that fertility in truly Jewish hands in contrast to its pagan mischances under *baalim*, tells its heirs in the crisis of the northern Kingdom 'He is your "I am" no longer'. The disclaimer – and on Hosea's lips especially – is arresting in the extreme. To crown the truth he called his third child *Lo-ʿAmmi*: 'You are not my people.'

That his mind was on the Exodus is clear from 12.9 and 13,4–5, where 'You shall know no gods but Me' seems drawn from what the writers of the Books of Exodus and Deuteronomy knew as 'the Ten Commandments'. It was that territorial heritage which was being whittled away before his eyes in the confusing crisis the northern Kingdom was undergoing as he spoke, under the menace of advancing Assyrians.

Menahem, who reigned between 745 and 738, had bargained away the villages of Galilee and – irony of ironies – men of Ephraim paid each fifty silver shekels, the price of avoiding deportation into slavery,[2] and so reverting into a bondage like pre-Exodus. It was an analogy that would often recur in the prophetic tradition. For what, long after Joseph, Egypt had been to them while awaiting Mosaic liberation remained the sharpest symbol of all other thwarting of their destiny.

The burden in Hosea's soul was that they and their rulers were doing the thwarting in themselves, their compromises and perversities. Their guilt in land-betrayal was the thrust of his case against the fertility cults – the 'mismarriage' of the land in their 'husbandry'. All reading – then and now – of Hosea's prophethood has to reckon carefully with the uncertainties that attach to it. One Jewish scholar held that one-third of its verses defied translation.[3] We do not know under what editorial aegis his deliverances were organized after he was taken captive in 722 when Samaria yielded to a siege lasting three years. Nor are there clues to their story en route to the canonical text we now possess. Some metaphors and allusions, vivid doubtless in their first context, can seem obscure to us. While there is no mistaking the essential theme we are pursuing here, the sequences in the present text are sometimes obscure and the transitions abrupt. How, for example, should we take the 'ovens', the 'kneading' and the 'dough' of 7.4–7, and the 'cake not turned' comment about Ephraim? Do we conclude that Hosea was himself a 'baker' as some have conjectured and not the 'priest' of other surmise? And what are 'the gray hairs . . . upon Ephraim' (7.9)? For Hosea himself the deepest source of them was the hidden dread in his great charge concerning 'not your "I am"'. For, if YAHWEH was withdrawing His Name from 'His people', if Israel was in truth no longer 'His,' then He no longer had a Name.[4] The supreme grief lay not only in their supercession but in His non-identity. If the Exodus was disauthenticated then he would be crying with Job: 'O that I knew where I might find Him!' In the Hebraic idiom, history undone would be theology forfeit.

Certainly 'the land devours its rulers' (7.7). In the years between 752 and 722 of Hosea's ministry, there ensued the aftermath of the death of Jeroboam II – whose excesses seem the main anxiety of Chapters 4 and 5 – the forfeitures under Menahem, the revolt under Pekah (reign 738–732), and the final Assyrian conquest in the last years of Hoshea's reign (732–722). Was all this 'the oven' while 'the baker was asleep' (7.6)? – or not asleep, but aligning vainly with Syria or eye-ing Egypt in a fruitless effort to counter the power of Assyria? If not a final disavowal of the mutual sponsorship between YAHWEH and Israel, there must be a hiatus, brief or long, within it, reading that *ehyeh* word of 1.9 with Exodus 3.14.

If its ultimate meaning is 'the One who lets be in Himself being', then the first 'place of the Name' in a people's liberation had now to be read in exile as the requital of disloyalty. The perennial problem of its conditionality assumed in Hosea's eloquence its most radical statement: 'I am not the "I am" you think I am.'[5]

II

How was the man Hosea led to this drastic reading of enigma in the very core of his nation's ideology? How could a 'people-identity', sealed in land-possession as the sacrament of election, have its warrant forfeited in land-surrender and exile? A history under divine aegis had once territorialized them in their Canaan. Could divine history now undo itself in the steady attrition, the final demise, that Hosea was witnessing of the northern Kingdom?[6]

The answer takes us to the central question of his prophethood – the meaning of his tragic marriage. How should we read those first three chapters and take the point of 'the woman of whoredom'? Is there one Gomer throughout or are there two women involved?[7] What was the reality of the 'marriage'? Was the compromised character (*zenunin*) of the union actual or allegorical, the 'prostitution' ritual or real? The debates of scholars are prolific and turn on conjectural factors about translation, redaction and the stance of readership. There are those who take the whole story as a literary contrivance to make a point, and not an actual experience of marital infidelity. In that case it is hard to explain the deep pathos of emotion that breathes through the whole book.

Others opine that the command: 'Go marry a "harlot" . . . ' (1.2) tells what Hosea was factually told to do as 'the beginning of the word of the Lord' to him. On that ground what source would there have been for any experience of marital betrayal as the burden of his analogy for the treachery of Israel to YAHWEH and the impulse to his own prophethood? Would it be credible for God to issue a command to him in those terms? Admittedly, as with Ezekiel, prophets thought themselves bidden to do strange things in the interests of demonstrating their meaning and being arresting with it.[8] But in Hosea's case here, how could marriage with an already known 'prostitute' ever generate an experience of broken faith to make any parallel with how he saw the situation between Israel and YAHWEH? On that hypothesis – aside from its inherent moral incredibility – could we have had any Hosea to puzzle us at all?

Despite the caveats of some experts, it seems truest to read the whole in the proleptic terms so common to Hebrew thought. All crucial events, like a marriage, have their whole future in their first 'eventing'. The vows that bind are ties that contain – 'for better or worse'. Hosea married a pure bride at whose hands he suffered unfaithfulness. Proleptically, he had married a 'prostitute' – a bride who let herself belong elsewhere. 'Children of whoredom' (1.2) could hardly mean that she was already a mother, otherwise how could she have borne them to him? (1.3). If we include them (as we must) in the same proleptic reading, the question arises when he gave them the grim names that carried the point of his reproach to Israel. If we are arguing that his perception about the nation arose out of his own anguish of heart, these can hardly have been their infant namings. Giving offspring signifying names was a common device of Hebrew prophets.[9] When things future are latent in things present, there is a certain telescoping of time sequence. The whole intention in the naming was its public relevance. On the premiss that Hosea was only *going to be* betrayed from within his own sincerity over Gomer, the children's dire names could only have been public when, tragically, they were becoming true. And they would become true only when their public meaning was required. It would be false both to Hosea's tragedy and to this exegesis to imagine that he was a mere 'fatalist' at their birth times. We must read them inside a proleptic situation. In being a betrayed husband he would, perforce, be a grieved father.[10]

Despite the problems that remain, only this way do we do justice to the principle of prophethood as ever entailing a personal privacy of emotion as the paradigm of where utterance derives and what it tells.[11]

Being on the suffering side of adultery was certainly the theme, if not the source, of Hosea's 'burden' about his people. 'The spirit of whoredoms' (4.12f) 'has caused them to err'. So also 9.1, and the whole thrust elsewhere of how the book yearns and admonishes. There are political echoes about 'horses and battles' and diplomatic manoeuvres with Syria or Egypt but these are only inside the ruling marital theme-imagery. Hence the restitution of Gomer as the symbol of 'mercy beyond judgement' in the 'redemption' of Israel. There are doubtless perplexities around the minutiae of Chapter 3 but a clear consistency in the theme of the unfaithful brought into reconciliation. For the ultimate passion of Hosea is hope and retrieval. It is not without reason that his 14th chapter is read in synagogues on 'the Sabbath of Repentance' between Rosh Hashona and Yom Kippur. The very 'cornfloor and winepress' Hosea had so ardently celebrated and whose calamity of dearth was the outward sign of the demise of 'covenant' through national 'adultery' – these must recover again in the embrace of chastened hope and ample grace. Whatever the roles of Gomer, in act or symbol, she is not 'forsaken'.

III

In the over-all Hebraic theme of 'the place of the Name' with its corollary of 'the name of the place', Hosea's prophethood captures, with sweet and sombre personal accents, the entire paradox it for ever contains. What is peoplehood under God and what its tenancy of the natural order, its ecological theology? Nowhere was the place/Name equation more passionately told than in Hosea's words and story. We carry forward the nature-theme of our Chapter 2, through its Judaic dimension in Chapter 1, into his abiding avowal/disavowal of 'covenanted peoplehood' which makes him a superb voice of its perennial affirmation/contradiction.

Any alert reader is quickly aware of how much Hosea roundly negates. *Lo-Ruhamah*, 'no mercy mercied', no more *'Ammi*, My people' (1.9). 'You are not My people; I will not be your God.' 'I will not have mercy' (2.4). 'No priest to Me' for 'lack of knowledge' (4.6). 'They have not known the Lord' (5.4). 'They say not to their hearts . . . ' (7.2). 'They do not return . . . nor seek His face' (7.10). 'I will love them no more' (9.5), and all in the pain of that idealized wilderness where 'I did know thee' (13.5). 'They will not find Him, for He has withdrawn from them' (5.6).

Such are the grim negatives that underwrite Hosea's message of judgement and supply the clue by which he reads the chaos and confusion of his time, the disarray of his rulers as Assyria looms on the near horizon of Ephraim and Samaria. Hosea's ethical alertness, we might say, is rooted in his sense of territory. Most signal of all is the naming of his firstborn, Jezreel. What, like some witch of Endor, did the name summon out of dark history! There was the play on words – *Yizr'e'l*, 'God sows' (the kingdom's name), *Yisra'el* 'God strives (or wins)' (the ancestor Jacob's new name). Darkening either, was the memory of Saul's forces gathering there before the calamity on Mount Gilboa to the south. There Ahab had criminally acquired, by Jezebel's guile, the vineyard of Naboth. There Jehu had slain Ahab's whole progeny in a bloodbath of revenge (2 Kings 10.1f). The place of these criminous names was clearly somehow indelible in Hosea's soul.

Yet the grim name he gave his first child as symbol of the coming elimination of political Israel could be also the echoing shell at which his ear could hear the response of benediction from those loved positives of 'corn and wine and oil'. They would 'answer Jezreel' and Israel would be again 'sown in the earth'. The other names of his children would be reversed and all would cry: 'Thou art my God,' in a new and now abiding betrothal (2.20–23).

So from all the hard negations in Hosea come the sure positives in which he is dominated by a sense of history. The disciplining of Gomer's waywardness is 'the wilderness' again (2.14) where compassions were joined with rigours. Even that 'valley of Achor' – one of the harshest items of ancient memory (Joshua 7.26) – can become 'a door of hope', so that Jezreel too, with its loads of iniquity, can hear the reversal of those cancelled names (2.23).[12] But the basis has to be no brief and casual 'repentance' like that in 6.1–4, 'the morning cloud and the short-lived dew' that cannot abide the heat of dawn. If the significance of *ehyeh* in

Exodus 3.14 is cancelled in 1.9, it is nevertheless the memory of the Exodus which undergirds Hosea's assurance of hope. 'When Israel was a child then I loved him and called My son out of Egypt' (11.1). That retrospect must be the spur to contrition. For, after their infancy and youth, there is no going back to Egypt (11.5) except as into another bondage which their first grim sojourn will symbolize in the Assyria to which they go as exiles, all the more tragically so by the recapitulation of what preceded Moses (9.3 and 6).[13] Hosea's unfailing 'natural theology' in the cycles of fertility nowhere replaces his steadfast appeal to people-history. For it is there that the whole thrust belongs, both of what he disavows of unconditional peoplehood and what he affirms of unfailing divine fidelity.

As a northerner, it is interesting how little truck he has with David and the united monarchy. Assuming the verse is integral (3.5), there is only one mention, perhaps because Judah in the south was still intact. 'While Judah still rules with God' (11.12), Hosea's whole emotion is bound up with his Ephraim, his Samaria. Insofar as 'Davidism' was the matrix of things Messianic, Hosea precedes them and all his hope is in the God of the Mosaic covenant for ever heralded and celebrated in his loved and poetic awareness of 'corn and wine and oil' as perennial evidences in the hallowed terrain.

IV

To that theme and its place in his literary style we must return. Meanwhile Hosea raises for us – in his own unique idiom – the bane of Israel's 'vineyard' destiny being politicized by the necessity of nationhood as more than peoplehood in land tenancy. This is his version of the issue explored throughout. Fields and agronomy, corn-lands and oil-yielding vegetation, grapes and olives are his delight and song: kings, rulers and 'palaces' his burden and despair. From Jeroboam II to Hoshea through wealthy profligacy and abortive policies, he lived under no stable régime to give Israeli polity a worthy expression. Admittedly Assyria was on the prowl but Hosea had misgivings of conscience about Israeli exercise of *real politik* as he read it through the travailing decades of his ministry. He would doubtless have registered the same unease had he lived under the Hasmoneans. In 19th century terms he would have been at home with the soil nurture of *Hibbet Zion*, an agricultural Zionism which Herzl thought a toothless thing, rather than with the latter's cult of favours from world powers.

Whereas Amos reserves his sharpest prosecution for social evils and oppression, Hosea marries his concern for the worship of God in the hallowing of the land with heavy disquiet about Israel's politics. He interrogates the whole tradition of monarchy. 'They have set up kings but not by Me' (8.4), echoing – if not indirectly citing – the demur puzzlingly recorded in 1 Samuel 8 preceding the royal anointing of Saul. In 13.11 he implies that Israeli monarchy was divinely conceded only in anger. This leaves little doubt about where Hosea would stand in the debate between Ben-Gurion style political pragmatism and an Elohist theology.[14] Ben-Gurion, too, was David named.

At its very outset, as the Canon now has it, the book (1.4) threatens 'an end to the kingdom of the house of Israel'. They will 'abide many days without a king' (3.4). How many days? and how far does kingless diaspora abide well by being such? The question has its point precisely because – against the tenour of his attack on monarchy – 3.5 adds that 'they will seek the Lord their God and David their king'. What, for Hosea, would turn on that vital 'and' linking the two 'seekings'? We can be in no doubt that the preaching of Hosea bears heavily on the whole issue within Jewry and Zionism about how allegedly divine peoplehood belongs with human statehood. The point is the more important since the very 'Proclamation' of the State of Israel declared that it would be 'based on principles . . . as conceived by the Prophets of Israel'. They, for the most part, were far from unanimous about how such principles were institutionally safe.

Significantly, Hosea's great hymn of future hope in 2.14–23 has no mention of a Temple nor of a kingship ensuring the restoration it promises. It foresees a 'betrothal in love' inside the benison of 'corn and wine and oil'. Trust in 'fenced cities' is part of 'forgetting their Maker' (8.14). Meanwhile going as captives into Assyria suggests a 'door of hope' insofar as that heathen power may symbolize the former Egypt out of which a new liberation may transpire. This seems to be the point of 8.13, 9.3 (with an obvious parallelism), 9.6, all read in the light of the historical differential in 11.5, and of the taunt, in 7.11, about royal diplomacy: 'They call to Egypt, they go to Assyria.'[15] The original Exodus could well be a symbol for a coming emancipation, as an Isaiah or Jeremiah might foresee and tell, but not by dint of monarchies of Israel. The salvation Israel will come to know will not be attained by her own powers political. Rather, for Hosea – back to his loved imagery: 'You shall call Me your husband' (2.16).

V

Thus Exodus rather than David dominates Hosea's retrospect of history while his main pre-occupation is with the land and its harvests, the human culture these crucially sustain as broadly pondered in Chapter 2 earlier. What we might call Israel *naturaliter* is more vital than an Israel political. He is a denizen under divine providence rather than a citizen under empire. He reads and receives his Israeli ethos as a man of the soil and the oil-press, not of corridors of power.[16]

There is, however, another great lesson from his story. It is one of critical relevance to all negotiation with religious diversity, namely the skill and sagacity with which he retrieves meaning from the *baal* worships and establishes his Hebraic theism the more squarely by so doing. His is a theology of 'redemption' of error from its own futility by rescuing it from its aberration. What he exemplifies this way abides through all such issues. It is also profoundly significant for how any wise 'quarrel' with Jewish exclusivism might perceive its task.

Hosea's strategy could well be illustrated from a quite different source. Hebrew prophets and psalmists were often scornfully dismissive of idols and their worshippers, reproaching 'eyes' that could not 'see' and 'lips' that did not speak (Isaiah 44 and Psalm 115 *et al.*), when their 'makers' would have protested that such 'eyes' were never supposed to 'see', these 'images' being representational. However, Mahmud Shabistari (d. 1320) – from within Islam – had a more perceptive stance. He wrote:

> Did the Muslim understand what the idol is, he would know that there is religion even in idolatry![17]

If not, fitly, a religion to approve, it might still be a religion to educate.

Hosea, in effect, retrieves from the fertility cults the point he requires, when daring to call 'God husband' as a language his people can discerningly use. Was not 'the land' as something 'married' – first, imagery-wise, to the Lord and then, by His beneficence, 'married' to the toiling, harvesting peasantry who thus reaped its life-sustaining fertility?

This overall divine/human truth of things – pondered for us in Chapter 2 – the *baalim* cults had dimly understood but only in a crude superstition that erected numerous shrines and by its 'sacred prostitution' degraded the truth of human physical sexuality. Hosea's culture was keenly aware of both the impulses and the scandals of this *mise-en-scène* around him, the former from his own Hebraic love of YAHWEH, the latter by the aversion it taught him.

Many scholars, rejecting the proleptic account of his 'marriage' as ever actual, have assumed that he could readily have contrived the parable from his context. It is not clear in what the 'whoredom' of Gomer – real or allegorical – consisted. Was it only in her perhaps being merely designated for temple rituals rather than actually so employed? Whatever the truth of her identity and her story with Hosea, Canaanite fertility rites enshrined a significance Hosea had to rescue on his own Elohist or Yahwist terms. There was always the fact of the Hebrew necessity to tell things distinctively and consistently with a sole worship. Resembling Canaanites and others was always a temptation to reject. But things vital were at stake both in the measure of resemblance no 'naturalism' could escape and in the monotheist, Hebrew shape that must be given to them. *Baalim* were multiple, obscene, pagan, degrading and wrong but that 'the land was *Beulah*, 'married' (as in Isaiah 62.4) was not to be gainsaid.

Thus, whether deliberately or incidentally, Hosea contrived at one and the same time to dissociate a pure faith totally from what it must only denounce yet, in so doing, retain the meaning it both told and falsified. 'A faith unfaithful kept it falsely true.' The pattern has a relevance far beyond the reach of Hosea's immediate world and bears powerfully on the exclusivism, as both 'true' and 'false', which Jewry in Judaism perennially exemplifies. Religious perceptions are less isolated than they often seem, or than they become when formalized into doctrines.

Of course, in the Jewish case, the dimension of history comes athwart the common ground of land and nature. Canaanites were not 'married to Canaan' in the way Hosea's Israelis were by dint of the memory and legend of Exodus.[18] Nevertheless, they had the same physical factors of ancestry, heritage and toil, the same energies that serviced harvests, the same precarious dependence on the auspices of land. Could Hosea have been open to a certain sympathy for these in his necessary and urgent reproach of what he saw as vulgarity and shame?

Doubtless there was – and is – a certain danger in the whole analogy of human economy as a 'marriage' with the soil and of divine bounty as a 'husbanding' in nature. How well Islam shrank from it with its insistent *tanazzuh*, despite the hymnic celebration of God over nature in the Qur'an.[19] Sexuality is always a problematic realm for analogy in theology – as ambiguous as the omnibus word 'love' in English. It is well that Hosea has YAHWEH say: 'I am God and not man' (11.9) yet, in context, the words only the more strongly underline the deeply 'human' yearning that cries: 'How shall I give you up, O Ephraim?' As in many moods of Hinduism, a sexual analogy for what under God obtains in 'husbandry' is minded for obtrusive phallic symbols, where sordid lust or sensuality belong. These are a far cry from the patient, modest, reverent caring toil of the farmer and from what the poet called 'the dream in the peasant's bent shoulders'. Even so, there is bitter point in finding 'a rape of nature' in the exploiting patterns of contemporary technology. *Hibbet Zion* and gentle love of the soil would be after Hosea's heart and close to his reading of a 'land and people marriage'.

The whole discourse that likens the earth-'husbandry' to the other sense of 'husband', and agriculture to sexual fertility, has to be kept within the control of the basic doctrine of creation as divine entrustment and so of creaturehood as responsible tenancy and hallowing custody. For both realms – the farm and the family, livelihood and intercourse – are set (for all three Semitic faiths) in that interpreting realm of divine generosity and risk.[20] It then follows that sexual fidelity in all its associative mystery can carry the truth of creative, divinely co-operative, creaturehood in all other spheres of divine bestowal of trust and liability. We may think that Hosea's engagement with the pros and cons of Canaanite cults was wider and larger than he knew but, if so, the reason was always the corollary of the reproach he had for them. The *baalim* might have a certain innocence but only as imperilling the final truth.

That truth was the sole, undivided, inalienable sovereignty of God, the sovereignty of which Jewry believed itself the sole, inalienable guardian. Theirs, in some sense, was 'the place of the Name' inasmuch as their land, as they possessed it, tilled and occupied it, thanks to divinely entering it, had become by their very habitation there the index to His power and mercy. Yet the meaning of the ambiguity around its fertility, with which Hosea wrestled, was that as landscape and terrain it yielded its fertility to more than them. That co-habitation is still the truth of it. How, then, would Hosea be prophesying in the current century?

VI

The question must take us to the other great dimension of his language and career, namely the intense personalism, the pathos of his heart emotions. They emerge in his very style of eloquence, the slant of his imagery. They argue the view we have adopted that Hosea's marriage was truly a fact of experience and no mere artifice of literary technique. Troth and betrothal and infidelity breathe through the emotions he attributes to God. His Lord, to be sure, 'is God and not a man', yet He tells His relation to Israel in the most laden human terms of yearning and distress.

There is the soliloquy of 6.4 – and again in 11.8 – as of one, in broken heart, obliged both to cling in affection and deplore in pain. As a mother in reminiscence the Exodus is recalled in wistfulness.

> When Israel was a child then I loved him and called my son out of Egypt.

'Then', in that far off story but what of now in the Ephraim I see? The 'infancy' bond comes again in 11.3–4.

> It was I who taught Ephraim to walk. I took him up in my arms . . . I bent down and fed him gently . . .

Was it the ignorance of childhood that did not know who gave 'the corn and wine and oil'? (2.8) In 2.1f. the young family, with their 'right' names, seem called on to 'plead with their mother' as a grieving husband might recruit from his offspring the healing of its rupture, if they have any remaining pull upon their mother. A whole theology of the Lord's relation to His people in the tenancy of their land is borne in upon Hosea, as a message of requital and reform, as it is born in him by his own marital and sexual biography of love and grief. Just as Amos came to the realization that YAHWEH was the Lord of history by putting together the rise of Assyria and the righteousness he already knew to be YAHWEH's as righteously requiting evils that could neither be condoned nor ignored, so comparably, in his different idiom, Hosea inter-associated his broken marriage and the yearning of his Lord. For both his and His had to do, whether in the territory of marital troth or the troth of national territory, with what had been given in loving trust.

The point seems to be captured in the reiterated theme of 'knowing' and 'knowledge' in Hosea's language. The word *Yada'*, used of both betrothals, means sexual experience between husband and wife, man and woman. Hosea uses it also to denote how Israel 'knows' or 'fails to know' her Lord. The sexual analogy, for all its boldness, could not be clearer.[21] It manifestly fits exactly the Israeli treachery explicit in the 'adultery' being enacted in the paganizing of their 'corn and wine and oil' and in the iniquitous politics of their rulers.

That the two belonged together was the reason why Hosea's metaphors about the latter – flaming ovens, wild prey-tearing beasts and worm-eaten timbers – were so grim and graphic (7.7, 13.8 and 5.12). Truly 'a vulture' winged 'over the house of the Lord'. For the 'harlotry' took form in rites – albeit celebrating fertility – that could provide occasion for ritual prostitution and so give rein to sanctioned sensuality which reproduced itself in the intrigues and mischief of politics and power. It was not simply that Israeli *amour propre* in Hosea read Canaanite rituals with innate hostility. It was that they had beguiled his own Israelites into a 'prostitution' of their destiny as YAHWEH's in His, and their, 'promised land'. In sum, they 'did not know the Lord'.

It has been conjectured that part of the reason lay in a fear lest their having been brought into the land as former strangers to it, by a Lord who had been originally their 'tribal God', meant that His worship did not fructify the soil. Did they, then, adopt Canaanite fertility rituals as a sort of second insurance necessary in their now agricultural economy? Such double 'protection' devices are far from unknown in other times and cultures. But what a faithless notion it was, given how 'it was I who gave . . . the corn and wine and oil' (2.8). They would need to know that YAHWEH was greater than their nomadism. Indeed, was it not in that very nomadism they had been shepherded into land tenure?

> Like grapes in the wilderness I found Israel. Like the first fruit on the fig-tree I saw your fathers. (9.10)

The One who had 'known them in the land of drought' would surely suffice them in 'their (new) pasture' (13.5). Hosea's burden was that 'as a silly dove without sense' they were so reluctant to learn it (7.11), 'the holy One in their midst' (11.9) was the enduring truth.

VII

In a prophethood conceived in the travail of his own emotions, Hosea had given abiding statement as to 'the whereabouts of God'. He belongs significantly in the logic and sequence of the present study. His theme of 'harlotry' as a metaphor in Biblical theology had a long impression on the prophetic mind. It recurs in many of his successors and becomes a note in many psalms. Isaiah echoed it memorably (1.21), it is frequent in Jeremiah and Ezekiel. It figures in recitals of Hebrew history of how 'they became unclean by their own acts and played the harlot in their doings' (Psalm 106.39).

It was, to be sure, an unhappy analogy to use of things religious. For it could so readily be turned around to scorn and scandalize. The elder brother in the story of 'the prodigal' could use it to vow no welcoming relationship (Luke 15.30). If copying Canaanites could be 'whoredom' they too could be wanton 'harlotry'. Such are the dangers of turns of even prophetic speech. The ultimate task would be to redeem the pagans from their paganism.

Hosea stayed within his vocation with 'the house of Israel' but, by his fidelity to 'the spirit of prophecy', he had given to the future that pregnant perception: 'I am not the "I am" you have in mind.' That assumptions about YAHWEH and how history might unfold His nature could need to be radically undone, amended, revised, enlarged, was a profound waymark in and for the Biblical mind.

The writer in the First Epistle of Peter could recall it to claim all that the New Testament was coming to mean. If those – Jews – who had somehow been 'no longer people of God' through sinful aberration, were generously reinstated, then those who had from time immemorial been perceived as 'no people' might, by a like compassion, be once and for all 'enpeopled'. Had Hosea unwittingly anticipated what 'God in Christ' would bring to pass?

> Who in past time were not a people are now the people of God: those who had obtained no mercy have now been mercied. (1 Peter 2.10)

The hard negatives of Hosea's daughter and son, *LoRuhamah* and *Lo'Ammi* are turned into the positive once more. Why not also, for the first time, an old 'absence by negation' from 'people-hood to God'? At once Peter reminds his readers in this new community that they are *paroikoi*, not 'parishioners' but, as it were, 'universal dwellers'.[22] It is intriguing that the word, with the kindred *parepidemoi*, is paired in the same way in the Greek of the Septuagint when Abraham, no less, is stating his claim to buy a burial place for his wife, Sarah. The psalmist in 39.13 was in the same human condition. In its haunting way the phrase 'strangers and pilgrims' – so much at odds with Israelite 'enlandizement' – tells a universal condition. In the New Testament, beyond the pledged tenancy of given territory and the destiny of singular birthing, that universal condition enters into the invitation of divine grace on the open terms of faith. Has Hosea conveyed us to the Christ-event as the potential of his great rendering of the 'I am' theme in the life of his people?

There is one final reason why the answer may be Yes. The intensity of his own personal emotion in the measure we have studied brought him into a strange intimacy with what – by its lights – he was constrained to see as the very yearning of God. He came to think of YAHWEH having, in transcendent terms, the griefs that were his own. His life-experience gave him the theme of his ministry. Perhaps for the first time in the whole prophetic Hebrew tradition, meaning was – as it were – incarnate in himself. What was essential in his word was the substance of his life. Prophethood always recruited biography. With Hosea they moved as one.

Chapter Four

'GENTILES'

I

It has always been urgent, yet also highly problematic, to receive and welcome others as 'human beings'. The term is commendably inclusive yet also blandly incomplete. For all of us humans are identified by particulars inseparable from our 'being human', the unambiguous recognition of which we expect and assume, the disregard of which we find disconcerting, if we are equable, exasperating if we are not. The toils and pains of racialism are notorious.

'Who we are' – by birth, language, place, culture and emotion – is synonymous with 'that we are' in the wide diversity of human-kind. Being anonymously human is the anomaly that can never be. While inter-human acceptance is crucial for society, it cannot sanely or safely avoid to be a mutuality across the otherness of the sundry humans we will always be. Caring for a mutuality alert to such liability will not do well to have some 'anti-' in its immediate consciousness, nor any disparagement, explicit or implicit, in the posture it brings to human exchange.

We encountered at the outset the elusive character of any definition of 'Semitism', or whatever the entity is that has so tragically incurred the hateful antipathy all too familiarly known as 'anti-Semitism'. We noted that 'Semitism' hardly exists except as denoting a sphere of linguistic studies or as drawn from those 'Semites' who are far more than, and other than, the 'Jewry' and the 'Jewish' for whom the inimical 'anti-' -ism is meant. How to deny, banish and defeat anti-Semitism is a high supreme task of inter-human society, going so long by default.

The corollary around a human mutuality about 'who we are' has to be the degree – and the temper – in which we exceptionalize ourselves. For 'exceptionalities' are part of identities everywhere. The burden of Judaic Semitism has always been to seek and require acceptance as 'Jewish' and not simply as human, and to do so uniquely as a truth of theology. It is a theology about an ethnic history which entails the discriminating concept of 'Gentiles'. These are officially defined as 'people who are non-Jewish'.

Jewry is distinctive in having its self-exempting descriptive for all the rest of humanity which constitutes a 'not-us' deep in the psyche of a 'people dwelling alone'. The reasons have been explored in previous chapters and the denominators – nevertheless common – of forebears, fortunes and foundings, of ancestry, territory and memory, on which their logic rested as election and covenant.

Hence the strong psychic and emotional impulse to see the non-Jew as a *goi* and other nations as *goyim* which Greek knew as *ethnoi* and Latin as *gentes*. The collective belongs more to pre-exilic Jewish history, the singular after diaspora. It is necessary to study the temper of this 'Gentilizing' of the rest of the world, both for its inner mystique in Jewish self-awareness and for the deep struggle the New Testament faith had in over-coming it and 'de-Gentilizing' its human world. The latter is the theme of Chapter 5 in the Christ-version of 'the place of the Name'.

It is significant that while the phrase 'from generation to generation' (so vital to Jewish lineage) occurs repeatedly in the Hebrew Bible, it is quite absent from the New Testament.[1] In the former *goi* and *goyim* occur almost four hundred times often in contradistinction to *'am*, used – as in Psalm 78.1 'Hear, O my people,' and in those Hosea passages – always about the 'elect' people, Israel and Judea earlier studied.

II

Goyim have played a perennial part in the self-awareness of Jewry. It could not be otherwise, implicitly in all Jewish external relations and explicitly during the two dispersions, Jewish and Christian, to be studied in Chapter 6, where the one thought its *'am* term was being usurped and the other the *goyim* term aptly becoming obsolete. It may be doubted whether the Jewish mind has ever duly reckoned with the *goyim* concept as a spiritual category in its perspective on humanity. It does not suffice to observe that, of course, 'the godly Gentile has a share in the life to come'. The re-assurance can seem patronizing as long as he is allowed no comparable part in divine peoplehood here and now, historically and universally. Whatever the ambivalence in the Jew/Gentile non-equation, there can be no doubting the enormous tragic burden it has entailed on the heirs of the 'covenant' that gave it being.

It is first necessary to appreciate the usage *goyim* as it occurs in the Hebrew Bible. For good or ill, hope or fear, inter-human proximities are inescapable. As if confirming this truth there are occasions in the Pentateuchal Books where *goi* is used for Israel, as in Moses' prayer in Exodus 33.13: 'Consider that this nation (*goi*) is Thy people (*'am*).' *Goi* tells each of 'the two nations' in Rebecca's womb (Genesis 25.23). Jacob's progeny and Esau's can share the term, as also, for example, when the blessing of Jacob in Genesis 35 by the new name of Israel assures him that 'a nation and a company of nations shall be of him' (v. 11).

But, steadily throughout the historical Books, in psalmody and the prophets, *goyim* are 'others', to be driven out in Deuteronomy 4.38, to be partitioned by lot among the invading 'tribes' under Joshua (23.4f) – a task according to Judges 2 left unfinished by that leader. Early yearnings after 'kingship' are – initially – resisted by Samuel on the ground that it would make Israel 'like the *goyim*' (1 Samuel 8.20). When the great king, David, prays he enquires 'what nation (*goi*) on earth is like to Thy people (*'am*)?' (cf. 1 Chronicles 17.21). Psalms 78 and 135 rehearse the conquests and deliverances by which YAHWEH protects His people and requites the *goyim*. Though occasionally even later the *goi* term can be used of Israel, its plural becomes more and more exclusively a synonym for all that is non-Jewry.[2] That the term could once be mutual may signify for more than etymology: its deep theological import in that unitary way might one day be retrieved.

Meanwhile, 'Gentiles', the rest of humans, persistently remain. Every identity is aware of 'others' and the sense of strangeness is often deep and prolonged but is there anywhere, save for the Jewish mind, a collective totality, not ourselves, so crucial to the inner consciousness that massively requires it and requires that it persist? Unless the terms are inexact Semitism consists in this 'Gentilizing' of non-Jewry and anti-Semitism a hateful register of the rejectionism it undergoes. The sense in which the two are co-lateral we have to explore in no way warrants the enormities which the hatred has contrived. These were the tragic burden that steadfast loyalty to sacred exceptionality was made to carry in the turmoil of the human scene. Where the burden fell was where invincibly the honour stood – the fidelity of the Jewish spirit to the assurance of its supreme destiny with YAHWEH. Was it darkly and bitterly this 'Gentile exclusion' which was read as fit for nemesis when, across the centuries, 'Gentiles' took their status into hate and guilt, in enmity at what they would not kindlier comprehend or – as *goyim* – dispassionately concede?

For it was clear from the outset that the exceptionality was not for inner prizing as some private secret. Its being was to be received. Joseph's brothers knew it in the turmoil of their enmity when the 'many-coloured coated dreamer' drew innocently near beyond Dothan, seeking where they fed their flocks, as Jacob had unsuspectingly directed him to do.[3] They rankled inwardly at their 'sheaves bending down' to his, at his fond father's preference for Rachel's first-born over their inferior mothering. They were 'verily guilty concerning him' like all anti-Semites are. But, there and then, contriving to think otherwise, all unaware how events would circumvent their treachery, they could not encompass.

This latent element of provocation, if such it be, is liable to be made explicit in certain psalms. 'He shall subdue the people under us and the nations under our feet' (47.3): 'the Lord is high above all people . . . let them praise thy great and terrible Name' (99.2–3): 'kings of the earth . . . let them praise the Name of the Lord' (148.11 and 13). When, as happily in for example Psalm 67, the glad theme is 'saving health among all nations', the aegis and source are always from a Hebrew benison, so that, if not fearful, then grateful, benediction is always in the one direction, from the 'Gentile' to the Israelite. When centuries later apostolic Christianity was able to recruit these passages with delight, it was because it saw them fulfilled in a unity where all were beneficiaries, all were debtors and all were instruments.

Such is the perversity of human nature that even Hebrew benediction did not readily reap the gratitude it deserved. All too frequently it was the sense of enmity that prevailed and could only prove reciprocal. The 'enemy' word comes some seventy times in one hundred and fifty psalms and sometimes – as in Psalm 2 – the confrontation when 'heathen rage' 'against the Lord and his anointed' reaches a derisory level quite oblivious of the political realities which the great prophets read only too well. 'Kiss the Son lest he be angry and ye perish . . . ' told a 'holy hill of Zion' only defiantly credible when physically so small, shadowed by mighty empires. Be the odds as they would, its being was to be perceived. Semitism in this psalmist's book was no negligible identity. It was the one 'YAHWEH had chosen for Himself.'[4] Its deep self-consciousness as divinely privileged meant a perennial burden stoically, yet ardently, borne in the context of a no less perennial non-Jewishness for which it was uncongenial and provocative.

III

Has this age-long phenomenon of Semitism been genuinely sifted in the ever urgent duty to expose and denounce the anti-Semitism it has so desperately undergone? John Lyly in his *Euphues and His England* (1580) observed how it was 'of the nature of that country to sift strangers'.[5] It is certainly of the nature of Jewishness to do so more, and the sifting down the centuries has brought to life and proof the darkest dimensions of guilt in the denial to Jewry of its essential human-ness. The question presses why a shamefully persistent anti-Semitism should have been so long and criminally sustained against an identity-in-community which so deeply exceptionalized its own humanity? There was never in Semitism what could warrant, still less justify, anti-Semitism but why has the negative thing been consistently so named? Why should it be that history's most consciously differentiated people have proved the world's most persistently persecuted?

It has repeatedly been urged, by Jews themselves and by perceptive

'Gentiles', that attitudes to the former are the very test-case of civilization and culture. Thus, for example, Ernst Fischer:

> The degree of a society's culture can be measured by its attitude towards the Jews. All forms of Anti-Semitism are evidence of a reversion to barbarism. Any system which persecutes the Jews, on whatever pretext, has forfeited all right to be regarded as progressive.[6]

Similarly, David Novak writes:

> The truth of every cause is validated or found fraudulent in the way in which it confronts the Jewish people.[7]

Such opinions, however, could be read as disqualifying any and every 'cause' that felt itself required to state its case or plead its reasons, if these entailed any critical analysis of Jewry or of Jewish relations. Ought exceptionality, so enforced, to comprise or enjoy a virtually inclusive exoneration that would equate all criticism with hostility?

The frequency of such claims that Jewishness is always and everywhere a test-case for human goodness is no doubt explained by the massive burden of Semitism in Jewish experience, the incessant exposure to incipient enmity.[8] In that light, it could well be condoned or approved. Yet, essentially, the truth remains that 'the truth of every cause' is tested by its handling of the human community at large, its will to human justice on every side. We are back again in the Judaic irony of both the necessity, and the ultimate impossibility, of reading humanity with an ethnic discrimination. For there is no exceptionality that can exempt itself from the radical interdependence of the human condition and the human neighbourhood. Ought the notion of 'the Gentiles' not somehow to rethink its legitimacy, the more so if we want to say:

> The reign of the Lord extends to all men, yet He chooses His elect nation. The devil, too, has his chosen ones. They are the Anti-Semites. He does not leave himself without special witness.[9]

The *Encyclopedia Judaica* in its entry on 'Gentiles' very truly observes:

> In general it may be said that the Jew's attitude towards the Gentile was largely conditioned by the Gentile's attitude towards him,[10]

adding that 'it varied greatly accordingly'. It was for their cruelty toward Jews that 'Gentiles' were condemned in the Talmud. This tragic tangle we have to explore later in study of the twin diasporas through the long centuries. Yet a 'Gentile' might not be taught the Torah. Deuteronomy 7.3–4, not to say Nehemiah, had forbidden inter-marriage – a rubric which had the religious sanction that only Jews were true monotheists and that 'idolatry was uniformly characteristic of all non-Jews'. Jews might 'for the sake of peace greet "Gentiles" on their festivals' but a 'Gentile' 'observing the Sabbath was punishable by death'.[11] To be sure he had a legal personality but could not be a legal witness nor have lost property legally restored. 'Gentiles' lacked, or were omitted from, the very thing which enabled Jewry to emerge, namely transition out of *benay Nuh* to *benay Yisrael*, seeing that birth and circumcision only became hallmarks of hereditary status via Abraham, himself born outside what his quality bequeathed.

It could not but come that this insistent 'othering by otherness' would be reciprocated. Tacitus long after Abraham had it tellingly in his *Historia*, volume 4: *'Profana illic omnia quae apud nos sacra rursum conversa apud illas quae nobis incesta'*, so that all that Romans held sacred, Jews held to be profane, while Romans found impure what was Jewishly holy. The steady inter-association of 'the Gentile' with the idolater became a prime element in Jewish Semitism from the time of the patriarchs, seeing that the Jewish people are where the throne of God rests. From this it might follow that a monotheism of singular ethnic custodianship must argue a political/religious nationalism. The issue – to be explored anon – exercised the Zionist mind from the outset, not least because of the tension created for it by its secular vision of the 'nation' to be created.

As for the 'Gentile'/ungodly equation, the Qumran treasures told its intensity.

> May you bring death to the ungodly with the breath of your lips . . . May
> He make your horns of iron and your hooves of bronze; may you toss like
> a young bull and trample the peoples like the mire of the streets.[12]

Allowance must doubtless be made for the frustration which dogged such minds in the aftermath of Maccabean failure, but the sentiment stemmed from inward perception of Rome and themselves. The sense of 'Gentiles' as 'pagans' engendered the conviction, variously argued throughout Jewish history, that only Jewish power was right for Jewish ethnicity, so making the latter somehow inherently subversive, despite the long and honoured tradition of suffering docility. The converse was the perception of 'Gentiles' as 'tyrants' notwithstanding the Roman tolerance of religious Judaism that made the Revolt so foolhardy.[13]

Whether in the ethnic or the doctrinal or the political the Judaic antithesis of 'the Gentiles' meant a subtle 'otherness' that almost approved the rejectionist response so that, in the origins of Zionism, the cry of *Die Juden sind ein Volk* on its part made the very point of the anti-Semites, namely that Jewry could never be fairly part of a European nation, being irreversibly 'other'.[14] The 'Gentile' denominator – always not shareable by Jewry – became a prescript for confrontation unless a total secularity could surmount it. For it was fastened in theology.

There is no separating of Jewish history from the absolute being. The Jewish people is imbued with God and, conversely, God is immersed in

Jewish history.[15] 'Gentiles', then, are no inconsequential, dispensable theme in Jewish thought. They belong within an entire theology and, were secularity to 'de-theologize' their Jewish meaning, what would be implied for Judaism itself?[16] Thanks to 'Gentiles' being perceived as the very corollary of Jews being Jews a situation of reciprocal consciousness prevails that has worked intolerable hardship on those who lived by its necessity. As Thomas Mann has it for his Joseph: 'The habitual knowledge that he was loved and preferred conditioned his whole being.'[17] What of the brethren's whole being?

IV

Being somehow inherently preferential with YAHWEH as how Jewry needed to be perceived by a 'Gentilized' world was corroborated by the social factors it entailed. Election with God somehow elicited the ghetto among humans. The Sabbath might well commend due space for worship but it sanctioned only Jewish obedience to what was 'made', i.e. fitted, for mankind at large. Its observance was more readily fulfilled in its own community when other identities defined themselves by other days. The dietary laws meant that mutual hospitality – that supreme sanction and surety of human community – was largely impossible. One could be intimate only in being private as a human neighbourhood. All sects and minorities, to be sure, intensify allegiance by narrowing the confines, but few with a Judaic perpetuity. The rite of circumcision left the mark of identity significantly in the flesh while the veto on inter-marriage, with other factors, made the menace of assimilation, by a strange irony, all the more suspect. How differently might Jewishness have known itself if it had not posited the world of 'Gentiles'?

The irony was deepened when anti-Semitism could be ambiguously detected in the very context where it was in fact being plainly deplored. Shakespeare's *The Merchant of Venice* is a telling case in point. It has often been decried as 'an anti-Semitic play', and few will deny that Shylock presents repelling features of vengefulness and spite. But could the playwright have him emerge as dramatically a 'man more sinned against than sinning', as noble in his broken-ness, without presenting so honestly the world that made him vengeful? '*The Merchant of Venice* reads finally as a most pro-Semitic play. Few can save much admiration for the likes of Graziano or the suave playthings of Belmont or those 'who spit upon the Jewish gaberdine'.[18]

Moreover, Shakespeare has Shylock make his superb gesture of defiance of those 'Gentiles' in the only ultimate terms that Jewry has, namely the inclusiveness of humanity.

I am a Jew. Hath not a Jew eyes? Hath not a Jew hands, organs, dimensions, senses, affections, passions: fed with same food, hurt with the same
weapons, subject to the same diseases, healed by the same means, warmed
and cooled by the same winter and summer as a Christian is? If you prick
us do we not bleed? If you tickle us do we not laugh? If you poison us do
we not die? And if you wrong us shall we not revenge? If we are like you in
the rest we will resemble you in that.[19]

Shylock's virile Semitism speaks a universal tongue and appeals to
things that tell eloquently against all vaunted exceptionality. Thus even
anti-Semitism is made to read its own image in the very Semitism it
maligns. On the very grounds that Shylock pleads, it is condemned
precisely where 'the Jew' seeks escape from his own privacy in emotions
he shares with 'Gentiles' because all alike are human. Shylock may be
thwarted on a technicality but there is a vindication even so – a vindication not of his venom but of his human identity where his Jewishness is
briefly transcended.

The play's depiction of the irony alike in the Semitism that affirms and
the anti-Semitism that denies Judaic self-perception – the irony latent in a
common human-ness – translates into many different realms that
Shakespeare's genius sifted for his theatre. It lives in the perennial cry: 'I
am a Jew as long as there are anti-Semites',[20] and in the logic of the Zionist
that only in being politically like all nations could Jewry safely be 'a nation
apart', or, if not 'safely', than 'defiantly'.

It extends into a deeper irony still, namely that the utmost will to exceptionality is for ever immersed in the frame of the common world. Even
apartheid, if we will to contrive it, will not attain immunity. The finest
achievements of political Zionism have not come without abiding debt to
'Gentile' factors – a situation readily recognized, for example, by the
historian Jacob Talmon.

> No Jewish historian, whatever his evaluation of the various factors involved
> in the restoration of Jewish statehood, can ignore the fact that Zionism
> would never have had a chance for success if centuries of Christian teaching
> and worship, liturgy and legend, had not conditioned the western nations
> to respond almost instinctively to the words 'Zion' and 'Israel'.[21]

The ultimate rescue from the Shoah came only in the inclusive human
cost of the invasion of the European continent from the west and its pene-
tration from the east. Dachau and Auschwitz were not overcome without
the Normandy beaches and Stalingrad. The sharp debate about whether
– and how – any earlier intervention might have availed only leaves the
tangle of war-policy and world scene the availing factor it attained to be.

Has there not always been a 'Gentile' dimension in Jewish benison as
well as Jewish persecution – Joseph's Egypt, Gath and Philistines in
David's strange progress from near banditry to splendid power, Hiram's

resources in the building of Solomon's Temple and the 'anointed' Cyrus in the renewal of post-exilic Jerusalem? In more than these circumstantial ways, has there not always been subtle inter-action between the elements in tension? The bold strategy of Hosea, studied in Chapters 2 and 3, in adapting the mind-set of *baal*-worshippers without their licentiousness and paganism sought, and found, what was negotiable in their positive favour as alert to fertility both of soil and sexuality. He might well be taken to hint for us now that great positives do well to relate themselves vitally to what they can never uncritically allow. Maybe the very 'Gentile' category is one that Jewry, for Jewry's own divine sake, could reasonably hold less absolute. So – crucial to both – a common humanity would seem to demand, and demand supremely in contemporary terms of global technology and economies in such disequilibrium. Chapters 9 and 10 must take the query further after due concern in Chapters 7 and 8 with the evidence of diasporas and Zions.[22]

V

The irony we perceive attending the whole Jew/'Gentile' distinction takes its most sinister form when the concept of 'chosen-ness' is borrowed for emulation, all too often without the intense moralism ultimately brought to it by the conscience of the great Hebrew prophets. Corporate egoism and self-will in many quarters can readily adapt the scenario of 'others as pagans' to warrant a myth of destiny. So one Encisco reasoned in the southern America.

> Moses sent Joshua to the inhabitants of Canaan, to Jericho, the first city in the promised land to demand that they abandon their city because it belonged to the people of Israel, in view of the fact that God had given it to them. When the people of Jericho did not give up their city, Joshua besieged them and killed them all, except a woman who had protected his spies, and after this Joshua conquered the entire land . . . all by the will of God because they were idolaters.[23]

Similar sanction has been invoked in such Biblical precedent.

Or perhaps a 'there is where' reading of eventful history has, like the Exodus, seemed to liberate into land possessing. To godly Boers in the 19th century the Vaal River could seem their national Jordan. The motif of fulfilling both territory and identity has been prominent in the whole northern American saga. Robert Frost could write, as we saw, and apparently with no sense of the dubious: 'The land was ours before we were the land's' – a sentiment belonging with Jewry from the time of Abraham. Recalling how 'we were England's . . . possessed by what we now no more possessed' Frost could have been musing like Israelites not yet fully out from the bonds of Egypt, 'weak . . . ' until they gave themselves to Canaan, to 'the gift outright' which was indeed 'many deeds of war'.[24]

Did not President Lincoln, addressing New Jersey Senators, refer to his nation as 'the almost chosen people'?[25] New Englanders, like Herman Melville the novelist, were enamoured of the theme. He called his countrymen 'the peculiar chosen people, the Israel of our time, we bear the ark of the liberties of the world'.[26] His readers know how Biblically laden was his imagery. In such sense of destiny via both geography and history, Jews were far from a 'people dwelling alone', while, thanks to this emulation, great numbers of Jews themselves inside the United States could happily find their final 'promised land' with no impulse either to Zionist reasoning or Zionist immigration.

When in these ways the 'Gentile' concept was, so to speak, turned on its head the question followed whether, in any and every event, all was an instinctive self-love akin to what the German philosopher Ludwig Feuerbach alleged of Jewry, in describing 'egoism as the principle of Judaism'.[27] In that case it could be seen as neither uniquely pretentious nor uniquely reprehensible but simply a peculiar version of multiple peculiarities across history. That way no 'Gentiles' would remain and, correspondingly, no 'Jews'. But multiple egoisms may be dis-equated and the Judaic still 'dwell alone'. Whether Zionism means it to be so remains its final indeterminacy and the long anguish of the Palestinians.

Yet the implications of election can have sinister borrowing as well as possible emulation. Such borrowing is capable of being the most damnable form of anti-Semitism by turning venomously into a pseudo-Semitism. Thus a notorious Nazi professor, a Wilhelm Hauer writing:

> We believe that God has laid a great task on our nation and that He had therefore revealed himself specially in its history and will continue to do so.[28]

What is menacing in such illicit borrowing is that its claim requires to be unilateral. 'Chosen-ness' cannot admit of rivals but must exclude all competition, the more so when it is itself imitative. Hence the total arrogance of Nazi-style Germanism, a volk romanticism which so fascinated Thomas Carlyle drawing on his studies in Johann Fichte and his successors. By the strangest of ironies it is then the Jews who become the 'excluded', the prime 'unchosen'.

There is one final twist to all musing on the notion of 'the Gentiles' as the alterity of Jewish consciousness. In what sense, or to what degree, has a 'renegade Jew' become a 'Gentile'? At least the great Maimonides hinted that he had. For the word well fitted what had to be disavowed, as was the case with the non observant 'son of the covenant' who profaned the Sabbath or married outside the nation or forsook the Torah.

There was always, and inevitably, this point at issue. On the one hand,

Jewish identity belonged perpetually in the covenant by the irreversibility of birth. Yet, clearly, 'always a Jew' was an idle truism given rank negligence of all that ethically and liturgically belonged with the faith and its practice. All faiths incur this problem of whether their 'faithful' are authentically such, but none so crucially, given the 'Jew by birth' warrant of covenant, when Sinai embraced its audience to the end of time. A Jew who held aloof from the congregation of Israel and went his own way became thereby 'as one of the Gentiles'. At times *Halakhah* characterized the non-observant Jew as 'taken captive by the Gentiles', not ethnically one of them, but one of them in effect. Could such an 'Israeli-Gentile' – if we may so speak – be 'half-positive' as some Rabbis thought?

It is an intriguing idea and perhaps opens the way for some gentle mitigation of a too long sundering by category. In any event, as *Pirke Avot* (5.21) enjoins, 'all argument' has to be 'for the sake of heaven'. That all depends on what 'heaven's sake' itself is for. Was Mishnah Sanhedrin not asking (4.5): 'Why was Adam created as a single person?' Was it not to teach that whoever destroyed a single soul, it was if he killed all humankind?' Saving one, too, could be as saving all. Could Jews come to embrace 'Gentiles' without ceasing to be themselves?

The question seems entirely academic yet the New Testament believes that there was a point in time when indeed it happened. How it did so, is the theme of the following chapter. The point of this one, as a bridge to it from the story of Chapter 1, and the intervening misgivings of Hosea with their strange relevance to both, is to serve as prelude to 'the place of the Name in Christ' where an inclusive community transpired. Its founding Jew/'Gentile' inclusion did not endure. Despite its Jewish magnanimity in its first apostles, it grew to be a predominantly 'Gentile' society as if to prove how insistent the distinction must remain.

Bitterly disowning all happier reading of the Jew/'Gentile' divide, Yeshayahu Leibowitz explains why with an acid irony: It is 'not as if the God of Israel were a Jew like the god of the Christians'.[29] To 'Judaize' 'God in Christ', except in antecedent story, would be as damnable an innuendo as 'Judaizing' YAHWEH, as if less than 'God of all the kindreds of the earth'.

If there was indeed a point at which, however contestedly, the Jew/'Gentile' distinction was effectively overcome in a genuine juncture of the two, the fact of it must bear hard on the difficult question of defining 'Semitism' which was faced in the Introduction. The genuine actuality of that juncture comes in the following chapter with its origins in Jesus. If we will allow it so, then the resulting New Testament Christianity can in no proper sense be described as anti-Semitic, yet it is precisely an inevitable identity between 'Christian' and 'anti-Semitic' which has been alleged – and more categorically since the Holocaust.

The enormity of the Shoah was the most venomous of all hatreds because it illegitimated people and went on to seek their elimination simply for being who they were. *Die Endlösung der Judenfrage* meant 'a world without Jews' for the devilish reason that they ought not to exist. Implacably, it willed their exclusion from human community. As such, it was the ultimate dimension of anti-Semitism. Anti-Judaism would have been some religious controversy like 'anti-socialist' or 'anti-conservative' are political alternatives. The Holocaust made anti-Semitism an utterly lethal executioner from which there was no appeal, against which there was no plea.

Given, by Auschwitz, Dachau and the gas chambers, that definition, anti-Semitism must surely make 'Semites' of all who disavow it, all who served to liquidate its machinery and end its horror. For by their total disavowal and their overcoming of it they became to it what abolitionists are to slavery.[30] If, then, anti-Semitism is seen to have found its ultimate delineation in the Holocaust the 'Semitism' term will need to be correspondingly re-assessed. It cannot honestly be circumscribed in terms that make Christians *en masse* – by definition – 'anti-Semitic', i.e. 'anti-Semitic merely in their capacity as Christian.

Yet, in some quarters, it is just this inherent identity between 'Christian' and 'anti-Semitic' which is alleged to be the fact. Thus, for example:

> The roots of Christian anti-Semitism need be traced no further than Christianity itself: Christians have been anti-Semitic because they have been Christians . . . Anti-Semitism is part of what it has meant to be historically a Christian.[31]

Or:

> Christianity's New Testament has been the most dangerous anti-Semitic tract in history . . . Without (it) Hitler's *Mein Kampf* could never have been written.[32]

It will be clear from Chapter 5 that this equation between 'Christian' and 'anti-Semite' is distorting the former and exclusifing the latter in the Holocaust and a Holocaust logic where there is no reprieve from disavowal. It completely ignores the profound Semitism of the New Testament, decries how deeply and confessionally grateful to Jewry the New Testament remains. If it is allowed, it necessitates a radical confining of what Semitism ever meant and must surely continue to mean – a meaning to which Christianity is no stranger.

This painful issue returns us to the whole significance of 'Gentiles' being 'non-Jews'. Indeed, of course, they are but why does the differentiating distinction have to belong with their human-ness? Negatives, anyway, like 'non-Buddhist' or 'non-Hindu' tend to be undesirable in being also without content and properly avoided now in intelligent dialogue. It is important that they should *not* play a necessary part in any designation.

Doing so has always been the problematic in the 'Gentile' word. If 'Semite'/'anti-Semitic' is thought to derive from 'Jew'/'Gentile' or if they be equated, clearly a travesty is made of all four. Yet this is what is liable to happen, if and when anti-Semitism, inclusively defined by the Holocaust, is aligned with 'Christianity', as has been the case in much pre- and post-Holocaust theology.

It remains, therefore, all the more urgent to understand in New Testament faith a signal effort to have Jewry and 'the Gentiles' inter-belong in a peoplehood to God where the one stayed duly present when the other, ceasing to be religiously other, was beloved in the Lord. If not that New Testament way how else? Never, if Israel is YAHWEH's 'bride', as the great Solomon Schechter has it, drawing on the Song of Songs:

'Behold thou are fair, my love, says God to Israel',

adding:

> You are fair through the giving of alms and performing acts of loving-kindness. You are my lovers and friends when you walk in my ways, as the Omnipresent is merciful and gracious, long-suffering and abundant in goodness, so be ye . . . [33]

Yet *Aspects of Rabbinic Theology* seems to sense that others too might attain these measures of divine imitation, if indeed all 'the hills of the Lord' are 'the tabernacles of God'.

This leads Schechter to the theme of the nations at large having been invited to the same destiny but having 'turned Him down'. Thus, if uneasily in all logic, he holds Israel's election as a non-exceptional relationship in order that a universal message might be conveyed. 'Adonai is Lord of all peoples' and it is not that Israel has an exceptional status, since the divine Kingdom is universal. Eminently fitting as this inclusiveness is, the question remains how it belongs with the 'bridal' analogy valid only for Jewry. Where, when and how were the nations offered the same dignity? Where, when and how is it known that they refused unless their paganism, often in fact sacramental in its sense of nature's 'mystery', alone signalled refusal?[34] Could the Judaic 'necessity' of 'Gentiles' be simply counter-partnering Judaic election, whether the criteria be ethnic or ethical? Or, in other terms, must election mean, either that an ethnic covenant is uniquely capable *qua* ethics, or that an ethical capability proves to be uniquely located ethnically? Or must the concept of 'the Gentiles' be an abiding riddle?

Chapter Five

THROUGH JESUS TO A
HUMAN INCLUSION

I

Scholars – Jewish, Christian and secular – have been minded to dispute it. Yet it happened, and happened, not by some invading zeal of 'Gentiles' clambering to be admitted, but by an inner decision of a wholly Jewish apostolate in the birth years of Christianity. Reasons for demur about the fact of it and – more – for its origins in Jesus will concern the story in the very telling and can be assessed afterwards. While it would be doubtful to describe Jesus as 'the founder of Christianity',[1] it would be more inapt to form some gibe to read that 'Jesus preached the kingdom of God and what ensued was the Church'. The point in those two phrases is better told by saying that 'the one consolidates the excellence of the other',[2] though we must add that, in long sequence to Constantine, the Church all too tragically betrayed its Jesus-genesis. It is what happened in the quarter century after the Passion of Jesus with which the Church's history is first concerned. It is intimately bound into his own story.

What happened, in seemingly haphazard manner with only a gathering conviction not a fanfare of trumpets, lay in how what they were telling about 'Messiah crucified' had so changed the whole Messianic theme that it not only could, but must, extend itself to 'Gentiles'. These were already drawn towards what Jewry had as 'proselytes', i.e. 'enquiring seekers', but deterred, for the most part, by the repellent ritual of circumcision which insisted on leaving its hallmark on their very flesh. The possibility of a Judaic 'connection' without that barbarity was the more appealing for its very tolerance of their susceptibilities.

Far more attractive than this negative gain were the great positives that said, in effect: 'You also may have fellowship with us' as ours is 'with the Father and His Son Jesus Christ'. The first initiative was the more reassuring for its very spontaneity, with no grudging element as from a half reluctant source. That clear note of the New Testament Letters and their wide, non race-directed destinations makes them appropriately bound into one Scripture with the Gospels those communities needed and ensured in the wake of that Gentile expansion. It is precisely this dual shape of the New Testament literature as we have it that warrants, and indeed demonstrates, where the mind of that epistolary world had its origin, namely in the Ministry of Jesus – the theme of the Gospels.

II

Deferring any case-making that might claim to counter this perception, explicit refutation is surely there in the Jesus we have from the evangelists. His words, we might say, 'sufficed to compel the recognition they preceded',[3] so that the repute the early Church gave to him he had himself created. We could well begin with those Beatitudes – well-known as their idiom 'Blessed be . . . ' not the 'Cursed' of other traditions. How gently out of all tribalism they are and capable of being everywhere morally descriptive. 'Blessed are the meek . . . ', 'the hungry after righteousness', 'the makers of peace . . . ', all in sharp contrast with 'Blessed be He, Lord God of our fathers and blessed are we the sheep of His hand . . . '. The Benedictions of the sermon discount, or otherwise defy, all nationality. For they are qualities whose incidence is not racial but moral, selective only on the will to heed their claim and know their logic. One does not need first to ask what race or language these 'blest ones' have. It suffices that they belong and move within the human world where they would not be who they are if they practised separatist ends and means. It is not only that they are inclusively described but also that their descriptives happen only in the doing and the living. Later in Matthew 5 the sermon has its: 'Be ye therefore inclusive (*teleioi*) as your heavenly Father . . . ' who is proven so in 'sending his rain on just and unjust alike . . . ' – a lesson reinforced in the same context by call to end the habit of restrictive greeting.[4]

What is so evident about the Beatitudes belongs also with the parables and their familiar formula: 'A certain man . . . ' One need not stay to ask: 'Is he Jew or "Gentile"?' Errant sons, clever usurers and lavish hosts are types all races know and come with sundry skins. 'What man of you?' is no flourish of rhetoric but a straightforward appeal to what any culture can appreciate and any folk link with their own. Only so was parable a teaching method, relying on a common stock of shared experience where radical new meanings might find hearing precisely because analogy had immediate register. When the first disciples stretched themselves towards 'Gentiles' they had ample impulse from the teaching Jesus, though it took more than his verbal medium to bring them to it.

There was never any Christian doubt as to the Jewishness of Jesus. How could there be when the Messianic concept lay at the very heart of Christian story and its New Testament document took it squarely and tenderly into Galilee and Jerusalem with unmistakably Hebrew idioms and memories? What manner of Jew has always been the vital question. Had he not deeply transformed by his preaching some of the root concepts of his own Jewish heritage? He spoke of God in terms that both inherited and left behind the covenantal privacies. These were widened into 'your heavenly Father' in terms that drew on the ultimate faith in a created order, where the flowers of the field or the ravens in the air had a significance prior to the thunders of Sinai and the 'pillar of cloud' conveying only 'chosen' ones to a 'promised land'. The land itself was read for its evidences in sowing and reaping, grazing and harvesting, as yielding meanings for the soul that could incorporate all and sundry in their open benison. In this way Jesus gave new measure to the land's 'promise'.

Covenantal tokens of God's mercy were thus read more in nature than ethnic story with the latter enclosed in the former. There was more than a hint of the perceptions Hosea had around 'corn and wine and oil,' as inviting the Jewish mind to 'inread' their own land-theology as eminently valid beyond its immediate Mosaic/Davidic setting when read inside its own Biblical doctrine of divine creation and world-wide human creatures. It would be fair to guess that this vision had imaginative source in Galilee itself, a cosmopolitan region of both rustic charm and deep social bitterness. 'One there is who knows . . . forgives . . . numbers your hairs . . . ' – that Aramaic formula so characteristic of Jesus – was both a reading of its landscape and a solace in its struggles.

There is no need to stress in Jesus' teaching a feel for the despised Samaritans with whom strict Jews 'had no dealings'. It took its place in his identification with those whom legal, ritual or social directives excluded from the society and the compassion of the duly righteous. His openness even to the 'renegade Jew' – that perpetual query around inviolable covenant – stood as strong precedent for how his apostles could duly reach towards 'Gentiles'. For his – and their – contemporaries knew only too well the analogy readily made between wayward Jews and 'Gentiles'. In his time and place, as zealots saw it, there was no more dastardly 'renegade-ness' than in a tax-gather for the Roman oppressor. The stories of the call of Matthew and the will Jesus had for the hospitality of Zaccheus served as clear warrant for what would become the behaviour of Paul, Peter and the rest towards such 'lesser breeds'. 'The new wine' of Jesus thesis about God burst the skins of the 'old bottles'.[5]

It is important to note, for example in Luke 15, how innovative, in these terms, Jesus was. Those three parables of the lost things, sheep, coin, son, are about how God acts and responds, and are directed by Jesus explicitly to Jewish authority countering both his teaching and his behaviour in those 'your heavenly Father' terms. He is responding to the charge of 'receiving sinners' which witnesses eloquently to the truth of him precisely in disputing it so pointedly. The early Church had no problem in replicating him and disavowing its own critics labouring the same charges. Indeed there is so much about the first Christians that replicates what had ensued in Jesus' ministry.

It is therefore no surprise that they were so interested in the past of Jesus or that there is a strong bond between the 'who and how' of Jesus and the theme and temper of the dispersing Church.[6] The story of how all began served to form the mind of what resulted. Its resurrection faith did not work to obscure the character of Jesus in so powerfully shaping its Christology. There is sober ground to say that what happened in Jesus and his ministry must have been of the sort to explain what transpired in – and as – the Christian community.

It was for this sense of things that Robert Browning reached in his poetic way

. . . withdraw your sense from out eternity
Strain it upon time
Then stand before that fact, that life and death,
Stay . . . till it grow the world on you . . .
. . . the Christ in God . . .
Knew first what else you should not recognise.[7]

That way the developed doctrine of 'the Word made flesh' was a truth growing out of historical relationship with the historical Jesus. The Resurrection established around him a people of a realized hope. He was one who taught a vision of God's people which his disciples came to embody in the community of faith about his divine significance as first expressed in what he preached. The heart of that preaching was a theme about God as One whose concern was with sinful humanity – a concern Jesus both revealed and made real alike in deed and word. It was the same concern from which the Church, in historic faith, drew its clue to the meaning both of his person and his death. 'God was in Christ' either way.

III

Faith did so only in the context of Messianic hope ambiguously at work and at stake in the immediate story. Here too the story in its immediacy and the faith of the Church in its emerging are integral, the one to the other. The Passion narratives, as we know them in the Gospels, write themselves in the setting of the early Church gathering round 'bread and wine' in cultic meditation around the grimly redeeming death of their

Master and finding themselves one in its mystery. 'The night in which he was betrayed' shapes their society as a liturgy in being the dire experience of their history. The Passion, ever fact and now ever liturgy, is on either count the impulse to community and its single seal. Where they celebrate is where they originate and where they do both they incorporate.

The Messianic dimension in the Jesus story has been the theme of endless debate, surmise and controversy. There is a sense in which its seeming to be enigmatic was the nature of its authenticity. It could not have been categorically claimed without incurring the endless contradictions about its nature. To 'be the Messiah' was a theme of radical ambiguity that had to be encountered and clarified in the very art of fulfilment. The story of the wilderness 'temptations' traces issues of economic plenty, apocalyptic miracle and political expediency, each of these in potential alliance with the others and fulfilling a confused gamut of hopes. It is illuminating to read their wilderness rejection against the back-drop of the cleansing of the Temple.[8] Jesus associated with the Zealots and, by cleansing the court not climbing the pinnacle, may have minded them to look for their satisfaction in his public action, only the more dramatically to repudiate it. For the entry and the cleansing held a Messianic interpretation of his mission yet disclaiming – in its final issue – the role they wanted him to play. All could be read as powerfully denoting Messiahship while patiently defining how it had to be.

That drama, leading to Gethsemane, if we have it rightly, had its reasons shaping steadily inside the course of his public ministry and stemming both from that ministry's experience and the prophetic imagery of 'the suffering servant'. That the latter was plainly in the thought pattern of the former is evident enough in the narrative as the Gospels offer it.[9] The hostility that Jesus met increasingly, despite the 'gladness' with which the common folk heard him, was so far akin to what the great prophets had known as 'the contradiction of sinners', sinners in high places, in the sins of power, of privilege and of perversity – all representatively human. As centuries before, so now – it was plain that truth in word did not painlessly prosper nor beatitudes persuade into their benediction. The wrongness of the human world does not yield to bearers of its healing word. Of these it exacts a higher cost than mountain sides as pulpits suffice to bear. There is a 'cup my Father gives' that sermons fill but cannot drink.

The 'retreat' of Jesus and his disciples far north to the foothills of Hermon makes, it would seem, a watershed where they confront the logic of a hard-pressed ministry compelling on them the Messianic focus. 'Whom do men, whom do you . . . say that I am?' The question was in no way rhetorical. How could it be in such a crisis? Where is all heading and is a suffering Messiahship what must be read there as its whole purport? The scene is loaded with the presentiment of Messiah's destiny, blunderingly hailed by Peter and sternly otherwise defined by Jesus' acceptance of his words: 'Thou art the Christ,' with the striking, immediate confidence about 'the Church' which will ensue to perpetuate the meaning.

It may be that the narrative only registers some *post facto* distortion in the guilt or guile of that perpetuating thing. To probe this will be our duty. If so, however, the *post facto* thing still needs explaining even as a 'prejudicial thing'. For fact it was. The thesis of its mistaken-ness has heavier onus on its hands than does its authenticity, while faith has to love the questions that beset it. For they attend on its prime quality as trust and love.

A Jesus in converse with his disciples wrestling with a Messianic logic discernible in his own ministry is a large part of the meaning of the faith in his Incarnation their long successors reached. For him, and retroactively for them, it was confirmed by the precedent of 'men of sorrows' who carried in their own persons the burden of a wayward world and did so, not out of some martyr complex, or cult of pseudo-grief, but as the price required by their loyalty to truth in the adversities their truth endured. Given the dependability here of the Gospel citations of 'the servant hymns', the language of 'offering', of 'ransom' and being 'set at nought', it is clear that Jesus drew from these precedents the shape of the Messiah his own ministry indicated he must be.

It is evident that the very form of the Passion narratives by the time they came to be 'scripture', drew heavily on the phrasings, even the literal details, with which those earlier prophet-sufferers had been described. The language that became the event's telling was already, as we have seen, the lectionary of the faith's liturgy.[10] What Paul years later would call 'having the mind of Christ' was happening in the very texture of the Gospels reporting the event. This inter-association of the very vocabulary of the prophetic tradition of redemptive suffering with the telling of Jesus crucified surely indicates how the Church saw in them common ground and that its seeing them so could not have happened had they not been reflecting their Lord's own mind – a mind to which they were closer both in time and sympathy than any late maturing scholarship could be.

The disciples at 'the Last Supper', for all their burdened incomprehension in that charged moment, could not fail at length to realize that Jesus had meant them to know his death as redemptive. The aura of the Passover with its timeless Jewish memory of 'salvation' would have them know that he was more than teacher, and no mere wandering charismatic soul who had stumbled into a sorry misadventure at the hands of ill fortune.[11] Rather he was 'Messianic' in the only, the costly, terms of 'new covenant' where 'the blood of his sacrifice was his own'.[12] The proof of that perception on their part was the centrality to their thought, their life, their liturgy and their narration, of that action in 'the bread and wine', in the life of their community. An awe of mystery remains around the person of Jesus, requiring to be searched and theologized by subsequent generations but it returns firmly to his own deed and word and these in their whole Messiah frame of reference inwardly discerned and consciously fulfilled.

IV

Being Messianic in those terms both sufficed and demanded to be taken as an event of universal reach. That was what ensued and ensued as no strange aberration but as the urgent logic born of its own nature and born so in the Jewish soul itself. It surely had to happen. For the old national, ethnic privilege, so long exceptionalized inside an inclusively created order of nature in human tenancy, could properly find itself fulfilled in being freely shared. For those first Judeo-Christians the impulse came from how Jesus had attained to be 'the Christ'. In the terms told in Gethsemane, ensuing on 'the Last Supper' and moving on to the Cross, the Messianic fact took in the human situation in inclusive sinfulness – 'the sin of the world'. It did not take in hand the defeat of Rome and so inaugurate a zealot, ethnic liberation for a Maccabean nationhood. Nor did it calculate on apocalyptic intervention to vindicate a desperate throw of eschatological dice.[13] Nor was it the final bid of desert austerity to unseat the hierarchy of darkness seated in Jerusalem.

In being none of these it was, in its suffering towards redemptiveness inherently set towards a 'de-Gentilizing' of humankind, not as somehow incongruously making all 'Jews', nor as unmaking authentic Jewishness, but as 'opening the kingdom of heaven to all believers' – 'believers' a category, a quality, an identity, capable of de-ethnicized, de-localized access, on the single ground of faith.

Perceiving the logic of 'Messiah-Jesus' to be this way and having this destiny was a wholly Jewish initiative, a generosity of spirit in a Jewish apostolate that read and told it so. There is no evidence in the New Testament that other than Jewish minds or 'Hellenized' Jewry took the crucial first steps of 'Gentile' inclusion. The narrative in Acts is elusive about the details of such a dramatic initiative. 'Men of Cyprus and Cyrene' who had 'preached to Jews only', began to speak to Greeks (Acts 11.19–20). The observation is almost laconic in its noting so pivotal a point in history but already around Stephen, an ardent Jew, tension with Jerusalem was brewing, while Philip beyond Gaza would be engaging with an Ethiopian. Tantalizing as his brevity is, the 'Gentile' narrator, Luke, makes no claim to 'Gentile' part in the implicit reversal of 'to none but Jews only'.

That all was 'native' Jewish impulse – if we may so describe it – is highly important. For the psychic strains in so radical a revision of themselves was no forfeiture but an 'obedience' proved tense indeed, as the sequel showed. Nor was the new perception of an inclusive 'people of God' any betrayal or false constraint. The story of Cornelius is there to show that there was much wistfulness for the opening to come, and come without that indignity of compulsory adult circumcision. But wistfulness was all that 'Gentiles' could bring. According to Acts 15.11, Peter put the matter in careful order: 'We believe that we (i.e. us Jews) will be saved even as they (i.e. Gentiles).' One would have expected the clauses in reverse – 'they' even as 'we'. What Messiah Jesus has inaugurated is not some essentially Jewish reality to which we gratuitously let 'Gentiles' come: it is an inherently inclusive thing which only had a Jewish setting for its nursery. At such a reading only Jewish minds could first arrive, as the great privilege of their unique story. That the mass of Jewry, after the Fall of Jerusalem could not, did not, see it so is the history we have to come to in Chapter 6.

It is precisely that tension which bequeathed itself into the curious tangle that waits for New Testament scholarship today around alleged privacies and openness inside the Gospels. In mind now is not the obviously wide embrace of Beatitude and parable already noted but passages which are – or seem to be – at odds with the range of Jesus ministry. On the one hand, 'I am not sent but to the lost sheep of Israel' and on the other, ' . . . this Gospel preached throughout the whole world' (Matthew 15.24, 26.13 and parallels). The former seems categorical about the geographical range of Jesus' own ministry and the latter presaging the times of the apostles, which would exactly fit the scenario in the Epistles. Or the former could be a test of faith in its immediate context and the latter, conceivably, a reference only to the Jewish diaspora.

It is evident enough that the Gospels were composed out of memories in oral tradition and that these necessarily reflected tensions inside the community itself. Moreover, the writings were from within faith and did not speak out of academic-style detachment from their contents. How could they? Yet, with patience and a due sense of their 'witnessing' role, it is feasible to negotiate these nuances without recourse to the evasive attribution of deliberate distortion,[14] which does scant justice to the overall picture the New Testament presents.

There was ample reason why the ministry of Jesus himself should have been geographically confined. The whole case here is that its universal opening turned on his Passion and was therefore apostolic. The encounter with the 'woman of Canaan' took place in the context of the northern 'retreat' and was for that reason exceptional. It is possible that the exchange was in test of her faith and that Jesus was phrasing the kind of response she was likely to expect from a Jewish rabbi and, thus, the kind of reluctance she would need to overcome. In the event she did have her desire, having risen to the logic with which she had been challenged.[15]

Elsewhere that 'God was able from stones to raise children to Abraham' was hardly the language of an inveterate racial separatist from whom Jesus had accepted baptism (Luke 3.8). Still more to the point was the reference in Jesus' famous sermon in the Nazareth synagogue to 'the widow of Sidon and Naaman the Syrian' that so angered his race-proud listeners' (Luke 4.26–27). There can be no valid reason to doubt that, for all the obvious territorial limits of his mission, there was a more than ethnic wideness to his sympathy – a feature that would be congruent with the homeland of his nurture in 'Galilee of the nations'.[16]

This issue of whether an open Church and Jesus in his ministry and Passion belong truly together leads on to the other debated question, namely whether that nascent Church really cared about its Jesus origins which some allege it ignored in its 'Gentile' pre-occupations. It seems an odd notion, given the very existence of the Gospels. These, to be sure, bear the influences of the world of the Epistles – the world that wanted them. Yet the perspectives dispersion brought in no way detract from their character as 'Gospels' rooted in a narrative and in no way treatizes of abstraction. The Epistles, though redolent of Jesus, are not themselves aiming to do the work they left to Gospellers – work proceeding meanwhile by oral memory and formation. They were pastoral ministries of nurture, serving scattered communities under sharp pressures and only lately learning to be 'Christian'. There is no argument calling in question 'inclusion through Jesus' to be sanely drawn from the dual character of the New Testament as documenting Jesus and shepherding the churches by pastoral correspondence.

A crucial and much misread passage in 2 Corinthians 5.16, where Paul writes about 'not knowing Christ after the flesh', has been taken to imply that Paul – and others – were disinterested in Jesus in Galilee and Judea. The plain import of the passage is quite other. It might be paraphrased:

> Truly we had worldly ideas of Messiah but we do not think that way any more. In Messiah now there has been what is entirely new. The old order of ideas Messianic has passed away: a new one has come about.

'Christ', better 'the Christ', was still for Paul and his generation a title, an office, and not yet only a personal name. 'The Christ and him crucified' was the heart of Paul's Gospel. The one crucified had only been so out of the travail of the active ministry. Paul, therefore, is in no dissociating from the reality of Jesus nor is he disowning interest in 'the earthly flesh', i.e. the manner of man that Jesus was. By 'once knowing him after the flesh' he is referring, not to acquaintance with Jesus *in situ*, but to the nationalist ideas of Messiahship, zeal for which had first so enraged him against the (for him as Saul) monstrous claims about a crucified Christ.

So read, his words do not foreclose the possibility – much debated – that Paul did actually see or hear Jesus in the flesh. Much depends on how we interpret his 'sitting at the feet of Gamaliel'. His role, according to Luke in Acts, in the events around Stephen would indicate that he had local and personal reach into the aura, if not the immediacy, of Jesus' story. His sense of being 'out of due time' as an apostle meant only that he had not companied with Jesus inside the intimate commission the disciples enjoyed. His apostolicity needed what only the Damascus road had bestowed but that commissioning vision may well have rekindled awareness of Jesus he had once, if remotely, possessed and, thanks to a Messianic affirming Church, was then passionately denouncing. For 'the heavenly vision' answered his desperate question with the personal name – 'I am Jesus.'[17]

It could hardly be that his whole 'obedience' to what the vision meant could be indifferent to the name on which it turned. While Paul's Letters were not involved in telling the story of Jesus' ministry there is ample evidence of its presence. Acts 20.25 has Paul telling the elders in a solemn moment at Miletus, the Ephesian port, to 'remember the words of the Lord Jesus'.[18] This he was himself steadily doing. The portraiture of love in 1 Corinthians 13 draws heavily on the Beatitudes and the character of Christ. What Paul has to teach the Corinthians about 'things clean and unclean', whether in ritual vessels or around 'idol meats', is clearly in debt to that of Jesus on the same theme. He claims that he is 'persuaded by the Lord Jesus' (Romans 14.14). Romans 12.14 echoes Matthew 5.44 and 1 Thessalonians 5.14, Matthew 5.39. His favourite parting words: 'The grace of our Lord Jesus Christ . . . ' surely include the benison of 'the grace with which he (Jesus) spoke' (Luke 4.22) no less than the drama of the Passion on which – and only after its significance could be understood – so much of Paul's own reading turned.

It is odd if not tendentious, therefore, that any case should have been developed somehow to decry the universal logic of Jesus' ministry and teaching by alleging indifference to these when the Church found itself incorporating 'Gentiles' in equal fellowship with Jews, or that 'Gentilizing' was somehow inconsistent with them. It is true that the Gospels are 'Passion narratives with antecedent preface', if we wish to phrase it so, but without the teaching there would have been no Passion and without their unity no Gospels. The fact of Gospels is the very demonstration of that unity and, with it, 'the mind of Christ' accomplished in the open Church.

V

It surely had to happen a grateful world would have need to say, in retrospect. Yet how problematic, even traumatic, it seemed to contemporaries on either side of the divide in Jewry which it occasioned. It was the

Jewishness of Jesus – always undoubted – via the Jewishness of his own disciples that gave being and shape to a wider 'Israel of God'. Like other dramatic movements in human history immediate details are less clear than the deeply operating factors. 'Some acts of some apostles' as that linking New Testament document set between Gospels and Letters had better been called, handles the drama with studied inattention until the initiative of embracing uncircumcised 'Gentiles' required debate in a Council in Jerusalem – a council that strangely focuses on dietary directions of a ritual kind rather than lauding a great venture with a salute of triumph. That very reticence may be significant as if a latent propriety had instinctively been sensed.

There was no doubt, however, about their 'ye shall do well', and the confident formula: 'It seemed good to the Holy Spirit and us . . . ' – not to the one without the other. There is the clear point to be made of apostolic authority approving, set however inside the only final warrant that mattered. It was, we must assume, a wholly Jewish Council and it was located in Jerusalem to which outspreading reach properly returned. Acts, to be sure, is a very far from comprehensive narrative and it may be urged that we do not hear adequately from the dissenting parties.

Even if these are not presented in the text with their own grounds and fears, there is no doubt of the divisive issue present in and for the Jewishness of all participants. It is plain in the struggle Paul and his kin underwent in working out the implications for both past and future. The inner conflict is witness to how radical the experience was. Could privilege be understood as, not foregone but shared, not forfeit but fulfilled? Was it appropriate to the inclusive Lordship behind creation and the human scenario that one people, one land, one testament should stay perpetually unmediated, precluded from ever extending its experience of divine vocation to those outside its birth and language? Ought it be for ever 'dwelling alone' in the mystery that was most decisive for its very quality, the enjoyment of its central destiny an abiding *non sequitur* for all else on the same human earth? Its thoroughly Jewish identity, despite the tension of its new interpretation, was clear from the sustained retention of Jewish psalmody, vocabulary and liturgical example. The very name of 'Christian' witnessed to its standing within the Messianic context. Doubtless the very tenacity of its Jewish frame of reference antagonized the more the Jewry that disavowed it. But these could have no complaint against the 'Gentilizing' as putting at risk the moral principles of the Torah. The New Testament Letters were diligent in the care for these against the odds of erstwhile pagan custom and habit.

In the last analysis disavowal, when it became convinced and near final, turned on that perception of Messiahship on which the Jewish Revolt hinged in the late sixties of the founding century. It was a revolt in which Christian Jews refused to share. For it was a signal verdict against the

Messiahship the new faith believed that Jesus had achieved. By a tragic irony, it was the trauma of dispersion after the Fall of Jerusalem that clinched the Jewish disclaimer of the Jewish validity of the nascent Church. It is idle to speculate how different the future of the Christian 'Jew/Gentile' inclusion might have been had the loss of the Temple not hastened Jewry, via the sages of Yavneh, into renewed consolidation around Torah and synagogue. So it was that two diasporas proceeded together, that of old Jewry dispersing from Jerusalem, and that of the apostolic Church fulfilling its perceived destiny – as Paul had it – 'from Jerusalem round about to Illyricum' with Rome beyond.[19] Yet a poet might discern some justice in their co-incidence, given the contrasted concepts of Messiah on which each moved, namely political liberation from Rome and 'Messiah Jesus crucified'.

It was the Passion of Jesus, read as the climax of his preaching mission, and the realization of the ancient hope, which translated into the human open-ness of the Church. Later in his retrospect, the fourth evangelist would state that case in the words his perspective could give to Jesus: 'If I be lifted up, I will draw all to me.'[20] The 'all' had to do, not with some compulsive salvation but an accessible one, in that faith would be the only, the available, pre-requisite. For, in its distinctive quality, the Johannine Gospel presents its narrative of a Jesus, as it were, already in the throes of where the Church came to be in relating with the – by then – non-acceding Jewry in their counter thesis. Such was the evangelist's authorial genius in seeing so skilfully that the sort of Rubicon Jesus, as the Christians believed, had required Jewry to cross occurred inside his ministry but as one they would have to take only in the sequel to his Passion and the coming-to-be of the Church.[21]

Hence that Gospel's structure as a succession of encounters in which initial incidents, calculated to arouse them, pass into discourses enshrining the Christology the writer's faith-community had reached. So, from Nicodemus to the 'man born blind', as 'occasion' for the discourses, the Christ of faith's theology speaks as in the Jesus situation where all historically belonged, but belonged with the destiny that theology understood. Only so can the fourth Gospel be intelligently understood, as holding in one, that story had led to a faith and that a faith had issued from a story and that these under-wrote each other. It is thus a deeply Jewish Gospel owing everything both to its Jewish loyalty and to the new dimensions to which it believed that loyalty had been called. The situation in the discourses was supremely told in the Prologue and renewed again in the long pre-Passion converse with the disciples, culminating in the Messianic testament – as we may well think it – in the prayer of Chapter 17 with its meditative summation of incarnate mission, so contrasted with the Gethsemane of the Synoptics.

The fourth Gospel is often seen as 'anti-Semitic' but, in truth, the reflective perceptions of the writer serve to clarify how enriching to both parties was the fusion of things Aramaic with those of the Greek tradition flowing from the Jew/'Gentile' incorporation in Christ.[22] Nowhere is this more evident than in its 'baptism' of the *Logos* concept. That Greek sense of a principle of order and rationality by which the real is the humanly intelligible was knit in one with the *dabar* of Hebrew faith. 'By the word (*dabar*) of the Lord were the heavens made' (Psalm 33.6) could be known as one with 'the Word was made flesh and tabernacled in our midst' (John 1.14). The imperative 'Be' of creation as divine handiwork thus became the 'indicative' verb of divine initiative in the Christ-event, joining the rational intelligibility of external nature with the place of historical disclosure of divine nature, so that the imperative behind our existence could be known in its quality as love and grace. So much was told in 'the Word made flesh'.

This *dabar/logos* – imperative/indicative – fusion of the Hebrew/Greek idiom made possible by the Jew/'Gentile' inclusion in Christ becomes the clearest index to many other discoveries of inter-relevance that took shape in the refining of Christian Christology. There is no need to regard, still less to deplore, this as some unhappy aberration from Hebraic loyalty or some blatant 'paganizing' of that pure monotheism.[23] The deep Biblical theme of divine 'agency', tasks humanly fulfilled on behalf of YAHWEH by His warrant and intent, was everywhere evident in patriarch, psalmist and prophet. That necessary 'humanism' of divine action in history was then concentrated and intensified in the Hebraic/Greek understanding of the personhood of Christ as the culminating and inclusive instance worthy to be formulated in the term 'God in Christ'. Here was no treachery to every instinct of the Jewish mind, only that mind in a new intensity of conviction, suitably aided by extra-Jewish thinking to mutual enrichment. Jew/'Gentile' inclusion in 'the body of Christ' proved to be, or become, a profound inclusion of their capacities of mind.

VI

Even so, the step which, according to Luke, was so unobtrusively taken by those nameless ones 'of Cyprus and Cyrene', proved occasion of great searchings of heart on either side of the divide. It would be unwise to take those of Paul the apostle as our sole index, central as the New Testament allows him to be in their exploration. On the withholding side, it seems clear that, by the seventies, the major factor was the material one of the forfeiture of the Temple and the partial physical exile from Hebraic norms. As noted earlier, an instinctive tendency to close ranks in self-defence or traditional self-conservation heavily conditioned Jewry against the 'new Israel' vision of their destiny. If only the initiative had been differently timed in their story, how different their response might have been. Or perhaps not. The Revolt, maintaining the Maccabean theme, had been a political assertion of Jewry as 'nation' while the nascent Christianity was none such. Rome had not been religiously harsh with Judaism. Reprobate procurators like Pilate might provoke it by their vagaries but it was a *religio licita* and need not have forfeited either its Jerusalem or its peace. But in demanding to be political, discontent with spiritual expression alone, it saw itself radically crippled. The Rabbis, salvaging all they could from that catastrophe, could hardly have accommodated what the Church proposed. In the meantime, in the decades between the Passion and loss of the Temple, the tensions that exploded in the Revolt were brewing ominously around the issue the Church presented. Whatever may be claimed from auspicious Roman roads and rule in fostering the 'Gentile' spread of Christianity, Jewish relations with Rome had decidedly adverse consequences for the hope of Jewish membership.

That contemporary circumstance only makes what actually happened on 'human inclusion' in open terms the more remarkable. Noteworthy within the New Testament writings, as indicating how a Christian Jewishness might express its new integrity, was the Letter to the Hebrews by an unknown, but clearly well versed, author. There is no doubting his Jewishness through images and analogies steeped in his defining world though remote from his readers now. Nor is there any question as to his point of departure from the suffering ministry of Jesus – the Christ 'who learned obedience in that he suffered'.[24] He appeals to a Christ crucified but enshrines that redemptive event in the imagery of Jewish priesthood 'entering the holiest' where the living cost of that event 'pleads' in the divine presence, not as to non-participatory remoteness but by what is already the divine self-expression. The 'sacrifice' that was anciently involuntary (as of an animal) and endlessly repeated in perennial ritual, is the 'priest's' from himself and belongs 'once and for all' in the time setting of the Cross.

The Letter, further, is able to recruit Abraham to exemplify how 'faith justifies' and the age-long Sabbath to foreshow the 'rest of the people of God'. The Letter is telling witness to how the 1st century Jewish mind could read, and fulfil, a total Jewish loyalty inside the new inclusive community the pioneers had ventured to embrace. The conviction they shared that the Temple, as 'the place of the Name' (whether or not still standing), had been succeeded by Jesus as the Christ. Therefore, in worship and sacrament and offering 'the tribes would go up', as to one in the midst where-ever they gathered 'in his Name'. And with the Temple went the cherished Jewish theme of the necessity of 'the land'. In the words of W. D. Davies, 'the territorial chrysalis of Christianity was broken open'.[25] The shore of Philistia at Yavneh would still be in 'the land' for the sages from Jerusalem rallying round the Torah and the synagogue while a dispersing Christianity could tell a theological loosening from territory by its very travels. Ties would remain in sentiment and heart, but they would express themselves in 'church aid' for 'the poor saints at Jerusalem'.[26]

It is in the personality of Saul/Paul that we encounter most intensely the issues belonging with Jewish participation in the open nature of the Church as derived from Jesus' ministry and the Christ-event to which it led. They are all present in the struggles of his emotions and his mind – the uniqueness and inviolability of the 'covenant', the writ of election, the irreversibility of the cultic law and its relation to the moral law, the reach of evil and the crux of redemption.

Such are the tensions that we find him positing a temporary withholding from faith on the part of his people, in order to 'let the Gentiles in', and the expectation of a later mass accession to faith of Jewry – thus contravening his own principle of deeply personal faith-decision. In Galatians he is even ready to read in 'the bondwoman Hagar' analogy for Sinai and the sacred law of Abraham's proper children. In the same Letter – against the grain of the Jewish 'seed' theme he so prized – he argues that 'Gentile' faith made 'children of Abraham', despite a 'promise' limited to Jews which could never be made 'of none effect'. He reconciles the paradox by pleading that the 'promise' to Abraham and his proper 'seed' was fulfilled in the faith each and all had in Jesus. In Romans he sees 'Gentiles' as 'branches broken off a wild olive tree', to be 'grafted into the 'good' Judaic tree (though evil by nature) to have the good sap infuse their in-grafted ones, though he has earlier included 'all under sin'. If the Holy Spirit at times lets his zeal disorganize his grammar, the same could be said of his logic.

All, however, is only a measure of how radically he strove with his 'Gentile' inclusive vocation to square it with inviolate election – an election which, for him in his apostolate, was also to be 'the minister to Gentiles'. That dual 'election' was the very core of his significance, as epitomizing in his own person that pain of the inclusion he served.

Perhaps the surest and most decisive dimension of his Christ-experience was his perception of 'the law as our pedagogue to bring us to Christ' (Galatians 3.24) – how its claim and its accusation of our failure denied us any truancy from the reality of evil.[27] In this way it was the very tenacity of his Jewishness – as explored in Romans 7 – that educated him in the central conviction of the new community, namely the utter necessity of redeeming grace in the converting of human nature. It was a truth from which no 'election' gave exemption. So it warranted and properly demanded a universal telling, the telling to which he was superbly dedicated. By the same token, there remained an abiding debt to the 'closedness' which had stayed potential of that realist education.[28]

For, though the law could only direct, accuse and condemn and not of itself redeem, humans would be in worse case without it. Its claims were truth's tribute to our calling and our dignity as meant for more than lust, envy, jealousy, pride, wrong and all the other sins which it identified and reproached. Thus, 'by the law came the knowledge of sin', yet not, via the law, the undoing of that 'knowledge'. It was this realization of the law's whole nature as disclosing the universally human situation of a moral vocation we inclusively 'fall short of' (and that culpably) which made Paul aware that no people were in privileged possession of its custody and none exempt from its indictment. For 'all had sinned and fallen short'. Paul's perception of the inclusiveness of Jesus and his energy in serving it in mission were the very logic of the realism about 'immoral humanity' for ever underlined in the Cross of Jesus – 'immoral', that is, not in any absence of law but precisely in the entire need of grace which law made so darkly evident.

That case was in no way quashed by the charge of 'anti-nomianism' often made against Paul. He was not against the law, only against the notion that law was all we needed. His sense of the indispensability of grace gave no occasion for wild doctrines of license to sin or of exoneration in wrong by absolving the soul while giving the body free range. No 'antinomian' would have struggled so earnestly for the moral probity and careful discipline of 'all the churches'.

The other deep significance of Paul is that his sense of mission to the 'Gentiles' came directly from 'God in Christ according to Jesus crucified' and not from a prior re-establishment of Davidic monarchy. This, in turn, radically revised the meaning of election. Many a prophetic vision had seen 'the nations flowing to Jerusalem' once a post-exilic kingdom had been restored. For high-minded Jewish souls were by no means oblivious of the universal debt entailed in their Judaic election. 'The nations', however, would need to await the final ensuring of Jewish hegemony after the pattern of 'the son of David', re-enacting the legend of their story's greatest poet-statesman.[29]

In Messiah Jesus crucified that expectation had been replaced. What so differently fulfilled it had not forfeited the vocation to the 'Gentiles' the prophets had nobly envisaged. It had simply achieved in it quite unexpected terms. Election as 'the blessing of the nations', far from being abandoned, was the more splendidly made good. In this way Paul could the more confidently find himself a loyal Jew. There was one other transformation of which he became also the symbol. It was that, whereas 'the nations would flow' to Jerusalem to shelter under the Davidic wing,[30] as indeed without it proselytes were already doing by ethical attraction alone, the Jesus thing would go out to 'fetch them home'. It would be world-seeking, as possessing a centre ready to take itself everywhere, as Paul did until his ecumenism made him a prisoner. Only then, under house arrest, did his hearers have to come to him. In this re-reading of the continuing mystery of election there was one notion he would have vigorously resisted, namely the popular one now current that Christianity was 'God for Gentiles only', or that somehow his reach into these and their world meant that Jews, the midwives of all else, were exempt from their own destiny. How could they be if, precisely when they were fulfilling it, they ceased to be present with it? To that notion of 'the two covenants' we have to come in Chapter 9.

There is a strange irony about the role of dispersion in the forming of faith. If, as we have seen, Christian inclusion derived from apostolic – and Jewish – perception and acceptance of Messiahship according to Jesus, then a readiness for the world, and journeying into it, were a due and right obedience. With its land and people vintage, the Judaic could only grieve over its physical and spiritual state of exile. For YAHWEH's 'foundation' was 'on mountains of holiness He loves' (Psalms 87.1–2). In the Apocalypse of Baruch (1xxxv.3) that grief finds typical tongue:

> We have gone forth from our land and Zion has been taken from us and we have nothing now save the Almighty and His law.

Into that world 'harsh and strange' our study has now to pass. Yet all that rabbinic Judaism contrived to be in its landlessness as 'only a people with a faith' might at length be seen to have been the definitively ultimate Jewish reality, despite the final despair of Zionism about any hope that was not in 'the land'. The next chapter has to explore that grieving yet achieving condition of Jewry in diaspora. Its long centuries and what issued from it at the turn of the 20th enshrine the age-long paradox of Semitism.[31]

Chapter Six

'THIS WORLD HARSH
AND STRANGE'

I

I can see no fruit in all their faith
But malice, falsehood and excessive pride.

A 17th century verdict about the Christian from Christopher
Marlowe's Barabbas in *The Jew of Malta*. By the late 19th century,
despite many yeas of 'emancipation' and an 'enlightenment', the
movement for political Zionism echoed the same verdict. In his *Der
Judenstaat*, Theodor Herzl, its first driving force, showed himself
convinced that the 'Gentile' world had long proved, and would always
remain, incorrigibly perverse in an irreversible anti-Jewishness where only
two impossible options existed for its Jewish victims. These were either
the recurrent jeopardy of persecution or an ultimate extinction by assimilation into non-Jewish culture and society.

Political Zionism, therefore, must insist on creating and pursuing a
third option, namely a virtual Jewish evacuation from the 'Gentile' world
into an autonomous nationalism which could resolve both sides of the
equation as a 'final solution'. By withdrawal from the hostile world 'harsh
and strange', Jewry would disembarrass it of their unwanted presence
and, by the same token, rescue itself from its implacable menace. Herzl's
theme might be read as a gesture of despair about any sustainable humanitas at least in respect of Judaic humankind.

We must reach in two following chapters the problematics around this
radical conclusion. The Nazism which would tragically underscore it still
lay two score decades away. In the eighteen-nineties there were intimations but for the majority of Herzl's immediate generation in Jewry his
clarion call seemed unconvincing. It was then a minority verdict that had
to promote itself in pioneer terms amid a Jewishness either apathetic or

sceptical as to its logic or its feasibility. For many it looked dangerously inimical to what they needed, as Jews, to prove as genuine 'nationals' inside the nations of their diaspora. The course of the story of Zionist case-making belongs later.

The point meanwhile is this founding perception in Zionism of an incurable incompatibility of the Judaic and the 'Gentile' in the same human society as history and the diaspora had made grimly clear. For Jewish experience to be 'involved in mankind', as 'mankind' when relating to Jews had persistently showed itself to be, had to be discerned as a failed story, a narrative of steady threat to authenticity.

In a strange way it could be said that this situation as to 'the fruit in all their faith,' proven in a 'world harsh and strange', tallies – if only ironically – with the founding perception of the New Testament. It is therefore the right place at which to begin in that Testament's relation to Jewish experience as Zionism read its people-history.

For a perception of 'sin' belonging to an entire world as something inveterate in society had been at the very heart of the New Testament text. 'The sin of the world', not attributable exclusively to any one sector, was the key to the Gospel that turned on the Passion of Jesus as the Christ. It was how the fourth Gospel diagnosed our common humanity, the human world in which he and his 'Beatitudes' could come to crucifixion. That story meant a steady realism about the human capacities for wrong, a strong scepticism, not unlike that of Zionist Jewry, about the range of human benevolence. If Semitism, in painful truth, was about this fact of suffering at human hands as 'the people of God', could God with His people be exempt from it?[1] Surely the way Zionism argued from things tragic in being Jewish at the hands of things evil in humans at large bore strong resemblance to how the Gospel read the wrongness of the world evident in the Gethsemane of Jesus.

The long siege of the Jewish soul and society should then be read as corroborating, in is own way, the radical realism about the human situation at the heart of Christianity. It is, then, the more strange that Christian faith should have been so far incriminated as the responsible source of the long Jewish tribulation from which Zionism sought its political remedy.

There was nothing 'anti-Semitic' in the deeply Semitic context in which that faith was brought to pass, nor any mandatory anti-Judaism in the genesis of Christianity. The impulse it had towards 'all nations' meant no exemption of the Jewish people. For in their very midst that impulse came.[2] On the contrary, Jewry had priority both in the initiative and its outreach. What later eventuated could perhaps best be explained as a mutual 'hardening of the heart',[3] explaining both the strictures in the Johannine Gospel and the maledictions in the Talmud.

This is in no way to exonerate the sharpness of John's Gospel in its equation between unbelief and sin and its perception of certain kinds of

Jews as of 'their father the devil'. Nor should it be forgivable because the Talmud reciprocated. The tensions were harshly mutual. John's reference to 'expulsion from the synagogue' (9.22) has echo in the Talmud where, also, Jewish Christians were seen as traitors and Jesus as 'a deceiver of Israel'. Its references to him were notably few, but also hostile, making him the bastard son of a Roman soldier named Panthera, and one who learned pseudo-miracles in Egypt by magic. He had been legally executed and his body had been stolen by his disciples who then invented a story about resurrection.

The intelligent student of the fourth Gospel has, then, to reckon with this mutual antipathy – not to extenuate either party but patiently to understand their situation. Its readers, like the community from which it derived, were still 'illicit' under the Roman rule, in contrast to the 'licit' nature of Jews in their Judaism.[4] The long and painful cost of Jewish powerlessness, the collective peril of 'contempt', still lay ahead, while in the first four Christian centuries a nascent Church, venturing into the untried perils of 'Gentile' inclusion, had strenuous pastoral tasks and exacting doctrinal themes with which to engage. The sharp animus of the Johannine Gospel has to be appraised in this context.[5] The preaching of the Cross was always insistently inclusive and its reproach was on 'the sin of the world' there epitomized, not on the 'sin' of 'these' or 'those' who happened to be around. It was never – for the New Testament – 'who' crucified Jesus, but always 'what'.[6]

It follows that there has to be, for each and all, an 'unhardening of the heart', seeking neither palliatives nor denunciations and avoiding myopic judgements.[7] It has been all too easy to want, either to circumvent anti-Semitic guilt or to join it too cavalierly with Christian faith. As with all deep issues the telling of their story becomes party to their passionate confusion. What is denied can too often be a hidden clue to what we resent. 'Gentile' inclusion being the crux of the story, John G. Grager, in *The Origins of Anti-Semitism*, elides it by insisting that

> for Christianity in its early stages, the real debate was never between Christians and Jews but among Christians. Eventually the anti-Jewish side won.[8]

Were there, then, no Jewish apostles ever? Was the Letter to the Romans only about 'internal' Christian debate with pagans? Could the Letter to the Hebrews belong to any 'anti-Jewish side'? Or 'winning' when it was so deeply reverential inside its Hebrew ethos?

Or, contrastedly, a Christian authorship for which

> The fateful causal relation between the Christian message and the death camps of Europe becomes manifest . . . The Shoah teaches the moral bankruptcy of the teaching of the Suffering servant.

Thus 'the resurrection contributes to the death of countless children'. A risen Christ yields an ideology of Jewish victimization.[9] Or again, a categorical verdict that 'Christians have been anti-Semitic because they have been Christians. (It) is part of what it means to be Christian.'[10]

These and similar voices of the ever categorical mood need an unhardening of the heart to control the blatancy in the mind. What may help to understand this is the fact – urgently to be stressed – that neither anti-Semitism nor Semitism have any credible meaning or existence if we are thinking in terms of the biological theory preached in the Aryan mythology of 'race' when the 'anti-' term was first made current.[11] For such theory of 'superior' and 'inferior' races, determined so by the biological factor, has no scientific legitimacy and no moral authority. It is the wilful fantastic.

The reasons for phobia and hatred of Jewry, in group or collective terms (i.e. not of persons who happen to be Jews but essentially for the reason that they are Jews), were socio-religious in their origin and character. By their socio-religious nature they certainly arrived also to be deeply ethnic, given the place that Hebrew religion itself devoted to the ethnic factor, the 'us and our children' theme reaching back to Abraham and Exodus. In a subtle way, this made the collective more vital than the individual member and somehow kindled a response that insistently engaged with that collective in ways that disengaged the parties from a self-to-self bond and engrossed it in the corporate 'other'. Thus Jews were 'prejudicial' because they were not 'Gentiles': 'Gentiles' were prejudicial because they were not Jews.

It is impossible to assign unilateral blame for this situation, though anti-Semitism, unknown as the term itself was till the 19th century, insisted on doing so. If we say with Jacob Katz,

> I regard the very presence of the unique Jewish community among the nations as the stimulus to the animosity directed as them,[12]

we have to realize that 'the very presence of the unique' aroused from the mentality of non-Jews a unique hostility, *not* from any objective deserts of Jewry but from what the symbol of 'Jews' signified to non-Jews. That symbol 'collectivized' an identity needing recognition, on its own terms, liable to be denied by what those terms *seemed* to mean to non-Jews. It was a 'Gentile' psychic predicament either way, the incidence of which occupied Chapter 4.

There is a painful sense in which it was all part of a radical, ultimately insoluble, issue of 'unbelief', an 'unbelief' between most Jews and Christians that was of such urgency to each that simply human relationships were occluded, or – if sought at all – could only be nothing more than a nexus for ever conditioned by a religious exclusion, either by the other, from being significantly inter-human.

Rabbinic Judaism, for its part, unlike its briefer Hellenistic phase,[13] did not engage in commendatory apologetic.

> The truth of Jewish teaching and the Jewish way of life was not a subject for argument . . . The Christians continued to be seen as heretics with whom no compromise was possible.[14]

Their Messianic 'pretension' could only be disowned. Jews were even ready to concede that 'they had killed Christ', in the sense that they held, and would for ever hold, dead – and buried – the 'Christian' Jesus and his/their pseudo Messianism.[15]

Post-Constantinian Christianity, for its part, felt itself reckoning, *vis-à-vis* Jewry, with a very specially informed, and therefore, adamant, unbelief in the sheer ruggedness with which Jewry through the centuries maintained its disavowal. Unlike Christian encounter with paganism, Jewry presented a privileged angle, via its Scriptures and its ethos, for which Christian faith could have no response not already refuted by its very content. It is little wonder that the search for human intercourse of mind, even when existent, stood pre-doomed.[16] Yet, finally, something honestly inter-human could be the only hope for either party caught in the mutual exclusions of their respective 'unbelievings'. These were in the making of mental 'ghettos', even before the power realm made a physical one of the Jewish party.[17]

In its gravitational way, history darkly perpetuated the implicit impasse. Once it was clear that Rabbinic Judaism was not consenting to any New Testament reading of its Judaic destiny and anti-Judaic Christian attitudes hardened, the former came to deny everything sustaining Christianity in the time contemporary with Christian origins, while the latter fell to decrying and distorting Jewish piety. Ironically it thus transpired that Christianity was drawn into a presentation, both of itself and Judaism, that obscured the very Jewishness of its own origins. There came to be a kind of self-betrayal, partly doctrinal, guiltily moral, of its own *raison d'être* in Judaic origins, so that the whence and whither of its own truth moved into darkening contradiction.

Nowhere was this more tragic than when polemic developed into the charge of 'deicide'. Angry Jewry might have allowed they had killed a Jesus in their own rationale of what had been, as reportedly in the Gospels, 'expedient'. But no intelligent Christian ever understood the meaning of the Incarnation as 'happening to God', in other terms than of 'God the Son', and of 'God in Christ'.[18] Only the ever transcendent Lord could ever have been 'made flesh' as 'the Word'. 'Deicide' was always unthinkable as a 'crime' for accusation, because it was inconceivable as a fact. 'Deaths of God' were never of that order.[19]

II

Jules Isaac's well-known study, *The Teaching of Contempt*, included the charge of 'deicide' made by Christianity against the synagogue as one on a sevenfold charge sheet. It argued the degenerate nature of Judaism in the time of Jesus, the sensuality of Jews, their culpable rejection of Jesus, their consequent rejection – as Jews – by God, their diaspora as retribution for Jesus' crucifixion and, finally, the demonization of ongoing Judaism.[20] All seven, he argued, could be traced in, or back to, the New Testament and its commentators.

Yet there were important senses in which Judaic/Christian relations owed their contra Jewish harshness to having for 'Bible' a 'canon' purporting to bind two 'testaments' in one. The Church claimed the right to hold Jewry liable for Mosaic law. Much decrying and burning of the Talmud derived from that presumption, inasmuch as Talmud and 'the oral law' were in unwarranted disloyalty, as the Church saw it, to the one lawful Pentateuch. On Jewish part they were the very form of Judaic inner fidelity, responding to experience of exile, in the Babylonian Talmud and to wider diaspora in the Palestine, or Jerusalem, Talmud. The Bible thus tangled the 'alien' communities in their mutual versions of alleged authenticity. The Church could oddly have seen itself as some kind of Josiah or Hezekiah, or an Isaiah calling innovators back 'to the law and the testimony' they were violating. The Christian ill-will in its deeply psychic enmities was nevertheless finding Biblical sanction for its attitude of corrective zeal.

Furthermore, its ongoing register of a prevenient divine purpose in Jewry, albeit now aberrant, meant that up to the 11th century, the Great Schism and the Crusades, official Christian ruling about Jews was one of conditional tolerance – a stance to which Paul's doctrine of a provisionality about Jewish 'unbelief' also strongly contributed. For, if they were one day to have that 'veil' lifted, an implacable persecution would not be sharing in the hope. As Gregory the Great saw it, to harry would 'not be of God'. Thus his 'rule' set the lines of all papal decrees or 'bulls' from early in the 7th to the 12th centuries. It ran:

> Just as license ought not to be allowed for Jews to do anything in their synagogues beyond what is permitted by law, so they ought also to suffer no injury in those things that have been granted to them.[21]

This 'license' to be 'submissively religious' has a strange resemblance to what Islam from that same 7th century would soon impose as the *dhimmi* system, except that Gregory held that there should also be 'persuasion by clear reasoning' whereby to help the wayward 'see the light'.[22] 'Things granted' and 'in their synagogues' were the crucial words' – living on sufferance under law, rearing their young and, under due surveillance, worshipping their Lord and fulfilling their religious Torah, their Sabbaths and their festivals. Given the absence of Jewish monarchy, it was a viability like that commended to exiles a millennium earlier by Jeremiah.

However, as evident even in the 4th century from Ambrose's dealings with Theodosius, official 'tolerance' might be grievously compromised by deviant bishops of local order and by unruly populace using laxity to practice violence. Jewry lived its 'tolerance' in sharp anxiety, being precariously exposed, whether under Islam when it supervened, or under a prejudiced Christendom. Even so, medieval tribulations were of a different order from the state-inspired pogroms of modern Europe, state-instigated as under Russian Tsars, or state-devised genocide of the Nazi-order in the 20th. Medieval mob violence contrived its malice but through the social loopholes too readily left by official policies, until the times of the Crusades.

Biblical perspectives in an ironical way also underwrote that medieval scene. The 'royal priesthood', 'priestly kingship' of the old order with Solomon 'consecrating' the Temple and the people called into kindred 'holiness' corroborated a case, at once imperial and papal. It yielded, via the prophets, the idea of a renegade people somehow made with 'unhearing ears' and self-deceived hearts, which the Church could invoke as explaining what, in churchly eyes, was otherwise inexplicable, namely Jewish failure to see the Christian meaning.[23] Hence again the charge that Jews were 'irrational,' and only obstinately given to their Judaic fidelity. Gregory's norm of 'reasoned persuasion' thus had its obverse, namely the 'insanity' of resisting 'sanity'.

Thus a Christian perversity took false rise from an alleged Judaic one, in the form of 'forced conversion', which – with its malice of mind – had a logic set to overcome what had proved wantonly rejectionist. That dimension of Jewish suffering had a root in the Christian emphasis on the urgency of right belief and the dire consequences of dying in unbelief. When Islam was on the scene the case for an element of force in the best interest of those concerned was partner to the *dhimmi* system.[24] Across the whole medieval stage there were sundry shapes of being 'forced', in simply being vulnerable, inferiorized, humiliated, or otherwise caught in a situation where acceding to the dominant brought respite, if not other advantage. Steadily and harshly, the whole scenario brought bitterness of soul and heavy social burdens to a Jewry shorn of its Temple ritual and scattered landless around an inhospitable world.

Moreover, at centuries' turn, or even otherwise, a register of passing time kept alive another Christian concept that critically affected Jewish fortunes, namely the role of their predicted 'mass conversion' prior to the return of Christ and the Last Judgement. Doctrines differed between Christians as to whether these awaited events were imminent or still a distant matter of patience. Either way, Jewry was drawn into Christian eschatology. If near, the more urgency to induced 'conversion', if far, Jews should at least keep the right to exist as Jews – provided they were kept from bringing Christians over to them – if only as a visible warning against unbelief and as a mysterious factor in apocalyptic hope, if the very climax and end of the world turned on their being brought into the Church.

In 1215 the Fourth Lateran Council laid down guidelines akin to those of Gregory the Great, and by these the western Church remained officially ordered until modern times. They contributed significantly to the emergence of the ghetto as the characteristic feature of Jewish life for long centuries. The decisions aimed to diminish social contact, to lay on Jewish survival criteria of Christian avoidance, save in restricted fields of economic necessity or convenience. Inter-marriage was excluded and Jews could enjoy no status, such as that of employer or official, that gave them any authority over Christians. Jewish worship was circumscribed, for example, by provision against new synagogues with limited repair of existing ones.

The effect was toward social segregation and the growth of an inter-alienation which – as we must see – only scholars with an intellectual or spiritual urge could readily disown. How the Lateran Council's rubrics worked, for ill or good, in the actual experience of Jews depended on unpredictables of the local scene and the attitude of lower clergy. They did nothing to curb the excesses of mob passion and something indirectly to incite them by sharpening a 'less than human' notion such as vulgarity was all too ready to indulge.

Meanwhile, the 11th century forays eastward in the guise of 'Crusades', for all their would-be chivalry, had attracted wild mob action en route and instigated much anti-Jewish emotion in the very act of ostensibly recovering the land of their 'undoing' – as Christendom regarded it. The ghettoizing factor became more marked, in that – in some cases – knightly financing of the Crusading took volunteers to Jewish sources of loans as society's usurers.

Slowly and inevitably the experience of being stressfully isolated both in psyche and community drew Jewry back into tradition in their Scripture, linking things immediate with a far past to identify themselves as age-long sufferers at the hand of human malice. Thus, for example, the Chronicle of Solomon Bar Simon turned in spirit to Psalm 83.12 with its lament of those long before who cried: 'let us take the houses of God in possession' and 'they have said: "Let us cut them off from being a people."'[25] History bitterly seen as re-enacting itself could ultimately bring the deeply wronged into the trauma of self-hatred – such being the way 'a ghetto of the psyche' may afflict the victim soul.

The sense of an inner reproach stemmed from a certain shame at a destiny of passivity. It was greatly intensified in later centuries and supremely as the ultimate burden of the Shoah. Given how the human psyche everywhere reacts, did this 'blame on the victim' also evoke the other feature that reached back into ancient history as that 'Remember Amalek' of Deuteronomy 25.17 – the implacable enemy who worked grim havoc on the wandering ancestors. Such quest into the past to make sense of the present was an abiding feature of Jewish diaspora through all the centuries until the 'emancipation' and then passionately in the will to Zion.

Yet even in the age of the Crusades and Judaic burdens of the 11th and 12th centuries there were bright features of scholarly contact and mutual deference with Christian Hebraists like Andrew and Hugh of St. Victor and their disciple Herbert of Bosham[26] who drew on the great Talmudist Rashi and his 'glosses' for their Biblical exegesis, emulating the famous Jerome in going to the Hebrew. It is intriguing to note how their very vocabulary echoed the crusading time – but not its physical zeal – in their partisanship.

These are the darts which the Jews level against us . . . they strive with the battering ram of their mockery to break down the stronghold of our faith.[27]

Nevertheless the contacts orally over texts they could mutually read without using each other's language save in the vernacular, were open to fair exchange, not least over Messianic issues. They shared the importance of the literal sense and were ready for 'uncatholic' ideas.

Whatever the practical value, for Jewish security, of its guidelines in 1215, the Fourth Lateran Council took one very 'uncatholic' step, and highly inimical to the well-being of Jewry, when it promulgated the dogma of transubstantiation to 'explain' the theme of 'the real presence' of Christ in the Eucharist. It not only committed sacramental faith to an impossible view of the nature of matter,[28] and a superstition-prone pattern of worship, it also exposed the Jewish population to calumny, false charges of desecration of 'the Host' and child murder. It gave a sinister angle to the concept of 'the blood of Christ' and played into the hands of long existing notions of magic and witchcraft around the mystery of blood in general.

The original Jewish claim that Jesus had deserved his death because of heresy – though long discreetly unvoiced – could be associated with the Christian ritual as what they would perpetrate anew when Christ's 'flesh and blood' became allegedly present again. Alleged acts of 'ritual murder', believers fantasizing in their version of 'the real presence' demanded to avenge as an ignominious crime. In times of plague – an untoward mystery in itself – scapegoating malice had free play and could be invariably directed against the old wrongdoers.

The chimerical deeds of which Jewry was accused were never witnessed by Christians but they could be conjured into reality by suspicions and hatreds bred from other seeds, whether in usury or social isolation. Jewish convert-apostates might also play a part. While Herbert of Bosham in Sussex poured over his Hebrew sources with a certain sense of awe, a priest in Norwich turned a child murder by some hand unknown into the legend of an annual child crucifixion which spread throughout Europe and was laid at the door of Jewish contempt alike for Christ, the Cross and the 'host' of the Eucharist.

The lust for relics, lucrative objects for local shrines to exploit, led to a crop of such charges in a useful martyrology inventing, or purporting to have witnessed, such deeds of infamy. A Jewish cannibalism came to be alleged in Germany to intensify the heinous guise they assumed in Christian credulity. Pope and Emperor denied the cannibalism as ever a Jewish practice but the Papacy let the child murder notion ride. It found full flow, for example, in the Hugh of Lincoln saga in the middle of the 13th century. Meanwhile the growing ritual of 'host-adoration' and the institution of Corpus Christi as a universal feast brought menace ever closer to the Jewish populace. When the 'host' became ever more visible and ever more piously venerated, the notion of its being defiled, stolen or tortured was ever more ready to hand for a highly charged, emotive and ignorant Christian populace. Jewry could be too easily, too crudely, incriminated. When Jews were expelled at various dates their dispersion served to spread their reputed crimes more widely.[29]

The calumnies and the slaughter fed on false accusation, even though the charge of 'blood oozing from profaned hosts', or mutilated ones (calumnies often fabricated) contradicted the vital doctrine itself.[30] That was only a bleak measure of how far desperate lunacy gripped the popular mind. Mobs were all too ready to avenge. The defencelessness of the innocent 'hosts' in the abuse of ritual had to be requited on the defencelessness of the innocent accused, and official disavowal was – or let itself be – powerless to protect them. Northern Europe was most implicated and its militant friars among the worst proponents of the venom in the outrages. When fears engendered by the Black Death in 1347–50 supervened no awe could for long stay the hand of the ruthless.

How should the mass medieval mind be read in its brutal proneness to demonic persecution? Ecclesiastical pretension must carry large blame. Its subtle instinct for dogmas drew a credulity all too power-bestowing in high places when a kind of monopoly magic attached to privileged ritual roles. For the vulgar throng, Jews became symbols for phobias on whom private guilts and grudges could be thrown. Jewish withdrawing into ghettos, comprehensible on genuine Jewish grounds, deepened suspicions by the absence of personal relations and sheer human contact. In his day distant from the 13th century, Martin Luther could write ironically of dietary seclusion: 'We let them eat and drink with us . . . we do not kidnap their children, nor poison their wells',[31] making a virtue of habits of hospitality Christians found no occasion to exercise while being libellous as well.

In such a 'world harsh and strange' it is fair to ask what legal status Jewry enjoyed. Historians seem much at odds about the niceties in answer. The circumstances varied from country to country in Europe. They turned on various statutes or decretals that amounted to a kind of 'serfdom', binding Jews under the control of baron, lord or king or emperor so that they became in some sense his 'property'. Was the notion inherited from ancient Rome and the Carolingian State? Prior to their expulsion from England in 1290, Jews were highly exploitable 'protégés' of the Crown outside the feudal pattern of other citizens and often 'licensed' as 'burghers' in towns. The style of King John – he of Magna Carta fame – can be guessed by his comment: 'If I give my peace even to a dog, it must be kept inviolate.'[32] With such auspices for their status as *perpetua servitus* (as having been 'crucifiers') the individual Jew may have found even expulsion less than wholly hostile, except that he would find similar patterns elsewhere.

French law of legal 'serfdom' went through many changes but broadly exceptionalized Jewish status as both a pseudo protection and a taxable usage. In the German realm the profits to be had gave ample ground to rulers to 'privilege' Jews adversely by having exclusive jurisdiction over their movements and their livelihood. It was the religious distinction which made possible the 'protective-humiliating' scheme of things, seeing that Jews were outside Christian Canon Law, oath-taking, property or residence rights, and court process of decision. Sadly even in forced migration Jews carried this 'legend' of the demonized, their being beholden in exclusive terms to Crown or Empire.

Ecclesiology conspired to victimize their sacred identity while state power burdened them with an ironically 'servile' status by which to exploit their potential as unique 'subjects', capitalizing on their being outside Christian normality. The irony could hardly be greater. Persecution could yield dividends by necessitating an ambiguous device by which it was a 'privilege' to be made 'servile'. When, as in France, in 1306, an edict of expulsion was enacted and Jews, many recently arrived from England, were dispersed anew, all debts owed to them were annexed by the French treasury. Over many decades, via Germany and the Low Countries, there was a steady drift of Ashkenazi Jewry into Poland.

III

One tragic feature – most evident in the saga of Spanish Jewry – was the bitter experience of many *conversos*, Jews who accepted to become Christians, as they did in Spain and Portugal in large numbers. Yet somehow an inveterate antipathy persisted that denied them the recognition their drastic revision of identity – not to say the inclusiveness of Christ – had surely warranted. It was as if the odds against a common humanity were fated to prevail. Jewry, so long pilloried as a spiritual danger, became in turn a social, even a racial, one. How could an identity so tenacious ever truly forego itself? Its will to do so could only be suspect: its Jewishness, as something *sui generis*, must for ever define it and, beyond all devices, be for ever greeted with antipathy.

Conversos were popularly dubbed *marranos* – a term akin to *Judensau* elsewhere – linking them despicably with 'swine'. With their new economic and social amenities, they were thought more threatening to 'Gentiles' than in their loyally Jewish days. 'You will find no rest among the Gentiles and your life will hang in the balance' their rabbis told them, as if to hear, across the long centuries, Theodor Herzl's cry: 'Palestine is the only land where our people can come to rest.'[33] When the newly shared identity of faith was legally in place, the incessant prejudice that was ethnic came to the fore. The supposedly integrated became the potentially subversive. Must they not be remaining inwardly Jewish – given the ever tenacious quality of their identity – so that a deep hypocrisy waited on both their accession *and* on the facility Spanish power accorded them. There was no sincerity in the Church's formula. Inveterate persecution had merely changed its tactics.

Riots broke out in mid-15th century Spain against the *conversos* fuelled – if not by suspicion – then by jealousy at the successes they attained. Oddly these were fed after 1453 by news of the Fall of Constantinople to the Turks, which kindled in the minds of some *conversos* that, with their ancient eastern foe laid low, new perspectives could open before them which might tempt, or be seen to tempt, them to more subtle secrecy.

It was, in part, in this context that the development began of the notorious Inquisition, in which the Dominicans were prominent. Despite the opposition of the Papacy to the Inquisition (as a Spanish exercise outside papal control), it had its callous, murderous way, with alleged secret practice of Judaism figuring largely in its brutal incidence. It operated by the use of torture, the practice of calumny and with venomous barbarity, from which no Jewish community across the domains of Aragon and Castile and the newly conquered Moorish Kingdom of Granada found respite.

It was the savage prelude to the expulsion of Jewry from Spain in 1492, an event as traumatic as any in the long anguish of exiles and dispersion. For Spanish Jewry had a history, both in length and authenticity of mind and spirit, as noble as any across the lands and centuries. The Sephardim had created their own Judeo-Spanish language, rich in culture and erudition, and steeped in piety and ardent self-esteem.

The desolation in those final years of the 15th century was marked not only in physical disruption and migration but the burden *conversos* carried in their efforts to return to Judaism, occasion for which varied precariously from place to place, on the vagaries of Popes and rulers and on the temper of cultures, pervious – or otherwise – to Jewish participation. There were cities and havens in the vast Sephardi migrations where their fortunes mingled, if in inner tension from time to time, with Ashkenazi Jewry in common enduring. The famous Isaac Luria, for example, of the Golan Heights, was the son of an Ashkenazi father and a Sephardi mother, and a vivid symbol of the psychic pressures of the ever restless quest for their true resolution.

It was a quest no less remarkable for its wide geographical dispersion. In the 16th and enusing centuries Sephardis would find themselves, fending for fulfilment across the Maghrib from Fez to Tunis, in Egypt, Palestine, Syria and Baghdad (recalling their ancient Babylon), in Ottoman domains from Rhodes to Constantinople, Smyrna to Salonika, in the sundry cities of Italy, into reaches of Poland and into the Low Countries and London. It was an uneven saga, with Fez, for example, devising the first ghetto for Jewish 'protection' yet appointing a Jew its ambassador in Amsterdam. The ghetto made its appearance in 1516 in Venice where, earlier, Jews from Spain had enjoyed a tolerable welcome, joining forces with Venetians of much earlier sojourn. Everywhere adaptability, the art of social and commercial 'navigation' in uncertain waters, were the mandatory skills, exercised with resilience and a readiness for whatever stint of opportunity or hostility might eventuate.

Despite the traditional Islamic norm of *dhimmi* status in the Ottoman realms, resourceful Jews were able to apply skills unique to them – mercantile and financial – by which to negotiate tolerable, if not even prosperous, existence. Prominent Jews exercised effective influence over successive Sultans, while leading women from 'high' families played a significant role as '*kalfas*', in charge of the Sultan's harem. In Amsterdam, Jewish merchants were able to profit from the growing trans-Atlantic ventures of trade, by, for example, the Ximenex of Antwerp. Such relief from hardship could cross to London, or be diverted to Italy where shipping and trading expertise plied in the Mediterranean. Leghorn was prominent and when, in 1675, it became a free port, Jewish merchants, who were the largest group of citizens, were able to spread their mercantile wings as far as Tunis and Smyrna.

The deep travail, however, of the diaspora condition is not well reflected in these elements of sanguine, even elegant, viability – always vulnerable and not extending far into the unfavoured segments of Jewry. An energetic and resourceful prosperity may have eased the religious sensitivities of those, unlike Shylock, ready to be satisfied with their 'Jewish gabardine'. It did not suffice to 'ease the sufferance' of others, who wore it with a dark intensity.

These cherished and told their Sephardism in a fever of kabbalistic

ardour and, later, the deep piety of Hasidism. It is significant that this religious fervour had its wellsprings mainly in the Judaic East. Mantua and
Ferrara and Amsterdam, as western cities might be broadly tolerable
havens for Jewish living, if not also for the Jewish soul (though Ferrara
had staged, in 1553, a burning of the Talmud). They could never satisfy
the yearnings of fiery spirits like David Reubeni of Venice, and the celebrated Nathan of Gaza. The former cast himself as a 'royal' Jew, urgent
to win back the Holy Land from the Turks and kindling, in a certain
Solomon Molcho, pretensions to Messiahship.

Earlier, the bitter departure from Spain had been read in such quarters
as a 'sign' of 'redemption' due to rescue a fugitive Israel. Nathan, an
Egyptian Jew, known as 'the holy lamp', espoused apocalyptic expectation of Messianic 'arrival', fed by the Kabbalah concepts of Isaac Luria of
Safad. In Lurianic doctrine, by the act of creation, God had 'exiled'
Himself into the recesses of divine being, whence only 'sparks' of divine
irradiation penetrated into the baser levels (sefirot) where humans dwell.
Only by Israel's meticulous Torah march to moral perfection would their
deliverance come. Hence the excitement of Messianic 'approach' and the
vehement fervour it aroused. When duly such a figure presented itself,
with Nathan's near delirious backing, in the fervid charisma of Shabbatai
Zvi (whose pretensions had begun in 1648), 'Messiah' was proclaimed.

Nathan, a far more credible figure than the maniacal Shabbatai, applied
his prestige and fervour to gain for this 'Messiah' a fanatically credulous
following, even though the Jerusalem and other Rabbis were dubious.
Such was the acclaim that they did not denounce or expose, despite the
liberties around the Torah that Shabbatai claimed and the exotic scenario
of redemption that he announced.[34] There were fantasmical notions that
he would take the Sultan's crown, gather 'pure tribes' mythically located
in the east, marry a daughter of Moses, and make actual the final redemption. Mass credulity followed his itinerary from Gaza to Aleppo and on
to Istanbul, despite his cavalier attitude to the sacred law, his denuncia-
tion of hesitant rabbis and his daring to pronounce on his own lips 'the
ineffable Name'. The rabble was beyond demur in its weird intoxication.

Nathan's corroborating calls across Jewry from Gaza to Prague and
Amsterdam brought a zealotry of fasting, ritual cleansing and scourging
to hail this Messianic 'Majesty'. When the Ottoman power grew alarmed,
Shabbatai was taken in chains, early in 1666, into, first dignified and then
hostile, custody, until eight months later he denied his claims, accepted to
be Muslim and was granted a pension of 150 piastres a day. Even with
this denouement, Nathan and his disciples contrived explanations in
refusing to admit their gullibility. More discreetly many rabbis, fearing
Turkish penalties, sought to banish the memory from the records and
pretend the fiasco had never happened.

Both sequels were measure of the tragic dimension either way. The supreme solace of Jewish existence, the hope of 'redemption', had been pathetically distorted and betrayed. All could be salvaged by incredible self-persuasion that Shabbatai had paid the ultimate price in a Jewish apostasy as prelude to his disclosing the glorious actuality, as if any kabbalistic 'hidden meanings' in the otherwise catastrophic could ever persuade any but the grossly deluded. Such desperate ingenuities over esoteric texts and their readings could, at length only degrade the very meaning of hope. Later ventures next century in Messianic fervour, though less spectacularly ill-fated, did nothing to relieve the mental yearnings they so dismally deceived.

Beneath all, lay the ever-present stress of inward selfhood over an identity so cruelly strained by psychic tension. *Marranos* reverting to their Judaism, Jews – either way – too often assumed to be equivocal, 'conversion' to the dominant ethos always, by its nature, problematic, a kind of social dubiety oppressively clinging to a most indubitably divine peoplehood – all these elements took their toll of private equanimity and left little escape from public travail.

Even the successes of the Jewish élite in the mainly Ashkenazi populations in Poland, Ukraine and Lithuania from the 17th century only left them the more exposed when the winds shifted, as they did, desperately in the uprising of the Polish peasantry in 1648. The obscurer Jews in the city shtetls were the still more defenceless. Jewish *savoir-faire*, skill in organizing large financing ventures and servicing the armies of the sundry powers in the Thirty Years War with both funds and victuals – these enabled Jewish practitioners to acquire both wealth and standing. Community affairs, religious and judicial, were under their control.

But, entrepreneurs 'in the middle' between 'Gentile' masters and their oppressed peasantry, they were readily 'sacrificed' by the former when the latter revolted. The massacres of 1648 marked a fatal landmark, a haunting shadow over the future of the ghetto. The prestigious titles and wide privileges the 'magnates' enjoyed served the common ghetto-folk little when princely favour was withdrawn and the mobs freed to prowl.

Given the oligarchic pattern that prevailed in the central European ghetto, the Jewish poor were powerless in their utter dependence on the magnates and under the yoke of the rabbis. The school of adversity was best relieved by popular recourse to the deep religious patterns pioneered by 'the Besht', namely Israel ben Eliezer (1700–60), known as the Ba'al Shem Tov, whose brand of charismatic devotion to prayer and aspiration stood outside the formalism and rigour of the synagogue and ministered to yearnings of the heart. He made vividly anew the role of the *zaddik* – no 'Messiah', but an 'initiate' whose sanctity availed to hearten and exemplify. The Hasidism that had birth this way brought a sense of the divine Shekinah into the heavy privations of the ghetto, despite the harsh resistance of the likes of 'the Gaon of Vilna' (1720–97) re-asserting Jewish *halakhah* in total authority. The physical and psychic insecurities of the ghetto were not spared the mutual repudiations of Judaic sects.

These deeply spiritual harbours of solace and inward courage availed little against the harsh physical and mental privations of 'the Pale' under the Russian Tsars and throughout the tribulations of a much 'partitioned' Poland. The dark story of those centuries from the 17th to the late 19th in Eastern Europe, so grim in the undergoing, so embittering in the telling, was the compelling retrospect of the Zionist conclusion concerning an incorrigible 'Gentile' world of rooted, implacable anti-Semitism from which there could be no effective residential escape.

Inside the long story of deprivation, periodic pogroms and perpetual psychic insecurity – outside the comforts of a spirituality which themselves attracted 'Gentile' scorn – two factors deepened the pathos. The one was the perceived failure of emancipation and 'enlightenment' to resolve the inter-human tension somehow ineradicable from the co-existence. The other was the unhappy non-success of Yiddish to sustain a unifying Jewish language affirming a unitary Jewish culture across the whole diaspora. The two were twinned in the one shape of tragedy.

As a promise of deliverance from 'a world harsh and strange' the story of 'emancipation' calls for no narration here. Its significance, for present purpose, lies only in its perceived 'denial from within'. Excepting the British and the American scene, where – by and large – Jewry has enjoyed tolerable human inter-community,[34] anti-Semitism, avowed or latent, put recurrently at risk the acceptance 'emancipation' supposedly ensured but proved inadequate dependably to guarantee. This evident discrepancy between hope and reality persisted despite the confident zeal with which European Jewry had espoused what it seemed to promise and vigorously pursued its fruits. The tale of 19th–20th century Jewish prowess in all the skills and arts and technologies is evidence enough. Somehow even these could endanger the inter-human openness the fact of them could only exemplify and empower. There was enough evidence across most European societies that an anti-Jewish malice aforethought remained. It was destined to descend into the enormity of the Shoah, where sundry other factors of global politics were fused into a catastrophic racialism seizing on all things Judaic as its sacrificial victim.

Pausing over the fate of Yiddish offers no relief from that horror but is yet symbolic of a kindred meaning inwardly known as dire forfeiture. We note in Chapter 7 the need in Zion's Israel to exclusify the newly nascent Hebrew. Yet, centred on Odessa – and later in New York City – Yiddish held the promise of an international Jewish culture, whose folklore and literature could help unify – and mitigate – diaspora. Among Russian Jews it was almost universal. From the late 17th century it had been the emblem of what Jews shared and that by which they were identified. In the 20th century it could boast a Nobel Prize-winner in Isaac Bashevis Singer.

Yet it lived under a sort of fatalism, close to the burden of anti-Semitism. Given European nationalisms, its old German hybridity became a stigma and thus a symbol of subservience. It availed, in a dark paradox, as a means to self-hatred. In the death camps, all its wit, its proverbial savour, its native genius, were forfeit, reduced to the tongue of grovellers stammering under 'the supreme race' of Germans. The hope it had cherished of being a cosmopolitan organ of autonomous Jewish culture died. The sort of vital asset without which no unitary identity can long survive, Yiddish had been a noble Jewish effort. Nazism destroyed it in Europe, extinguishing its inner hopefulness.

A minor casualty – it might be said – in so overwhelming a people-elimination as the Shoah in that second quarter of the 20th century. The Nazi will to exterminate some six million Jewish victims of its twelve or so years of European aggression and conquest, for the reason of their Jewishness, appals the human imagination like no other enormity. Perhaps its direst aspect is the near unbearable obligation to undying memorializing, never some 'lest we forget', only 'how shall we remember?' Zionism and the State of Israel are a partial answer. Their antecedents anti-dated the Shoah by some half century, but what the Shoah told has to be read as their ultimate vindication. That 'how?' about remembering does not lie only on contemporary Jewry. It weighs darkly also on the conscience world politics must bring to the shape of the Zionist answer. For it was out of the assessment of the 'Gentile' world as irretrievably 'anti-Jewish' that the modern will to a recovered Zion was born and passionately sustained. The Shoah had supremely confirmed that verdict. The unforgettable emotions would perpetuate the indelible assurance about the necessity of Israel. Must it also perpetuate irreconcilable enmity on another soil and time?

Chapter Seven

ZIONISM – THE REALIZED QUEST?

I

'You mighty ones that do His bidding' (Psalm 103.20) would be an ambiguous salute to the positive story of Zionism in the modern world. The controversialist, Yeshayahu Leibowitz, cites it to explain how 'Jewish fidelity requires great fortitude'. He was using an odd freedom of exegesis as the context has to do, it would seem, with the angels of heaven. He was no admiring zealot for Zion, describing the reason for the pursuit of a Jewish state as merely the fact of Jewry being 'fed up with being ruled by *Goyim*'.[1] That sentiment was a far cry from the ardour of a Theodor Herzl or the vision of an Ahad Ha-am.

'Ye that excel in strength' – as translation of the Psalm runs – was far from descriptive of those early pioneers unless we measure it in respect of the massive obstacles they had to overcome. Instead they were reduced to paying sometimes almost obsequious court to the powers that then were, offering to manage the finances of the Ottoman Caliphate in exchange for some liberty of Palestinian settlement, or laying subtle siege to Bible-loving custodians of British imperial power. Such powers were in the saddle in those testing decades of the Zionist dream.

Nor were the pioneers unambiguously 'doing YAHWEH's bidding'. The concepts of a Jewish nationalism by which they were driven were a far cry from the piety of those who could only 'wait in devout patience for the Messiah', or who were well content with their own diaspora identity and security as Jews and saw themselves compromised, if not threatened by the idea that they were strenuously to be involved elsewhere. The long sequence from the First Zionist Congress to the current régime of Ariel Sharon in all its twists and turnings tells in retrospect the hidden load of daunting tragedy in the whole Zionist enterprise, the paradox of the vexatious and the splendid in the task in hand. For Zionism was proposing to

96

disqualify the most prolonged condition of Jewish existence and the tenacious survival power it had demonstrated, namely diaspora. Measured in these terms, its founders and fulfillers were indeed 'mighty ones' fitly summoned to the art of praise. Their strength was duly evidenced in the very odds they faced and in their capacity to argue that as long as defeat was never conceded it could never happen.

The purpose of this chapter is to seek a due esteem of 19th and 20th century Zionism as a sustained Jewish venture in fortitude of mind and resolute political will, capable at critical junctures of producing personalities apt to the need of the hour and equipped to symbolize its meaning.

Given the undoubted 'quest' in the will to Zionism, 'realized' is certainly the right descriptive. The State of Israel is an evident *fait accompli*. A succession of *faits accomplis* have punctuated the story of its attainment and, short of the direst calamity shattering more than itself, the State is irreducible. No realistic Palestinian policy imagines or demands its expulsion into the sea. There is no liquidity about Israel in those terms. The State has come to stay even while its geographical definition is grimly lacking. That territorial indecision, while – as we must see – no small part of its ambiguity, remains an anxious issue without undoing the State's existence. Indeed undefined *de jure* borders are the substance of its reality *de facto*.[2] At every point its leadership has been able to conjure actual certainties out of implicit predicament. As we saw spiritually in Hosea, things proleptic – a sort of 'present/future' tense in political grammar – long characterized the Jewish mind but none, surely, so confident as Theodor Herzl's cry in 1897: 'At Basle, I founded the Jewish State.'

The Hebrew title of 'The Jewish National Fund', *Keren Kayemit le-Israel*, purposely echoed the Talmud's phrase about 'The Eternal Fund of the World to Come', about acts of merit acquiring heavenly reward.[3] However 'secular' aspects of its nationalism might be, there was no 'perpetual futurism' about the Messianism latent in its own fervour. It was no Maimonides and his kin insisting that any Messiah who comes or boasts a present tense, is invariably a false Messiah. The adversaries of political Zionism might use that argument to disavow its presumptuous impiety in their eyes but in its own terms it moved with an urgent, present destiny. The goal might be a thing of distant hope. Its summons to action meant an immediate energy. It is evident on every ground that the first factor in the realization of the quest was the process of realizing what the quest had to be and this way the founding impulses shaped themselves into a passionate repudiation of diaspora and a romantic espousal of nationhood. In *Rome and Jerusalem*, published in 1862, Moshe Hess drew his vision from the struggle for Italian unification. He was not writing about the Vatican and Jewry but about a Jewish emulation of Mazzini, with a doctrine of national identity realized in the kindred land by an assertion of corporate will which repudiated – in the case of Hess – the facile notion of 'the universal', whether of a religion or a culture.

As his contemporary had it only 'auto-emancipation' could suffice. Leo Pinsker's manifesto of that name was a voice from the Russian side in the same sense – the conviction of men who were now convinced that 'Jews would always be strangers' in the world of non-Jews and must renew themselves as a nation in their own right and under their own power.

Once converted to this conviction, the Viennese Herzl, with his *Der Judenstaat*, published in 1896, became its most ardent voice, urging mass emigration to Palestine as what Jews must do and what non-Jews must facilitate. If, as the poetry of C. S. Lewis has it, there is 'the very part of love which must despair', such 'love out of despair' would be the love for recovered nationhood.[4] As Herzl had come to believe, Jewry were 'a people' whom 'an enemy had made such without their will'. Events from Paris to Odessa had persuaded him that anti-Semitism threatened Jewish extinction within two generations – a fate only to be averted by evacuating the lands that were minded always to be menacing. If his thesis was prescient – all unawares – of what Hitlerism would mean, it is also clear that he had no happy experience of diaspora such as denizens of Washington or Brooklyn would enjoy in a context they could readily call their sufficient 'homeland'. For Herzl, in his time and place, Jews were perpetual 'outsiders'. Emancipation which was not 'auto' was a mirage or worse. Europe made Jewry unassimilable except on impossibly un-Jewish terms that made for an 'inner slavery'.[5] They could neither integrate nor co-exist. They should 'nationalize' their entire psyche and reach for statehood on a sacred soil, emulating their persecutors in their own strengths.

Herzl's career and his pamphlet could be truly described as meteoric, alike in eloquence, ardour and influence. His brief career – he died in 1904 warning of any lapse of nerve or wisdom 'when he was gone' – was the first, perhaps the clearest of the many Zionist examples of the role of personality in historical events.[6] Central to his thinking was the establishing of a 'presence' on the ground but in legal, not nefarious, terms. He assiduously sought Ottoman favour in contrast to the subsequent embrace of powered seizure in the minds of Vladimir Jabotinsky and Max Nordau, to whom we come elsewhere. Herzl held that existing purely agricultural 'Zionists' precariously tending the soil, only ill-served the necessary goal and that on two counts. They depended on sheer local goodwill and they lacked the state-intending courage. *Aliyah*, or 'going up', needed in some way to be seconded by the political world it was leaving precisely because it sought a polity of its own.

It was all a secular reckoning in that Herzl's thought on the holiness of the land was pragmatic. Its 'legend' – so vital to religious Zionists – was an asset in the campaign to re-possess it rather than a mission of piety. Either way, it did not seriously reckon with 'an existing population' – a failure which would prove throughout the bane of all that ensued. In the twin essentials of creating a 'colonizing' presence in a 'mother country' and of being shrewdly political Herzl had chartered the 'realization' of Zionism out of the other 'realization' that the 'Gentile' world would for ever disallow a Jewish legitimacy on Jewry's necessary terms.

II

Both 'realizations' were carried forward by Chaim Weizmann, a figure likewise exemplifying the capacity of Zionism to produce 'the man for the hour'. In the changed circumstances of the nineteen tens and twenties, Weizmann's contribution was to secure from the wartime British Cabinet in 1917, the famous – or infamous – Balfour Declaration, registering 'great power favour' towards 'the establishment of a national home in Palestine for the Jewish people'. He had achieved by a prolonged and persistent process of persuasion and negotiation, at precisely the moment when the collapse of Ottomanism was impending, the hope of a political legitimacy supporting a growing landed presence. It was a feat which only the patient diplomacy and the subtle stature Weizmann exercised could have accomplished. He knew how to handle Jewish awkwardness in the United States – a burden Herzl never carried – and how to offset the strong misgivings of British Jewry and how to maximize the sympathies of Anglo-Saxon Biblicists and, most of all, how to manipulate the crucial issues of wartime crisis and capitalize on the pro-Zionist potential they afforded.

Weizmann could readily be 'promoted' to the (first) Presidency of Israel by Ben-Gurion in 1948 as a way of signalling that the 'British option' stance he had so fruitfully exploited needed to be relegated to the past. But in its time and through the ensuing confusions of the Mandate period his acumen and his role had been indispensable to the rule on which Ben-Gurion was launched after independence. History cannot afford senti-mental gratitude when self-realization moves on.

Even so, Weizmann's diplomacy and personal *savoir-faire* ensured that during 'Britain's moment in the Middle East', it could be held – if only ambiguously – to the fostering of that 'Jewish homeland/state'. For the Balfour Declaration underlay the League of Nations Mandate and the Jewish Agency could hold the mandatory power to a Zionist reading of its double meanings. The 'realized quest' we are studying had willy-nilly to pursue its way by firmly exploiting all that ambiguity had left deliber-ately contestable. When between the wars, i.e. 1919 to 1939, Palestinianism had perforce to contest the same ambivalence in the name of its own nationality the peak of Weizmann's role passed but his part continued to be vital.

The riots, conclaves, passions and inconclusions of those years leading up to the establishment of the State of Israel were an unlovely story, giving an odd turn to Herzl's phrase about how 'an enmity made us a people'. For it was out of a grim episode of enmities that a political Zion came to state-fruition, and grim it has remained in being the State it is. Yet there was a positive resilience in the energy and the strategy by which it was achieved. Weizmann may have entitled his memoirs as *Trial and Error* which could no less have been named 'test and triumph'.[7] His diplomatic skill and personal stature were vital in the final 'wobble' around the American recognition of the new State. For ensuring its prompt announcement was decisive for its success.[8]

At that critical point and in the ensuring of the partition vote itself, Israel's birth had apt auspices – if we may so speak – in the ambassadorial midwifery of Abba Eban at the United Nations. Another 'man for the hour', his presentational skills and his ability to ensure prime media time for their deployment contributed greatly to the success of the Assembly vote. During a hazardous time he became the acceptable face and voice of Zionism, where and how they were both needed at the heart of decision making in a world forum. His persuasive eloquence and his personal lobbying among crucial parties to the vote and the intense manoeuvres preceding it did signal service in the final stage of the long quest for statehood. He was inspired by a clear sense of the Jewish will to autonomy in political and cultural terms and cultural purpose. Israel would be among Arab, Middle-eastern peoples: in his view it had no intention to be one. For him there was a proper justice in an international assent. Israel was to be among the nations, not an inter-Levantine creature, thinking to be Arabized. By his ideal it would no longer be 'a people dwelling apart', yet 'apart' it would be from the broad identity of its own context.[9]

Meanwhile, firmly rooted in that chosen geography, the supreme 'man for the hour' of independence was equally firmly in the saddle, as leader of the Israeli Labour Party and its first Prime Minister. David Ben-Gurion brusquely jettisoned the Weizmann mode. He was not allowed to sign the Declaration of Independence for which his diplomacy had been so long preparing the sure path, while Ben-Gurion would come to be described as 'the Jew who left the Zionists behind'.[10] Pragmatism was at the core of his leadership, signalled immediately in the fact that he accepted the Partition vote while not accepting the given boundaries, which were left for further decision. The same virile realism prompted him to see that the new State must be recognized in the Jewish diaspora as having consigned 'Zionism' to history – Zionism, that is, understood as the campaign to create it – lest continuing to think in the old terms should jeopardize the role of the achieved reality.

Tension developed between Ben-Gurion and diaspora personalities like Nahum Goldman over the primacy of Israel as Zion accomplished. Jewry must henceforth be 'Israelocentric'. The establishment of the State had radically changed the world-role of the Jewish people. Diaspora Jews should now identify by sharing in person in the ingathering. It was in this sense that he abandoned the name 'Zionist' unless it meant now living and working in the land. The only post-1948 fulfilling of the term was by immigration and – as he put it – 'writing a new Torah with engineers, farmers and kibbutzniks'.[11]

There was a certain rough arrogance about this stance and Israel's acute dependence on the resources and the politics of the continuing American Jewish diaspora was never in question, despite the tensions his philosophy caused. His robust 'Israeli-ism' filled the need of the time. He was ready enough to give his pragmatism a religious – or irreligious – ground, making secular sense of 'the chosen people' concept. 'The Israelites had chosen God positively.' 'The land' was 'the land of the championship of God'. Judaism was nothing if not 'connected with the physical existence of a nation'. 'The Jews could be considered a self-chosen people.' His belief in God meant 'their native genius', compared with which Arab nationalism was a cultured pearl in relation to a real one.[12] The land, which belonged to Jews and to Jews alone, with their autonomy at length achieved inside it, had liberated them to be the selves which, in diaspora, they could never be.

The stamp which his personality imprinted on the new State stored into its future many vexing issues which his assurance concealed but until time and tiredness overtook him he remained the genius of its politics, the symbol of its temper, moulding a successor like Golda Meir in his redoubtable image. She was certainly of his mind when she famously remarked that 'there were no Palestinians', meaning that they did not exist as a political expression but only as a 'tribal' entity. She merely made explicit what had always been the robustness of Ben-Gurion's statehood requiring the political 'de-legitimizing' of the other. The necessary corollary of the astute and virile assertion of the Israeli competitor territorially was a designation of monopoly in ideology to be steadily made good in concrete fact.

There were potential flaws in Ben-Gurion's posture in relation to Jewish diaspora which his theory so roundly disqualified but he was signally successful in his political mastery of the 'religious' factor. The vexed question as to whether – or how – Israeli nationalism was 'religious' could be left pragmatically indecisive, so long as the religious parties were effectively 'in the palm of his hand', even though the price might be their bargaining penchant for budgetary favours. Zionism had had to be 'secular' to get going at all and it might be thought 'presumptuous' in doing so. Yet the first Ashkenazi Chief Rabbi could argue that godless men were at times the instruments of God.

When the first Minister for Religious Affairs suggested the revival of a

Sanhedrin – even to adapt traditional *Halakhah* to modern needs – the proposal fell by the wayside over disagreement about its composition. Ben-Gurion was glad to see it stillborn. His Biblicism was happier in the campaigns of Joshua than the minutiae of Leviticus – a realism eminently right for the occupant of the saddle of the fledgling statehood. Power, as Thucydides argued, was the supreme condition of civilization and Ben-Gurion would have been congenial to his chronicling. It was this powerful blend of pragmatism and opportunism, exemplified in the leadership of Ben-Gurion that presented to the world the positive face of Semitism as his Zionism enshrined it. The ever latent ambivalence about its version of Judaism remains the permanently open question.

III

Inevitably – in the given time and place – its necessary militarism bore the stamp of the same opportunism. Former Generals and/or 'freedom-fighters' became Prime Ministers – Begin, Shamir, Rabin, Barak and Sharon, in their marked diversity of peace-making or peace-disdaining roles. Opportunistic warring, as in the days of Levi Eshcol and in 1982, could be in seriously strained relations with the political mind, either enhancing or jeopardizing the State's well-being. The Cabinet and the Knesset have sometimes been parties to the fact after it had been virtually accomplished. This was part of the genius of the Israeli will. The instincts by which Ben-Gurion had successfully achieved the victories of 1948/49 tempted him into the folly of the Suez Campaign of 1956, a nefarious episode in collusion with the Anglo-French conspiracy from which all three parties had ignominiously to withdraw.

In 1967, however, military opportunism, in the second defensive war of the State's survival, accomplished – to its own amazement – the most signal of victories, one that, more than the persuasions of ideological Zionism, gathered into a near consensus of approval the sentiments of the wide diaspora. The unexpected triumph was greatly aided by the inept-ness of the Arab States – a circumstance altogether right for the energies of a watchful and then a vigorous pragmatism. The emotions of that week in June 1967 celebrated a 'realization' both fulfilling and fulfilled.[13]

It was possible for Michael Elkins, the BBC correspondent, to predict at noon on the Monday that victory in Sinai against the Egyptian forces was assured. A pre-emptive strike had first destroyed the air-strips and a second aerial sortie eliminated the hapless planes unable to take off. This left the ground forces stranded helplessly without air cover in Sinai. Their 'assured overthrow' left the Israeli army at ease on its other fronts so that, when Hussein of Jordan decided to ignore the wisdom of neutrality and intervened, the capture of the Old City of Jerusalem became a reality, against all pre-conceived odds and expectations when the war began. Likewise, by a combination of resourceful intelligence and military speed, the Golan Heights became the prize on the Syrian front.

The hero of that north-eastern seizure was Moshe Dayan, an almost legendary figure of military prowess and state-founding zeal. With his famous eye-guard and his diarist daughter, Yael of famous Biblical aura in her naming,[14] he personified the martial virtues of the new and forthright Semitism of those defining years in battle and belligerence. From his days with Palmach and his defence of Degania in 1948, to his role in the 1973 repulse of Egypt, he embodied the necessary flair by which the State imposed itself on the terrain and on the calendar of history. By his gallant retrieval of his dead and wounded men and his boldness in relying on his own intelligence and taking his own field liberties beyond the writ of his Commander, Yitzhak Rabin and the ever prudent Premier, Levi Eshkol, he emerged as a kind of 'Nelson' of Israel.

Though operating in the days of Labour Party dominance there was in his expression of being Israeli an almost Jabotinsky-type ruthlessness about an inevitable destiny to suppress the Palestinian will to resistance. Israel could have no truck with conciliation until the enemy was cowed and quiescent. In his sequence of roles as Chief of Staff, or Minister of Defence or inside a 'kitchen cabinet, or inflicting reprisal on border infiltrators, he combined a certain sneaking respect for Arabism – and an ability in its language – with a quite stern dedication to the task Israel had in hand, namely to ensure that victory was won and seen to be won. Leaving the foe no military option meant that a status quo Israel controlled could sit out all eventualities to advantage – given American assent and American means. These could be ensured without any dutiful attention to American advice.

Yet his very representativeness in these Israeli/Semitic terms was accompanied by a strange sense of fatedness to succeed only by the warfare that had to supervene and to persist – as long as might be – given the intrusive nature of the Zionist purpose. Thus his very realism held in tension the achievements he exemplified in politics and war, namely the human disquiet that, for sensitive minds, bitterly attached to them. It was as if he unknowingly anticipated the desperate impasse of the years that would follow his generation. His capacity for entering into what it meant to Palestinians could not admit relinquishing the burden of pursuing the business falling to generations called and bound to war, though he was instrumental in the preference for acts of war that attained military ends rather than merely signalled a power to intimidate. The 'other' needed to be psychologically inferiorized but it was even more important that he be physically contained and subdued.

It was not surprising that what had guided his mind and leadership in the fifties and sixties generated a certain pessimism in the seventies at the growing contortions of Menahem Begin's Cabinet from which he resigned late in 1979 to die some two years later, just ten days after the assassination of the President of Egypt with whom he had negotiated the peace agreements. The subtlety and potential duplicity of Begin's distinction – in Palestinian issues at that point – between granting autonomy over limited areas *to* the inhabitants and not *of* the territory *per se*, displeased him as an empty quibble.

Begin, though in his contrasted idiom, was another in the sage of Israel's Zionist pride of whom it could be said with Shakespeare: 'Our virtues lie in the interpretation of the time.'[15] His ruthless role in the tormenting of the Mandatory power, his exploits at the King David Hotel massacre, his staunch defiance of Ben-Gurion and the Haganah in the episode of the *Altalena*[16] – might have made him seem an unlikely candidate for supreme political office, nurtured as he was in the sharpest Jabotinsky tradition and long almost a pariah after the launching of the State, as one never reconciled to the ideological implications of partition.

Yet in the Ben-Gurion years and beyond he had played fairly with the constitutional system, biding his time until occasion spelled opportunity. There was a tenacity about his doggedness in negotiation in the Carter years, a capacity to concede and not to concede by riddles of linguistic usage that served Israel well. For given that the entire situation, both at short range and long, was inherently one of pragmatic 'developing' and given, too, that diplomacy is always somewhat 'tongue in cheek', Begin's cautious discharge of Likud's access to power could be read as no less contributory, in its sagacious way, to Israel's goals than Ben-Gurion's vigour three decades earlier. For Begin's career held together in its ardent terrorism and its political tenacity the twin elements of Zionist necessity both in the gaining and the sustaining of the vital statehood.[17]

During his time of office the pace of 'settlement-creation' moved ever onward, making any later evacuation inherently impossible and so steadily pursuing the philosophy of virtual 'annexation' consistent with his life-long commitment to ultimate indivisibility. Begin had lost both his parents and a brother in the Shoah and read the entire non-Jewish world as inimical to Jewry. For him 'there was no guarantee that could guarantee an international guarantee'.[18] Thus he both personified and implemented the world-view in which Herzl's Zionism had been conceived. It was he who annexed the Golan Heights and made even tenuous peace-making a process of near exasperation for those who dealt with his doggedness. Yet, as the nature of his achievement, it served Israel well in a world 'harsh and strange'.

How should historians read the story of his resignation and personal collapse? Was it explicable as the price of heavy health problems and the stress of vexing times? Or was it, more deeply than Dayan's misgivings, an index to the conscience of the Zionist quest itself? It would appear that his Cabinet in 1982 had been trapped by the hawkish Sharon into the tragic invasion of Lebanon, with its toll on the image of Israel and its dire cost in the agonies of a neighbour land and the camps of refugees. 'I cannot go on' was his only explanation in the late summer of 1983 and he never enlarged further. Was he a human casualty of the anguish of the Zionist quest, a victim of the long burden of a militancy with no other vindication than the duty it imposed?[19] The war, he had assumed would last two days, still had months to run. He was bitterly accused of squandering Jewish lives, a reproach which broke his fortitude precisely where, in ardent nationalism, it had drawn its strength. Of all the symbolic figures in the dramatis personae of the story on the stage of Zionist Israel in its still-unfolding 'acts', none is more eloquent than Menahem Begin.

IV

His career and character suggest that the course of thought about 'the realized quest' turn, from its point at Begin's passing from the active scene, to the 'peace dimension' ever present in the intrepid narrative of 'the conflictual'. Its most telling moment as a keeping of the conscience came at the high point of the 1967 capture of the Old City and the soldiers' rapturous access to the Western Wall. According to the recollection of Uzi Narkis, the Chief Rabbi of the Defence Forces proposed they go beyond where Dayan had halted them, enter the sacred area and blow up the Dome of the Rock. Chief Rabbi Goren was over-ruled and had to be satisfied with a ritual use of the traditional 'horn' beside the Wall. The memoir adds that he told Narkis: 'You will enter the history books by this deed of yours.'[20] An Ariel Sharon, at that point, would have let the Rabbi have his way. In a moment of stupendous triumph the ultimate religious euphoria would have carried the day and ended with explosives thirteen centuries of Islamic stake in Jerusalem. That there was a mind to prevent it and leave Islam in site-possession may have been massively deplored in other Zionist quarters but it remains a signal evidence of Zionist nobility of soul in the very flush of victory.

Though often only in minority terms or edged out of policy-making, the fact that the quest for Zion has always been served by vital conscience remains its finest asset. Those with the primary will to peace were the early 'federalists', like Judah Magnes and Norman Bentwich, who were ready to express their compatibility with the Palestinian people, not in territorial partition but in political co-existence somehow expressed in a dual statehood. Their concepts, however, fell foul of the basic Zionist premise that Jewish power in a Jewish territory was the indispensable requisite of their emphatic closing off for ever of the 'host-nation' delusion. In any event, it seemed clear, despite early glimpses of some 'unison', that the ideal had no realist prospect from the other side.

Therein, of course, lay the basic contradiction implicit in the Herzl dream. There was no viable marriage between political success and moral innocence. It was, therefore, all the more praiseworthy that there remained in the field a school of thought that continued to struggle for the justice they knew to be crucial for the conscience of the whole enterprise and contend against the pragmatism or the wilful negligence of the issue that dictated the course of events. It was no small task to 'hope against hope', while steadily discerning 'in its own wreck the thing it contemplated'. They continued to strive for their ever diminishing perception of some emergent factor that might redeem the situation and reverse the ebbing tide of hope.

It was, in part, the very fact of the ongoing success of the pragmatist pursuit of state and power that complicated the quest for peace. For it entailed a kind of compound interest whereby success demanded its own consolidation, achievement only being the more achieved as it held its ground and reinforced its will. Furthermore, the Palestinian will to relate in mutual terms, whether inter-religious, intellectual or social, was made hesitant by the persistent sense of political inequality as the Israeli hold on events increased. There was a fear that genuine dialogue could not be 'in good faith' as long as authentic solution to the major political stakes remained unreached. Amicable exchanges in other realms might be interpreted to mean that all was well or that a status quo, perceived as unjust, was being finalized by default.

After 1967, the peace activists found temporary succour in the political dimensions of the concern for a Jewish statehood that preserved a sound Jewishness in numbers and in ethos – a concern shared well beyond their activist philosophy of peace-pursuit. Given that the post-1949 Israel had a limited non-Jewish minority after the events of the partitioning, and given, that the further territory acquired in 1967 was so heavily Palestinian – and that with a highly distressed population – it would be well to trade territory for genuine peace. Thus Israel would preserve her ethno-cultural Semitic identity as a more homogeneous society. Abba Eban in those late sixties was a notable advocate of this reading of the bargaining potential of the unexpected acquisition of territory in 1967. His case-making certainly helped the peace advocates with their moral emphasis on a truly Semitic conscience in terms of love of neighbour.

Sadly, however, the advocates of land for readier defence (the Jordan being the best – and the natural – frontier) slowly won the counter argument and peace-advocacy had to fall back on the ultimately human plea of a feasible compatibility, made the more urgent by the depth of frustration and near despair into which the second *nakbah*, or 'disaster', as they called it, had cast the Palestinians and out of which they had no adequate leadership to draw them.

The peace task became all the harder in that the 'land for peace' argument proved, for Israel, a broken reed, not only on defence grounds but by the perception, later championed by Benyamin Netanyahu, that Israel could envisage *both* security and homogeneity.[21] A comparison of statistics, whether by natural progeny or immigration, could argue a population situation issuing favourably for the Jewish State. If the land question and the ever maintained ambiguity about its given frontiers had thus to be also a calculus of human souls, a numerical as well as a territorial competence for the air in which to breathe, the task of the peace-seekers became ever more tense and prejudiced.

Yet resolutely they have persisted and stayed fortified by the conscience of the great Hebraic prophetic tradition, the Micahs who had spoken of 'dealing justly' as a clue to 'walking humbly with YAHWEH', and the Isaiahs who had accused the impulse to 'lay house to house and field to field until there be no room'. In measure, too, they had succour from the Israeli legal establishment, in courts where redress might be successfully argued against arbitrary confiscation of land and property, against detention without trial or denial of planting rights, water rights or the right to travel or have access to academic tuition. Expert use of legal means to the mitigation of personal hardship was available to Palestinian lawyers and, thanks to the strength of Israel's court system frequently helped to ameliorate some of the rigours of the 'occupied territories' and to keep the quest for peace paramount in the common mind, whether by highlighting what would otherwise have gone by default, or by witnessing to things 'rotten in the State' that might arouse and deserve the international reproach on which all peace-makers rely in domestic struggle. That so much of what afflicted Palestinians under 'occupation' violated Geneva Conventions and UNO resolutions gave the Israeli judiciary significant 'aid and comfort' in its juridical stake in the human objectives of the peace activists.

To be sure, legal safeguards against the abuse of human rights could always be circumvented by plea of military necessity or by political action to close any loopholes that jurists had utilized. Israel's confrontation with civil unrest and *Intifadah* had features in common with statehoods everywhere. What was distinctive in her story has been the depth of her prophetic tradition and the vigour of her justice system as together inspiring and enabling a resolute will to peace among some citizens, despite the bigoted excesses of some Zionisms and the long frustrations in the elusiveness of the peace they sought.

In the weary years of deferment and recrimination since Madrid and Oslo, it is possible to read that phased 'peace-building' as a trap by which Palestinianism was drawn into a virtual surrender of its most basic legitimacy as well as being made somehow responsible for policing and ensuring Israeli-favouring terms. Many assessors on either side have so argued with current history sustaining them.[22] Yet, whatever cynicism is traditional to politics, the peace-mind in Semitic Zionism remained a steadfast heir-in-spirit to the supreme ethicism of the prophets and a strong private and communal conscience in the comings and goings of the national scene.

Its most dramatic moment and its most devastating tribulation came in the great peace-rally in 1995 when Prime Minister Rabin was assassinated almost with a song-sheet in his hand. Yigal Amir, the assassin, symbolized all that in the other mind of Israel was adamant against their reading of the Jewish soul. The deed which threw State and people into their greatest heart-searching had been virtually seconded – in verbal terms – by much of the venom of political rhetoric that had preceded it in vilification and a 'teaching of contempt'. This only served notice on peace activists that their utmost prospect of hope could only be pursued at the dire risk of civil war.

Their vision and their validity could not be blamed for a situation so daunting in its odds. Nevertheless, with the lawyers who seconded them in the courts and the literati who echoed their pleas in poem and story, they sustained a long battle to fulfil a Semitism with a righteous will, that had a mind for the common humanity of a single, conceivably 'holy', land.

They were present, too, in the ranks of the Defence Forces, witness, for example, the compassionate emotions of soldier-diarists in the June War of 1967,[23] and a press report of September 2001, of some sixty high school students refusing to do military service on the West Bank and on the Gaza Strip, citing as 'racist' and 'violatory of human rights', the duties to which they were being sent. Facing at least two weeks in gaol, the teenagers sent an open letter to Sharon, declaring that their conscience forbade their taking part in oppression, land expropriation, house demolition and execution without trial. An IDF spokesman responded that they had a right to their thoughts but had to do what they were told.[24]

Despite the certainty of imprisonment, recruits and reservists have held to their conscience-light, rarely finding any favour in so doing from the official 'conscience-committee' to which the IDF refers such aberrant 'God-wrestlers' with the meaning of their name as Israelis as old Jacob once learned it at his Peniel. The exemption of Yeshiva students and other religious personnel from military duty – much resented by the kibbutzniks and other secular Jews – meant that these were not called upon to make moral and perhaps costly decisions about the justice of their State's ordering of its régime.

Happily, realizing the quest for a renewal of contemporary Semitism had readier fulfilment in the gentle realm of language than in the angry arena of conflict and diplomacy. The story of Israel's superb renewal of the Hebrew tongue and its baptism into the vocabulary of modern life is the glad, the salient, achievement of national self-fulfilment, Hebraism lives anew in the rebirth of Hebrew out of its Talmudic sanctity into the open forum of a modern culture.

V

The renewal of Hebrew as the national language of the new Israel was a gesture of fine genius. For, as many Zionists observed, the State was no esperanto entity, some newly concerted political diction addressing the world as some novelty of invention. It was politically rekindling its Davidic sovereignty which befitted conversing and transacting both its letters and its sciences in the speech of ancient psalmody, suitably tuned to its modern business in the world. Herzl may have told his dream in the vibrant German of *Der Judenstaat*, while Primo Levi would tell a lively Jewishness in a later generation in a noble Italian prose and poetry, but the sundry languages of a European nurture could be no adequate expression of the new reality. From Russian to French they were too loaded with the traumas and tribulations of history. Moreover, their continuing currency inside a reconcerted Israel would perpetuate the diversity of origin from which the several *Aliyahs* had been drawn. Sephardi and Ashkanezi would maintain their religious duality inside Israel but the ambition had been to add all that might flow into 'the covenant' of the land from Arab and African territories for whom no European language would have sufficed to tell their migration. All homecomings had to affirm themselves in the true meaning of their arrival, hard as the grammar lessons might be. The rules and vocabulary of Hebrew would confirm, in the very arduousness of the education into fluency, the adaptation of the psyche and the heart to the new allegiance.

The success of the great linguistic venture both as fact and symbol was the more remarkable, given the deep roots of Yiddish in the tradition of European Jewry. That speech had articulated their humour, their grim tenacity, their heartfelt pathos through many generations and established itself in the affection of countless users. Nevertheless, it had to give way to the more ultimate, the change-confirming language of the Tanakh and the Talmud, of patriarchal narratives and prophetic summons. As the Muslim Qur'an knew well to say, Jewry were 'the people of the Book' and reconstituted peoplehood demanded the nation's literacy contrived anew from the Book's tongue.

The transition so many immigrants into Israel made has been the more symbolic in that Yiddish was so far the sign and tongue of dispersion, having developed from its origins in German dialects in the 10th and following centuries, while it has no status inside Israel.[25] It lived with and through the wider dispersions across Poland eastward and southward through Ukraine as far as the Crimea. It reflected in its whole ethos the culture of the rural *shtetls* and the city ghettos where, by dint of religious separation, dietary laws and the Sabbath, medieval and early modern European Jewry had its social being. It was, therefore, the verbal currency of that burdened diaspora condition, the language of a 'world harsh and strange'. The Israeli Askhanezi might be so termed from the Yiddish word for 'German', but for all their significance as a major community, their Yiddish could never be adopted into the life of the national Semitism of the new/old homeland in the making. Nor, indeed, could the Spanish of the Sephardi. Was not Yiddish the major language heard, unheard, in the anguish of the Shoah, breathing the unutterable desolation of a people's immolation?

Even so, Yiddish literature held a precious legacy for the new Hebraists in Israel via the assimilation into Hebrew of much of its quality and, most of all, the tales of the famous Rabbi Nachman of Bratislav, inspirer of many Israeli Hebrew literati striving to create a new excellence in the celebration of identity. There was, therefore, a notable forfeiture in the decisive abandonment of Yiddish, serving also to represent the receding of the ghettoized diaspora that language had so far symbolized. For Yiddish, in the German if not in the Eastern European, context had been

> seen as a deliberate corruption and desecration of German, a secretive and lying code and as a particular threat to the new pan-German political identity.[26]

On every count, therefore, the new Israeli Hebrew language renaissance was the more tellingly renewing all that Zionism meant.

It had, however, a less happy implication for the unity of the Israeli population. The surviving Arabic-speaking Arabs had a perpetual reminder of their 'alien' character. To be sure, Palestinian academics, clergy and lawyers perforce became language Hebraists just as Israeli academia developed lively studies in Arabic literature, but ordinary folk, farmers and traders, were sadly disadvantaged in their dealings with Israeli officialdom with its ever more tedious restrictions on their daily living. Moreover, however bilingual the State might partially be, the supremacy of Hebrew soon lent itself to indulgence, in song and story, of that ancient 'Amalekite' imagery concerning Palestinians, the object of inveterate hostility.

The great pioneer of the renewal of Hebrew was Eliezer Ben-Yehuda who named his first born son, Ben Zion, vowing he should hear no alien sounds. A Lithuanian by birth, Ben Yehuda was fired by the dream of a Hebrew fulfilling its Biblical destiny as the bearer of contemporary culture fitted to grace 'the land of promise' no less creatively than the dogged 19th century settlements rescuing its soil from stagnant swamps. Maybe aptly, he drew inspiration from a Hebrew version of Defoe's *Robinson Crusoe* that came to hand in his boyhood. He came to believe with driving passion that a recovered nationhood – long before it was in sight – demanded its ancient speech. This, against much prejudice, meant retrieving the language from the monopoly of Yeshivas and the religious mind, working first in Vienna and then in Algiers where, perforce, he used Hebrew to converse with local Jews. Dogged by ill health, he reached Palestine in 1881, acquainting his bride with Hebrew as they went, to be startled at Jaffa by how 'Arab' all appeared and how Arabic was all he heard. His first Hebrew-using contacts in Jerusalem were Orthodox using Talmudic Hebrew.

Steadily he adapted, foregoing his name Perlman, and initiating an early Hebrew journalism in which he fell foul of the suspicious Orthodox who accused him to the Ottoman power which in turn imprisoned him. English intervention rescued him, though his pioneer newspaper, *Ha-Tzvi*, stayed awhile banned.

These adversities he turned to opportunity, working on a pioneer Hebrew dictionary identifying Hebrew words and terms with cross referencing and much ingenuity and resourcefulness. It remained a labour until his death and shortly after amounted to seventeen volumes. The compilation preferred European sources to Arabic for word-coining and Ben Yehuda favoured the Sephardi diction. The battle for its currency was far from easy in the face of heavy prejudice and veneration of the sacred. There was resistance even from sponsors of German in institutions of German connection. From the beginning of the Mandate the standing of Hebrew was assured when the Mandatory Power agreed to a trilingual usage. Theodor Herzl's easy assumption that the new 'State' as and when contrived could be a polyglot entity had been banished – by none more tellingly than by Ben Yehuda – from the fulfilling of his 'dream'.

As with all pioneering, Ben Yehuda's Hebrew has had to yield to much innovation and adaptation since his day, conceding influences he would not have approved, from Russian, still more from English, and even from Yiddish, but he had wrought, by his determination and zeal, the essential future in word and song of the recovered Zion.

Zionism, we might say, was made fully transactable in soul and body, trade and power, society and sovereignty, by the resurrection and the life of Hebrew, liberating it from the implied servility of alien or uncongenial speech, outside the ever reciprocal partnering of what is 'to the manner born'. Thus the Hebrew literature of Zionism in its artistic creativity has been the amenable servant of the political enterprise, showing an indifference, if not hostility, to the national and personal role of Palestinian society and culture. There has been little trace of any post-Zionist dimension in the sense of Ben-Gurion's idea that once statehood had been achieved, there was no further point to any 'Zionist' quest for it in the long familiar terms. The only exception would be the curiously called 'Canaanites', like Yonatan Ratosh and their journal *Aleph*. Urgent to abandon the Judaism of the diaspora and to belong in ancient 'Canaan', they cultivated a sense of Eretz Kedem alongside Eretz Israel, as the domain of 'this Hebrew nation' distinguished from Jews at large. They came to its old/new territoriality more in the sense of 'space' than of history, seeing 'return' as a land-destiny rather than a time-destiny.

Yet, as with all Zionism, they belonged and they wrote from a position of power and powered acquisition and therefore had an ambiguous 'feeling' for 'Canaanites' other than themselves. Their love-affair with 'nativeness' may have affected their style and vocabulary but did not lift them into a genuine empathy with 'the other' and, thereby, into authentic art. Other aspects of sharply contrasted ways of life persisted and always, there was the latent fear of pan-Arabism.

Despite the many odds and the steady obstacle to inter-human feeling set by the military and political imbalance of their situation, writers like Amos Oz and Smilanski Yizhar were able to portray with penetrating realism the privations inflicted on Palestinians. They were also honest probers of the troubled conscience inside Israeli militarism.[27] From such pens the new and vibrant Hebrew language drew inspiration not only from its cruel racial entanglement but from the Biblical landscape. For example, Amos Oz writes how 'you cannot kill the olive' (though official policy can well uproot groves of them). For the old ones 'grow bitter in tranquillity' (and also in insurrection) in their ability to thrust through the earth and draw up the scant moisture that hides below the stones.[28]

Other writers, however, used their Hebrew writing prowess to renew the endless 'war with Amalek' tradition, notable among them, Moshe Shamir, one-time member of the Knesset for the Tehiya Party. He and his kind saw the Israeli/Arab strife as between 'culture and the desert'. They were still, in their generation, 'at war with Amalek', sustaining an ancient vow. One, Ahron Davidi, dubbed Arabs the grossest, least productive race in the world, while Shamir's *Tahat Hashemesh* ('Beneath the Sun') has a character, oddly named 'Balfouria' whose boy-friend vents his disdain on 'unwashed Arabs' and exults in 'absolute' separatism fully in the Jabotinsky tradition.[29] The title laid the stress on 'blood, land and sun' in the idiom of the *sabra*, redeeming with sweat and bent brow what these conspired and attained to make inalienably separatist. The same theme came in two works – 'With His Own Hands' and 'He Walked in the Fields', which became popular celebrations of that dour dimension of Zion's twinned recovery both of tongue and territory. In these writers the renewed self of land and literature found voice and echo in the mood, if not the primal eloquence, of the famed 'Song of Deborah'.

VI

The poetry of H. N. Bialik, the other pioneer with Ben Yehuda of the new Hebrew epoch, offers expository transition to another kindred dimension of Zionist achievement in the economy of land possession which took the double form of steady soil/soul culture in one unison, and the excellence of Zionist technology fulfilled in its laboratories and experimental initiatives on every hand.

Aliyah, or 'going in to possess', had always been the basic requisite in the Zionist mind, the urgent thrust in its will. The sundry sequences of *Aliyahs* marked its progress in what might happily be termed 'ground zero', i.e. that 'without which nothing'. The establishment of a physical presence, humanly rooted in the soil, was the *sine qua non* of any ultimate success, the heart objective of all Herzl's and Weizmann's ventures towards the diplomacy that might gain for it the vital freedom and the political permission. The very soul of Zionism fused with the very soil of the terrain, being crumbled – if only metaphorically – in human fingers, settled in human camps and furrowed by human ploughs. 'The dream,' as Ezra Pound elsewhere had it, was 'in the peasant's bent shoulders', and not a 'pathos' but a passion.[30] Jewish humanity, like the probing, drinking roots of the olive, must tenant the sacred earth.

The poetry of Bialik, in sharing the characteristic with others such as Abraham Shlonsky, gave to this re-colonizing of 'mother country' an expression of deeply 'female' imagery. Whether consciously or otherwise, it seemed to be reaching for the Biblical idiom of Isaiah 62.4: 'Thy land shall be married – Beulah,' its name. The new nationalism, in Judaic form, could tell itself in eroticism, as it eloquently did in Bialik's verse. Was he – we might ask – recalling the tender yearnings of the Book of Hosea, the prophet of the northern Kingdom in the troubled 8th century whose own marital anguish seems to have been the setting of his vision of the nation as 'the unfaithful bride'?

Hosea stands among all the prophets as the most alert to the feminine analogy of the relation of Israel the people to Israel the land. In that quality, he also achieved the boldest *tour de force* of prophetic rhetoric by recruiting the imagery of the pagan (and wayward Israeli) fertility cults to disqualify them completely.[31] They contained in perverse, promiscuous form, the golden truth of an *eros* in the meaning of Judaic covenant, as of a 'love' between YAHWEH and His people, enshrined in a love between soil and soul in their tenancy pursued as a 'fertility' both of agriculture and of righteousness.

There may be due question about how closely we should take Zionist poetry consciously back to Hosea in these erotic terms, but the intensity of the kibbutz bond with the soil, the ideology of a devoted husbandry, are not in doubt. There were Marxist, socialist ideals, to be sure, and the secularity was often of the brusque Ben-Gurion order, with little patience for the kiss of sanctity. Nevertheless, that soul and soil had to be 'wedded' into fruitfulness was not in doubt.

By the quality of its ideology of nationhood, the prowess of Zionist recovery of a territorial expression is evident on every hand. It told itself in an impressive versatility in almost every realm, except the ever elusive goal of a political and emotional compatibility with an ineffacable Palestine and its Palestinianism. The flowering of Israeli poetry and Hebrew literature had its counterpart in the driving energies of Israeli archaeology. The fascination of Biblical soil and story which, long before and during the British Mandate, had inspired the Palestine Exploration Society possessed no less the souls of a rediscovered Zion. The secrets of Masada were revealed by the labours of Yigael Yadin and the 'Zealots' Last Stand' on that grim bastion of Herodian *superbia* famously recruited by his exploring skills for the heartening of Israeli Defence Forces in their symbolic baptism.[32] Elsewhere, in and around Jerusalem and across the cherished landscape, archaeological expertise pursued its sacrament of repossession, if also at times arousing Palestinian suspicion of other and nefarious intent. Not even the far past could be exempt from the tensions of a bitter present but – as the playful might say – the new Israel left no stone unturned to affirm itself in vigorous and competent entry on to a destiny wedded to every dimension of its past the spade and its techniques could decipher and proclaim. Whether Joshua at Jericho, or Deborah at Megiddo, or Samson at Timnath, or David in the Vale of Elah, all were rightly to be sifted in token of an urgent identity sited story could renew. Archaeology could be no less a negotiable asset to lively self-authentication than a resurrected Hebrew discourse. For story was what territory had always held in trust.

The self-fulfilment of Zionism in such peaceful terms was equally sought and found in the prowess of a sustained technology. Its salient achievement was the acquisition – unique to the Middle East – of nuclear power to be the ultimate sanction, if ever need arose, of the irreducibility of Israel.

That competence, however, owed itself to patient decades of laboratory experimentation in all the realms of applied science. From the early days of pioneers like those of Rishon-l-Zion, experiments in agronomy, chemistry, animal biology and technical management of natural resources, have been crucial to Israeli philosophy and land development. In the ever vital issue of water supply Zionist skills have written their competence into the terrain in magisterial style, despite the ever attendant political problems besetting the scientific. They saw themselves from the beginning as in proud contrast to what they read as the primitivism of Palestinian soil-possession and husbandry. The prophetic vision in the phrase: 'Thy land shall be married' – echoing the tender Hosea – they took upon themselves as eager nuptials celebrated by practical intelligence.[33]

Darkly, all the deep lyricism of this land/people marriage – the glad draining of swamps, the poetry of orchards, the vistas of citrus groves and the yield of vineyards into expert wineries – suffers the bleak scarring of the landscape, the uglification of the loved terrain and, more recently the shame and futility of a wall of alienation arguing a malaise no land nurture can redeem from the inevitable politics by which all re-tenanting was conditioned. Even so, the lyrical love of age-long 'Next Year in Jerusalem' wistfulness has not been denied its manual satisfaction, if in the menial role of the tractor and the irrigation pump. 'Labour' has been an honoured word in Zion, all politics apart.

With certain significant exceptions on the western hills of Jerusalem, there has been no striking architectural attainment in a recovered Zion to vie with the energies expended on things waiting to be unearthed below a cherished past. Contemporary domestic construction has been too bastion-minded in the swelling suburbs of Jerusalem. Happily, however, under the imaginative mayoralty of Teddy Kollek, earlier the spirited aide to Ben-Gurion, the Old City received, post-1967, a worthy furbishment, fulfilling in Zionist terms the mystic Muslim ideals of *Fada'il al-Quds*.[34] Its old walls have been made negotiable on foot like the walls of old Chester, its sewage system modernized and many of its covered suqs repaved, and its ramparts illuminated by night. 'How amiable are Thy dwellings, O Lord of hosts' – ever the spur to Jewish yearning – can at least be told in the physical terms available to civic pride.

The supreme physical expression of the realized ambition for a Zion renewed is the Yad va Shem Memorial to the victims of the Shoah, its very title echoing the kindred 'place and name' formula in which the founding Judaic sense of 'land and Lord', as studied in Chapter 1, was enshrined. 'There will I dwell,' for 'in them I find My delight' in psalm and prophet had long defined the unison of folk and fealty, of vineyard and vine-dressers, of habitation shared by God and His people, so that divine identity and people custody both ways were co-affirmed.[35] Now in the Shoah Memorial that 'place and name' inherence, either in the other, took form in a symbol where so many nameless ones were somehow 'named anew' out of their anguish and out of the cruel oblivion in which their tribulation had meant to cast them – and all on the soil where, despite their constant menace in diaspora, they covenantally belonged.

In the depths of its deep inner mystique, Zionism knew it had made good its quest in the sacramental meaning of that gaunt, forbidding edifice, with its ever-burning flame, its chimney and its blackened walls, its telling of dread-loaded place names and its ever haunting shrine-role as the mandatory point of visitation for all comers to Jerusalem. 'A place and a name' for a Jewry so grimly desolated and denied in the Shoah stand as the grimly sublime token of a Jewry in fidelity to itself – a fidelity only enabled to attain the token by the constancy in the vision of Zion renewed.

The impulses to a Jewish nationalism, for a 19th century Zionism, came half a century before the rise of Nazism in Europe, some of them against the very confidence of a trusted Enlightenment. Not many in Jewry then envisaged, still less approved, the fundamental and abiding distrust of 'the Gentiles' on which the founding Zionists proceeded. Even so, what ultimately transpired in Hitler's Germany tragically confirmed the logic that had driven their wills from Hess and Pinsker to Herzl and Jabotinski. It was as if the Shoah, in its terrible conclusiveness, had validated all that the most forthright Zionists had said about an irreducible anti-Semitism endemic in the non-Jewish world.

It followed that a Zion, realized in the crucial form of an Israel as both state and nation, was emotionally sanctioned by a seemingly vindicated philosophy of perennial distrust elsewhere. Of this, in all its otherwise urgent necessity, the Yad va Shem Memorial became the abiding symbol. It memorialized a Semitism which, somehow, could alone be its own guarantor and guardian, a Semitism never allowing itself to be vulnerable again. Thus the very idealism of its quest was pursued by a vigilance that could never renounce its posture of suspicious self-reliance, however dependent it might still need to be in material terms on resources, mainly from the United States, which it could not of itself command. These it would need to ensure in the context of a wider Semitism. On every count, the Zionist quest could be reviewed as a thoroughly interior success.

Yet, by the same reckoning it moves in that success as an entity under arms, with a citizenry caught in a psychosis of anxiety required thereby to live like an armed camp, the abode of an ever elusive rest on its undoubted laurels. 'The final solution' which Herzl proposed to his dubious generation for the ancient dilemma of being Jewish in a non-Jewish humankind has issued into an impasse tragically like, yet decisively different from, the old frustration he willed to escape.

By dint of location and an 'existing population' there were elements of Greek tragedy in the drama of accomplished Zion – the fate of transcendent meanings and heroic figures in the web of circumstance. The justice a Palestinianism had full warrant to plead, and its ineptitudes in doing so, left no occasion for an Israeli attainment, thus far if ever, of the essential goal in its interior Judaic sanction.[36] It is as if Israel and Zionism in their unison must say with Shakespeare:

> Our wills and fates do so contrary run
> That our devices still are overthrown.
> Our thoughts are ours, their ends none of our own.[37]

– reading 'ends' as how, thus far, 'purpose' has eventuated, all question apart of whether it could have done otherwise. Tragedy darkens all.

Marc Chagall and Rabbi Ben Ezra (he thanks to Browning) will give better shape, in Chapter 10 and epigraph, to the pathos of this conclusion. The immediate Chapter 8 in sequel to 'the realized quest?' must undertake what history has no less to interrogate as 'the great forfeiture'.

Chapter Eight

ZIONISM – THE GREAT FORFEITURE?

I

The Zionist establishment of Jewish statehood after some eighteen centuries of abeyance in diaspora may be truly saluted as supremely exemplifying the spirit and staying power of Jewry and their Judaism. The achievement was a salient theme of the 20th century. Should it also be described as a tragic forfeiture of a more enduring and more ultimate destiny? The Jews may have brought Semitism once again into the stream of political history in a noble gesture of particularism and independence, but has the price of doing so – in the event – proved an undoing of their genius in the tragedy into which it fell?

'In the event' – we have to say. For there was always the hope of an entire innocence, indeed a beneficence, in the Zionist enterprise whereas, in time and place and statehood form, there could only be also wrongs and sorrows darkly waiting on the visionary ends. The Semitic re-entry into 'free history' brought it also into the entanglements, moral because also political, implicit in doing so, requiring it to be, by the strangest paradox, a very 'Gentile' thing.[1] The Jewish mind would often say that YAHWEH was the God who could be spoken of only by telling stories. What story, then, does a century of effective Zionism tell of Him and of His 'Semites'? Is the question fair and right? Or how else could 'the story' have been, seeing that there were always factors outside Jewish control?

In his *Se Non Ora Quando* ('If not now when?') Primo Levy wrote three years before his death in 1987:

> I am convinced that the role of Israel as the unifying centre for Jews is now – let me stress now – declining. It is therefore necessary for the centre of gravity for Jews to . . . return to the diaspora Jews who have the task of

reminding our friends in Israel that within Judaism there is a tradition of tolerance.

Never himself a Zionist, he was a highly esteemed survivor of the Shoah and a tireless searcher of the survivors' task of faithful memory and a mentor of his Italian Jewish community through the darkest Fascist years. In the same novel he has a character explain how 'from the promised land no call reached him'. It did not 'warm his heart'.[2]

'Centres of gravity' for religions may well be in constant debate and even rivalry but Primo Levi's verdict spoke out of a profoundly Semitic unease. Failure to 'warm the heart', however, is no prescript for disallowing the logic in the mind and – as we have seen in the previous chapter – political Zionism could mount both a telling case in reason and one passionate in the soul. What then of Semitism was in forfeit? Where do misgivings take origin? Where was the history culpable – in the conceiving or the fulfilling, in the ideology or the pragmatism? Does the long retrospect to Hess and Pinsker, Herzl and Asher Ginsburg, identify a vision destined for ever to contain a contradiction, so that 'it had been proper to have conjectured at the purpose of God much sooner'?[3] Or was it that imponderables then hidden proved incorrigible to their successors denied the innocence of pioneers? 'If we will it,' Herzl had written in *Der Judenstaat*, 'it is not a dream,' but as his own exertions proved there were other 'wills' liable to qualify 'the dream' and make its realization quite undreamlike.

'Conjecturing at the purpose of God' was hardly the language of the founding fathers of the Zionist movement but they were certainly 'conjecturing at the purpose of Jewishness'. In retrospect it seems clear that there was a double, and fatal, flaw in their conjecturing. It had to do with the ever ambiguous relation between the territorial statehood and the ongoing diaspora. The tensions, emotional and spiritual, in their respective logics have never been resolved. The flaw, secondly, had to do with the inevitable conflict latent in a project of statehood which could never be both unilaterally and justly attained, seeing that it could only succeed in its intended terms by a parallel sequence of injustice, oppression and tragedy.

To identify a double flaw and to express it in these terms is, by a strange irony, an index to the very genius of Judaism as – in Arthur Cohen's elusive phrase – 'exercising freedom to intend transcendence'.[4] In 'a historical and theological introduction' to Judaism he sees Jewry as at once 'natural and supernatural'. It is inside this double descriptive that 'the double flaw' of a Zionist Semitism must be seen to arise. On the one hand, in this writer's view, 'the natural Jew' is 'situated in nature', reacts to cultures and belongs in history in broad human ways. Yet, so doing, he has to 'break out of this fate into destiny', as 'not only open toward God but the one to whom God has opened himself'. By covenantal status the Jew is lifted from 'the fatality of nature' into 'the supernatural vocation' that belongs with the assurance that God has called Jewry to Himself, so 'confirming in them' this transcending possibility.[5]

Given this theology of Judaic identity, the question follows how diaspora and Zionism serve it, whether either or neither? Some accounts of each have long disqualified the other and the issue abides around their inter-play. How, in these divine terms, is the destiny of Judaic community feasibly achievable among other nations with their notions of themselves? How far is it sustainable inside the exigencies of state-founding and state-sustaining in an arena of explicit conflict over land-right and human rights? Can a theology of election and covenant be interpreted and pursued in a form that has no escape from being coercive by dint of the physical patterns it must pursue? Will its given 'supernatural' character be for ever forfeit to its 'natural' self?

To such questions are we led if we accept Arthur Cohen's thesis of the nature of Semitism but to disavow them would be to evaporate the mystery when Zion and diaspora alike would cease to be recognizably either Jewish or Judaic. Only in their Jewishness are either problematic, whether for their own self-reference or for the cultures and politics of humanity at large.

II

We need not stay long here over the logic of contradiction in the theory of Zionism between a perpetual diaspora and an essential political territorialism. The previous chapter noted the strong sense for diaspora which initially Zionism had to counter and overcome. It was part of the case made by Reform Judaism that the long diaspora had demonstrated how marginal the political dimension of the faith had duly been. It had shown its durability more decisively than in the brief centuries of Jewish monarchy from Saul to Zechariah and under the Hasmoneans. Was it not in the very resilience of diaspora that Jewry had found its *raison d'être*, rather than in Herzlian counsels of ultimate despair of 'Gentile' neighbouring? Would it not be out of the very prosperity of diaspora that any statehood could either emerge or survive?

Nor were the anti-Zionist misgivings merely of this practical order or of comparative history. They stemmed from a deeply ethical anxiety. If, for example, the Jews had . . . 'an inherited, innate ability to give the world an ethical consciousness, or in the symphony of the nations' to 'play the ethical melody',[6] how would this obtain in the inherently angry, even brutal, scenarios of a political order fated to violence in a human context of legitimate resistance – a resistance the political enterprise would itself generate? Might not the whole venture – for lack of a supremely restraining wisdom – fall back on to an almost Essene doctrine of 'the two spirits', in which it would become emotionally necessary to demonize all Palestinians and so give a radical – and perverse – grounding to the cause that must defeat them?[7]

Nobly resisting this dark logic, as peace-lovers in Israel would do, must mean that a deep moral dilemma could root itself incorrigibly in the very counsels of the State and make problematic the entire role of religion in the life of the new national society, setting a Judaic ambivalence at its very core. It is not argued that the anti-Zionist mind foresaw all that would ensue. For the shape of the future and the exigencies of world politics lay concealed. But there was an innate fear – out of deeply Judaic thinking – that the vision, in realizing 'the dream', might engender a nightmare. What if the need to demonize the physical 'other' in the Palestinians or, contrariwise, to bring them inter-human relation, should bring about a domestic quarrel inside Jewry itself and Zionism find itself engaged in the only war it could never win, namely a war between Jews?

It was thus that 'the call of the promised land' did not 'warm the heart', not because diaspora Jewry was slothful, 'at ease in a local Zion' of their own,[8] but because there was genuine apprehension in the mind about the spiritual entanglements of a Jewish nationalism in unavoidably invasive terms. However mitigated by the sincerest expressions of peaceable intent and feasible innocence, these misgivings were deeply reinforced by the virile realism of the most forthright exponents of the things in view. These pioneers of the Likud mind knew well enough what had been meant by the two rabbis who had been sent on a fact-finding mission to Palestine after the Basle conference of 1890 where Herzl said that he 'founded the Jewish State'. They wrote:

'The bride is beautiful but she is married to another man.'[9]

The analogy was worthy of the prophet Hosea, though negligent of how else he might signify. If that were so, there would need to be either divorce or rape. Vladimir Jabotinsky saw Herzl's *Altneuland* as a place to be forcibly acquired via what he called 'the iron wall' (or more properly 'an iron fist') as the prior condition of negotiation. Zionists would indeed parley with 'the Arabs' but only when they had been subdued to the point where they would capitulate to the terms Zion would impose.

It was not clear from the 'wall' analogy where it was to run, so that the notion of forcefulness concealed what has remained the stubborn issue of partitionability. Pleas for 'the recognition of Israel's right to be' always leave it indeterminate as a geographical expression. The Jabotinsky 'wall' could easily be on the Euphrates. For he included what became the State of Jordan and as a 'Revisionist' fought hard to retain it. His 'wall' was a metaphor, not for demarcation, but of the 'impassible', the time where resistance must stop.[10] He scorned the idea that Zionism needed a 'soft' approach as if it could be some 'silent conspiracy'. It must pursue a rigorous racial policy of excluding alien elements and asserting uncompromising claims in near fascist terms. *Homo homini lupus.* There is a necessary wolfishness in human affairs. He wrote:

> A sacred truth whose realization requires the use of force does not thereby cease to be a sacred truth. This is the basis of our stand towards Arab resistance.[11]

He wanted 'no alien minorities that would weaken national unity'. Did he ever appreciate that his logic might apply conversely when he wrote, of a Zionist Jewry:

> For such a race the very idea that it will accept the authority of an alien element is organically disgusting and detestable.[12]

Or, perhaps, the very thrust of a reciprocal rejectionism fortified his resolution as to where the die must fall. Certainly 'bi-federalism' was no viable, only a deviant, idea.

His contemporary, Max Nordau, was of similar mind. Though as we saw in Chapter 6, there could be a wry tribute to the Jewry of the ghetto, 'emancipation' had forced Jews into a Maccabean re-entry into political nationalism uncompromisingly racial and territorial.[13]

To begin with these stormy petrels of post-Herzl Zionism in study of its arguable 'forfeiture' of the wise Judaic mind is only to characterize the strands in the ensuing story of kindred self-fulfilment or self-violation of Jewishness, hinging on what that 'self' should be, as Zionism so profoundly set it at stake. For with the story of heroic attainment and sustained discipline of will we traced in Chapter 7 there goes a parallel story of chicanery and scheming, of subtle cunning and the double mind. It emerges at so many points and unwinds itself in a tally of situations where what satisfaction may admire is also what integrity must lament.

Instances only must suffice from a narrative endlessly retold and bewilderingly tangled. The deliberate double-dealing of the Balfour Declaration in 1917 became notorious. As being then in the seat of power, the British were culpable but the elusive phrasing was all the scheming of the contriving Weizmann who wanted to avoid alarmism in a nevertheless workable warrant for feasible settlements. The subsequent Jewish Agency was insistent on an exclusively Jewish reading of the Declaration's intent when, in the twenties, it became the text of the British Mandate. 'A national home in . . . ' became entirely 'a national state of . . . ' in disallowance of any positive relevance to the Palestinian case it supposedly 'safeguarded'. It might be pointless to want political means to be mindful of moral ends. For, in A. A. Cohen's language, this was 'the natural Jew', on behalf however of his 'supernatural destiny'.

The cost would always be the connivance of the latter with the former.

It stayed so in the onward story. After the Arab uprising of 1936, Ben-Gurion told the Executive of the Jewish Agency:

> It is not in order to establish peace in this country that we need an agreement (i.e. with the Arabs) . . . but peace for us is a means. The end is the complete and full realization of Zionism. Only for that do we need an agreement,[14]

in that it would facilitate the ongoing theme as only temporarily 'agreeable'. It was Ben-Gurion's version of a Jabotinsky scenario. His attitude was brutally pragmatic. Only, he thought, when 'the Arabs were in total despair' would acceptance of Eretz Yisrael be conceded in what he owned would have to be for them 'a craven peace'.

It was likewise with his acceptance of the partition proposal that same time of the Peel Commission – not that Israel was ever divisible – but that arguably now the State could come into being without any Jewish/Arab agreement, i.e. Zionism would be immune from any Arab veto. From London he wrote to his son Amos:

> I am certain we will be able to settle in all the other parts of the country, whether through agreement or in some other way.[15]

Whatever others, Palestinian or British, might assume, 'the rest would come in the course of time'. The present could always be feloniously in fee to the envisaged future.

III

This subtle elusiveness persisted in a situation somewhat akin in the period after the truce that temporarily intervened after armed encounters of 1948 and indeed has never yet been formalized into a peace. Ben-Gurion saw them as 'useful' for the time being and nicely serving Israel's purpose, while the world was left thinking that there was no progress because 'there was no one willing to talk'. Indeed, few aspects of Semitism in its Israeli expression are more deplorable, in political terms, than its relation to the United Nations as – however fallible – the crucial organ and forum of international opinion. Zionism, by definition, was aspiring to be 'among the nations' yet, the US apart, it held their inter-state counsels too often, if not in contempt, in bland disregard. This aspect was the more intransigent, in that in juridical terms, the State owed its very being to the establishing vote of that very body.

The UNO was, to be sure, the legatee of the former League of Nations whose 'Mandate' to Britain it had in sequence as having derived from a Balfour Declaration which had no legal status and was merely an expression of one power's 'good favour'. Thus the new state drew its sanction from the historic vote of November 1947, to whose authority it had looked and under whose wing it had legal birth. It was, therefore, the more unseemly that it should have come to regard it as a virtual enemy, to discount its frequent Resolutions and to ignore its often common mind about the claims of justice and human rights, or about the very provisions underwriting Israel's own existence.

An early and dastardly example was the murder of its envoy, Count Bernadotte, one of whose assassins survived to be the State's Prime Minister. Did it presage a day when an assassin's hand and a certain cast of mind in Israel would murder the State's own Prime Minister? It was an affront to the international body whose blessing it had avidly sought and courted a bare ten months earlier. Was it to be read as the dark face of Semitism in political passion? It was a crime but also a symbol. Long forgotten now and buried in a long history of fact-creation, it dramatically signalled what was to become the inner theme of the whole, namely Israel's unwillingness to let its territorial dimensions be finally agreed. When it shredded UNO Resolutions they had chiefly to do with the issue of 'settlements' being made on areas still *sub judice*. The open question about boundaries could be kept diplomatically open, whether by stalemate or procrastination and in the ensuing situation a physical piecemeal answer be achieved in Israel's favour.

In pre-mandate and mandate years it had always been an urgent policy of Weizmann and others by all means to insert a presence both to affirm the claim and also to anchor its making good, in step by step sites and occupancies that could later coalesce and so build into islands of actuality. That policy had contributed significantly to the mapping of the 1947 partition zones. The killing of the envoy mediator in 1948 had largely to do with the peace-plan he had in hand which – especially on the Latrun salient on the vital access to Jerusalem – would preclude its absorption inside Israeli borders. There was also the now long forgotten item about the internationalization of Jerusalem. Count Bernadotte must die to keep the territorial future crucially an open question.

If what we saw in those years was a basic unreadiness to finalize the borders so that 'Israel's right to exist' could be asserted, still in no way an open question essentially, while staying an open question geographically, it would seem that what has obtained since the nineties is a basic incapacity to finalize them. For doing so in any terms short of the Jordan River would incur the risk of civil war inside Israel, the settlements being irreducible in their resistance even to Israeli governmental will and Army action, and/or the will to such a policy being impossibly divisive of Israeli society. Has the story then reached a point where peace is no longer negotiable on the Israeli side seeing that no government can realistically contemplate a policy that promises to end in civil chaos?

Can it then only wait oppressively for capitulation from the other party? Hardly. What Ben-Gurion and his generation found so desirable and satisfactory in the UNO partition decision was that it certified an Israeli political right to be. It validated statehood and paved the way for its declaration, with international consent. It assumed, but was not crowned with, acceptance of its enmapped limits. These became the subject of armed conflict.

The same partition vote had similarly conferred a right to exist on the other territorial party, namely a now truncated 'Palestine'. It is a tragic irony that the decision which partitioned the land disrupted the identity of that 'Palestine'. Being *de facto* if not *de jure* the incoming party, Israel, was capable of unitary acceptance of the proferred identity – if as the nucleus of more. Palestine as the truncated party was not. It was required to concede the moiety of its historical existence. As old as the Philistines and older than its 'Palestinian Talmud', confused and badly led, it repudiated its partition, refusing not merely, like Israel, to admit the lines, but their being drawn at all on its national soil.

How 'national' was it then? The question is a subtle one. It has often been claimed by Zionists that there was no authentic Palestinianism, unless as a pale echo of the Israeli one conjured out of nothing to oppose it. This misreading was the point of Gold Meir's famous observation 'There are no Palestinians.' She could not mean that they did not statistically exist: she meant that they were not a political identity. Her verdict eminently suited the Israeli book but it was invalid. The Palestinian dilemma was to reach the political self-declaration which Israel was able to achieve overnight when the Mandate legally ended. For Palestinians it would be the task of painful decades, as something to be affirmed from inside a patronizing Arabism and only slowly asserted in an international community reluctant to concede or, as long with the US, derisively against it.

The absorption of a truncated Palestine into the State of Jordan after the truces of 1948/49 continued until 1967. Only a little before that second date did a Palestinianism begin to assert itself independently – though 'independent' it could never be thanks to the entanglements of the Arab world. It was tragically stimulated by the disaster of that June War when the River Jordan was reached by the Israeli forces, all Jerusalem acquired and the surviving 20 per cent of the 'West Bank' occupied – but not annexed.[16]

It was further advanced by the infernecine war of 'Beds and Feds' in September 1970, when the State of Jordan forcibly disallowed the use of its territory for Palestinian resistance – ends that transgressed its own authority – and virtually exported the trauma of Palestinian 'guest-status' from its own midst into Lebanon. Through all ran the tragic misery of dispersed Palestinian refugees, some now for the second or third time, housed to languish in camps under the auspices of United Nations agency of relief.[17]

In this lengthening maelstrom Palestinian nationality found itself politically, but inevitably in 'terrorist' terms, as long as world opinion stayed oblivious of its claim and while a now re-affirmed Israel had no occasion to address the latent question of her final boundaries or reckon with any 'Palestine' in juridical terms. She could look back with pride – for all its moral compromise – to its Suez venture of 1956, conniving with Anglo-French folly around the canal's nationalization and usefully securing guarantees about its important back door in maritime terms at Sharm al-Shaikh and the Gulf of ʿAqabah. The year 1956 was its first war of aggression with 1948 its positive battle for survival. The two dimensions might be said to have merged in the June War of 1967, though the resounding 'pre-emptive action' was aggressively contrived.[18] When the humiliating débâcle of 1967 drew from Egypt six years later the partial rehabilitation of Egyptian morale in the autumn Yom Kippur War of 1973, Israel was able to ensure the security of its southern flank by a 'peace' with Egypt that effectively left the Palestinian cause still further driven into forlorn self-reliance. President Sadat, to be sure, had believed he had secured effective 'linkage' of his 'peace' with 'solution' of the Palestinian issue and an end of settlements, so that he had in no way betrayed his Palestinians.[19] Begin, from the Israeli side, would ensure that 'linkage' would be a stillborn notion in the womb of time.[20]

Any statehood vision, still more its 'declaration', remained dreamily elusive for Palestinian nationalism, reduced to a desperate policy of intermittent violence as its self-frustrating plea for recognition, its 'renunciation' the perpetual veto on any perception of the legitimacy for which it pleaded. Meanwhile the tribulations of refugeedom persisted to keep the political impasse tragic, while its incidence in Lebanon put intolerable strains of the fragility of the Lebanese political order of things.

It was then that Israel embarked on what proved to be the ugliest mood of Semitism in the invasion of Beirut. Wounded and irritated, but in no way essentially jeopardized by Palestinian 'will-to-be' and perceiving a situation of sectarian division inside Lebanon which might be exploited to advantage, Israel invaded its northern neighbour. There was no question of its military capacity for victory, its power, if so it were, to reach Damascus also and Aleppo. What was dubious was its wisdom and its ethic. It would seem that saner minds were inveigled into the invasion by Ariel Sharon and by an exclusively forcible vision of how Palestinianism might be eliminated.

Initially the theme had been to 'impose quiet' on a twenty-mile border depth to protect exposed residents in northern Israel. Sharon persuaded the Cabinet to permit a 48-hour, 40 km. attack which he then turned into an all-out invasion using tactical developments on the ground as his excuse.

> Born of the ambition of one wilful, reckless man, Israel's 1982 invasion of Lebanon was anchored in delusion, propelled by deceit and bound to end in calamity.[21]

The long occupancy of Lebanon by Israeli forces did indeed ensure the expulsion of the Palestinian (PLO) forces to Tunis, though in unremitting defiance. The gamble of some Lebanese collusion backfired with calamitous consequences for that country's equilibrium.[22] Some eleven thousand were killed and there followed the brutal massacres of the camps of Sabra and Chatila, far outweighing the wartime atrocity of Dair Yassin at home in Israel. Israel finally retreated to an occupied buffer zone in the south of Lebanon, held only to become for almost twenty more years a training, proving ground for the martial exploits of Hamas prowess in enmity to Israel.

The enforced exodus of Palestinian armed resistance into Tunis accentuated the problems that had arisen of a physically divided Palestinianism ever since 1967, between 'West Bankers' and the leadership. Under no pressure to attend to those ever undrawn borders, Israel was free to 'occupy' and steadily 'Judaize' what some of its mentors might one day perhaps barter for peace and others would contrive perpetually to retain and at length exclusify. Those alternates took a variety of political permutations inside the Byzantine complexity of Israeli sects and parties and politics until the onset of the first *Intifadah*.

The ultimate moral and political obligation inherent in the very concept of juridical partition could stay in deceptive default, to the lengthening false comfort of the Israeli soul, the steady abeyance of the sort of vital integrity which only a lively 'Peace Now' movement upheld. Israel could be broadly soothed into a studied hiatus in the definition of its own image, the definition that had been required in its acceptance to be 'state-ified' in partitioned terms, with the other party trapped in frustration and a justly alienated mind.

Meanwhile that other party would be slowly struggling to re-present itself before the international community, for ever hobbled in doing so by the ambiguities present in inter-Arabism, too often 'wounded in the house of friends'. When might the world concede that it had legitimacy, that its 'violence' could give way to a peaceful self-image that had not thereby forfeited its right? Was it able to speak with a credibly single voice? That must turn on how far, and when, Israel was ready to trust its word and cease to provoke the extremists who kept to a voice raucous and hateful. When and how might it safely 'proclaim' its 'statehood', embryonic as it must remain, as long as Israel stayed unwilling either to believe it as a neighbour or concede it as a fact?

The broad stream of Palestinianism by 1988 affirmed its recognition of Israel's right to be, 'within borders secured in being defined' and only defined when they were mutually secured. That paradox had always been the situation. Would, could, Israel rise to clinching it and if so, when and by what mechanism? Was there sincerity and could it hold? In a diminutive stretch of common territory would not a Palestinian State be a potential menace, a source of constant unease, a seed-bed of conspiracy? And what of settlements incorrigible, and ex-residents yearning out of abject poverty to return? Had not history in fact itself foreclosed its own correction as futile and forlorn? Had Israel become, in effect, party to an irreversible scenario of tragic victimization for which she would not be held guilty but for which there were no amends consistent with her own statehood or integrity?

IV

This retrospect brings us to the nineties. Its pathos is memorably told in the Palestinian statement at the Madrid Conference of 1990 to which Prime Minister Yitzhak Shamir came with an all too evident reluctance but which led, circuitously, to the Oslo accords. The statement ran:

> We the people of Palestine stand before you in the fullness of our pain, our pride and our anticipation, for we long harboured a yearning for peace and a dream of justice and freedom. For too long, the Palestine people have gone unheeded, silenced and denied, our identity negated by political expediency; our right to struggle against injustice maligned; and our present existence subdued by the past tragedy of another people. For the greater part of this century we have been victimized by the myth of a land without a people and described with impunity as the invisible Palestinians. Before such a wilful blindness we refused to disappear or to accept a distorted destiny. Our Intifada is a testimony to our perseverance and resilience, waged in a just struggle to regain our rights. It is time for us to narrate our own story, to stand witness as advocates of truth which has long lain buried in the consciousness and conscience of the world. We do not stand before you as suppliants, but rather as the torch-bearers who know that, in our world of today, ignorance can never be an excuse. We seek neither an admission of guilt after the fact, nor vengeance for past inequities, but rather an act of will that would make a just peace a reality.[23]

In its cadences, almost echoing Abraham Lincoln or its 'dream' with Martin Luther King, it did not read – or sound – like Yasser Arafat but, whosoever's the hand, it was a noble statement both of retrospect and intent, neither lame nor vindictive nor despairing. It read as a dignified indictment of a United States that had stayed long on behalf of their protégé in an unheeding stance of bare 'anti-terrorism'. Most of all it was an impassioned charge against the Israeli pursuit of a partitioned heritage who would not come to agreeing where the frontier would be (if partition really was the name of the story) and meanwhile camped increasingly where the other party was destined to be and doing so behind a policy of excluded negotiation or an ambition that cherished indivisibility. It was poetically right – if emotionally distressful – that it should have been left to a Palestinian pen to draft, in those Madrid terms, the Israeli charge-sheet.

The Madrid Conference with American consent and an inclusive participation was a notable waymark but too public a forum to yield negotiated success. The secret talks in Norway, with a careful phasing of steps and a pledge of final completion on a given time-scale, kindled ardent hopes and proved a trust-building achievement destined to seem, in retrospect, a hollow or a treacherous thing. The nearer it seemed to bring the reality of Palestinian statehood the more the recalcitrant elements in the Israeli imagination asserted their anger or disquiet.

The Gaza Strip and Jericho were ceded to Palestinian control with six enclaves following, equipped by Israel for Palestinian policing and administration, and elections went ahead for a Palestinian Parliament, though genuine freezing of settlements tarried inconclusively. Despite continuing severities, like the virtual exile to the snows of Hermon of a hundred and more alleged Palestinian activists, Rabin's government found itself riding a tiger of zealot-like hostility which brought the fourth decade of the State of Israel to the most appalling depth of self-awareness in the assassination, by a Jewish hand, of its own Prime Minister and a hero of its martial deeds in self-creation.

It could not be deplored as an individual act of private barbarity. It had been, as it were, 'monitored' by sectarian assassination by word and innuendo, a bigotry eager for the 'iron wall' thesis of the Likud tradition. These had portrayed Rabin as 'traitor', cartooned him in Nazi dress and reviled his cautious espousal of the hope of peace. His murder – even the ease with which it could be contrived – revealed how dire was the mental and spiritual condition inside Israel, how precariously poised its very capacity had become for any further measures under Oslo.

In due course, with Likud tactically distancing itself from the deed, the subsequent election brought Benyamin Netanyahu to power to preside enigmatically over a slow repudiation of what Oslo promised. Though some 80 per cent of the city of Hebron was transferred to Palestinian control, the fewness of the implanted zealots ensured how brutally confrontational that nest of history would remain.[24] Like the murder of Count Bernadotte in 1948, the murder of Yitzhak Rabin in 1995 demonstrated that there were elements of violence in Israel determined never to negotiate towards a peace of the definition of borders which would be remotely acceptable to the Palestinian side. The State was effectively hobbled by its own cruel indeterminacy yet deeply moved by other elements earnestly committed by its moral conscience to seek and ensure its peace. But could any government contemplate civil war within as the price of doing so? In the event, the Likud mind would directly – or indirectly – prevail, directly by regaining power in 1996, indirectly by constraining even Labour leaders to 'mark their mark' as in no way gullible or naive in any peace ideology.

There were two grim examples of the latter when, prior to calling an election, with undue delay after the Rabin murder,[25] Shimon Peres proved his 'dove–hawk' capacity. While pressing on with Israeli withdrawal from major Palestinian towns, he sent more than one hundred activists into virtual isolation on the winter snows of Lebanon, where they were tutored in disruptive tactics by Hizballah forces in the buffer zone. The harsh militarization of the Hamas segment of Palestinianism was dramatically set forward.[26] It was as if the quest for peace, in the given depth of division in Israeli society, could only be pursued with gestures that bartered away its hope of success.

The second evident occasion of such quandary was the same leader's decision to bomb the Lebanese Hizballah resulting in the massacre of Cana with more than a hundred fatalities including personnel of the UNO Base, long employed in striving to safeguard the peace of Israel's northern border. Three years later another Labour Prime Minister would succeed in withdrawing the Israeli presence from Lebanon that had elicited the armed Hizballah presence – itself a legacy from the invasion of Lebanon in 1982.

When Peres lost the election it was said that Netanyahu had a 'map in the mind' that left further implementation of the Oslo Accords in virtual abeyance. The principle of gradualism in those agreements was praiseworthy, given the urgent need to build a long-shattered mutual trust but it also facilitated the opposite end. Deferment in the time-scale heightened distrust and left vigorously pursued occasion for rapid settlement-planting, which, in turn, left long-term PLO hopes elusive and, with their failure, the sinister popularity growth of the extremists outside the PLO.

The formal elections early in 1996 of a Palestinian 'Parliament' and of Yasser Arafat as 'President' could only mean a highly ambivalent achievement of tragically gathering stalemate in which the near hollowness of these advances would be evidently at the mercy of that segment of Israeli society which, like the Lord in the mood of Psalm 2, 'would have them in derision'. For the ultimate flaw in the Oslo plan – as some acutely foresaw at the time – was that it virtually made the Palestine Authority liable for the policing and ultimate eliminating of Palestinian extremists. The gesture by Israel in equipping and arming local forces for this purpose had this element of cunning, as well as magnanimity – the latter of great asset in the international arena.

While settlements went forward and much else provocative in the emotional area – and even by dint of archaeology[27] – the conciliatory measures were deprived of their full promise. The task of Palestinian control was made steadily more problematic, as well as odious by degrees, the more Israel deferred the basic elements of peace that had to do with 'agreed borders', viable statehoods both ways, withdrawal from settlements within those agreed, the return of exiles, and some sharing of symbolic Jerusalem. It was an odd and cruel dilemma to be duty-bound to curb one's own belligerents, when Israeli policy was conniving with their provocation and had land initiatives of her own. Arafat had been manoeuvred into becoming, as it were, a hostage, with Israel able to determine whether or not 'he had done enough', and to bomb and deride him if they decreed he had not.

The tragic comedy of this situation came late in 2001 when Sharon's coalition government bombed out of function the police structure from which it was requiring the suppression of suicide-bombers who, in their heinous way, were answering Israel's own denials of hope. Sharon's 'turning of the screw' was pathetic to behold, yet ruthless – a Gaza airstrip bull-dozed, 'presidential' helicopters destroyed and their erstwhile user thoroughly humiliated and immobilized in near assassination, until 'he had done enough'. It was a strange and ugly gloss on the Jabotinsky concept of 'the iron fist', the more subtle for being applied – not as he once thought – to produce a treaty of surrender but to grovel under the terms of one imposed. Retrospect may come to identify it as the sourest face, in this mood, of Israeli Semitism.

If late 2001 was only extracting from the potential of Oslo what it had artlessly conceded and which already 1997 had kept in view, there had intervened the Camp David saga of the summer of 2000 in the fading weeks of President Clinton's bid for the honour of clinching 'the final fulfilment' of Oslo and Ehud Barak's pledged conclusion of peace.

What was the truth of that second famous Camp David where the PLO was said to have forfeited its last and best chance – a chance which the second and far different *Intifadah* would bitterly weep for as a supreme folly? Was 90 per cent of a 20 per cent (Palestine-wise) West Bank really on offer, with ensured 'de-settlementizing', genuine control in the abeyance of Israel armour, with an economically viable achievable agriculture, water resources, well-digging, olive planting, an integrated road-system and feasible connection with the Gaza Strip, international relations, and a lifting of Israeli veto on financial assets of the PLO?

Hardly, in many areas dubiously, in no areas definitively. All of them hinged, in part, on the return of refugees which Israel could not begin to negotiate. There were limits to the viability of a further three million more of population, and a necessary veto on the implications of their presence out of the long and bitter tradition of resentment and enmity and their threat to the homogeneity so crucial to Israeli identity. In the light of this realism could Camp David have been acceptable, conjured against the clock, and shortly to be followed by an Israeli election where all the portents said that it would produce a régime bent on rescinding it?

For perpetually in the analysis was that dimension in Israeli society holding a version of Semitism for which, whatever the vicissitudes of partition-theory and a policy of borders, the land (the land on this view already 'partitioned' at the River Jordan in 1921) was essentially, politically and emotionally, indivisible. By their measure, Zionism could never have been embarked, from the beginning, on a strategy of co-habitation in statehoods. Those who read their Zionism otherwise had – perhaps finally – failed to dissuade or deter them. Yet there was a scenario by which the reproach could seem to belong with a Palestinianism that had not been able to betray its refugees. Whether they should have been left in grimly prolonged refugeedom was not Israel's responsibility. It lay squarely as a human problem on the Arab soul. But that the tragedy had historically overtaken them in the forties and the sixties of the 20th century was the human consequence of Zion. The permanence of their exile – if such it be – must stand as the ultimate verdict on the fact, and the cost, of homecoming effectively and conceptually spelling a home-denying.

V

The foregoing, as only synoptic and based on the focal issue of defining agreed borders, has made no attempt to do narrative justice to a complex story. The aim has been to ponder a Semitism which, in Zionist form, has been required by its own logic in practice to forfeit its own ideology told in theory. But has the survey been unduly harsh, disallowing or discounting aspects of resolve and high purpose studied in Chapter 7? Indictments can only be fair if they stay balanced. What of the democratic status of Palestinians inside Israel, the citizens' rights, their members in the Knesset? What of the lively conscience, the vigorous efforts of the peace movements? And with all these, why not a present suspension of judgement given that so much is 'on the way' and deserves to await some future vindication? If not naively sanguine, observers should not be premature.

There is wisdom in such counsels, unless the means have already suborned the end. Abba Eban in his time of office would often plead that way. He wrote after 1967:

> There was a deep seated conflict . . . discomfort in Israel about the idea of ruling a foreign (sic) people. But, in the policy and doctrine of Israel, this

was regarded as a temporary paradox that would somehow be resolved in the context of peace.

He added that Israel was not an 'Esperanto' country writing its history on a clean slate.[28] Yet, a year later, pleading the fact of conflicts ever since the Mandate years, he told the United Nations that 'there was nothing normal or legitimate to return to', thus, by a form of words, eliding the whole question of centuries-old Palestinian presence and arguing as if only recent wars had created the issue.[29] He forgot that much in history can be cheaply resolved if only one foreshortens the perspective. What if the long-pressed, staunchly-pressing, will for peace were to have only the solace of splendid failure, frustrated by the weight or the venom of other counsels?

Much in that question turns on the strange postures of Judaism in the emergence and the ongoing shaping of the State and on the deep failure of official religion in the spiritual realms of political wisdom and personal well-being. Orthodox Judaism in Israel, ever engrossed on using its parties' bargaining position in the Knesset to extract maximum favours for its own purposes and insisting magisterially on a monopoly of religious law, has demonstrated a total failure to bring a perceptive, critical spirituality to bear on the evolving situation and the intensifying confrontation with the Palestinians.

In this it was little aided by the long Biblical tradition of 'anathema for Amalek', the ancient and ever vilified foe who had allegedly impeded transit into 'the land of promise'.[30] The theme of 'them that hate us' and 'the hand of our enemies', which Luke included in his Gospel as 'the song of Zachariah',[31] could all too readily underwrite an inability to register any common humanity in a bitter situation. It would be left to young soldiers to sense a kind of 'I know you in this dark' emotion around the scene of combat in the Six Day War,[32] while some Rabbis were reading the state of armed conflict as divinely 'providential'. Thus the Orthodox writer, Haim Peles:

> The people of Israel are presently in such a state that a formal peace with the Arabs will bring about assimilation in the Semitic (sic) region. Consequently we may see in the state of war between us and the Arabs the hand of Providence.[33]

It was – for that cast of mind – 'such a state' as it would be providential to perpetuate.

An obvious area of this spiritual failure of the religious mind in Israel was that of restraining, or at least refraining from, the reversal of victimization which was so deep an issue for the very vitality of Zionism. At long last, the centuries 'harsh and strange' had given way to a situation empowered to affirm its own dignity, to inflict – if need be – not to be inflicted by, what, elsewhere, Shakespeare called 'outrageous fortune'. Zionism had been born, not only to end forever 'host nations' and their unpredictable moods, but to allow Israelis to assert the emotional mood of their own sovereignty.

Palestinian resisters of their country's being forfeit to that danger, too obviously incurred at Israeli hands untutored by the compassionate precept about 'loving the stranger', could see the precept as only grimly ironical.[34] Rooted in the land for generations, they had been made 'strangers' there as indigenes such as Jewry had never been during their alien time of Egyptian sojourn. Exodus memories, renewed in the Passover ritual as an exit out of slavery, could not fit what should be required of them as now the 'pharaohs' themselves. In any event, was there not a reading of rabbinic law which required Jewish power, when it was enjoyed, to enforce the Noahid law on the 'Gentiles' inside such Judaic statehood?[35] Happily, the broad secularity of Israel – as well as divergent rabbinic reading on Noahid obligation – obviated any such infliction of Israeli power on non-Jews. The factors that governed the use of Israeli empowerment were political and Zionist, not Talmudic and theological.

The real point, however, turns on how the very achievement of Zionist statehood, and the cost of its maintaining, sharpened Jewish particularism and constricted the capacity of Judaism to be inclusive in its sympathies. The necessities of a Joshua redivivus quickened the will to separatism and Orthodoxy lived the years in inward looking zeal for its own domestic pieties and privilege to the tragic neglect of spiritual discernment and vocation. It failed to inspire a lively or gentle conscience in any effective form.

Exacting and devious as the ways of the religious parties have been in Israeli politics and irksome in their incidence on daily life, there has been an important sense in which the Ben-Gurion cast of mind wanted it so. Yeshayahu Leibowitz quotes him as 'wanting the State to hold religion in the palm of its hand', and telling Leibowitz:

> You demand . . . the separation of religion and State. Your object is that the Jewish religion reinstate itself as an independent factor so that the political authority will be compelled to deal with it. I will never agree to the separation of religion from the State.[36]

There is a double irony here. On the one hand the State had a tedious and burdensome rabbinic establishment complicating both its constitutional workings and its social order, on the other it had an official religion neutralized from any effective moral intrusion into its counsels, a hierarchy producing no Savonarola to monitor its soul, no William Temple to call its social order towards a divine will. It would be left to religious scholars and sages to cherish the conscience of Zion. Martin Buber lived on the same Jerusalem street as Ben-Gurion but their political premises did not coincide and it is said they rarely met. For all the labyrinthine tedium involved by rabbinical politicizing, Ben-Gurion had the political luxury of a religious officialdom content to extort its self-serving demands rather than hold the State liable for spiritual ends laid down by godly conscience. 'A kept mistress of the secular government', religion in Israel did 'not radiate the light of Judaism even to the Jews'.[37]

The tale of its exactingness in the will to impose rigorous Sabbath rules, its urgent censorship, of social mores, has often been rehearsed. Readings of 'thou shall do no labour' on the Sabbath could be carried to bizarre lengths of mechanical gadgetry that made a mock of sanity and reverence. More unhappy was the near exclusion of Reform, and 'liberal', Judaism from the formation of the Jewish mind about Arabism, justice, conscience or personal faith initiatives. Mixed prayer services (of men and women) at the Western Wall have been refused, while the exemption of Yeshiva students from military service offends the secular mind. Effective monitoring of the counsels of statehood would have to come from consciences little aided, and long obstructed by, the official voices of Judaism in Israel, with their will to monopoly over the very definition of 'being Jewish' – a monopoly exercised via control over marriage, divorce and inheritance.

This was only consequential on the ambiguity inherent in the original philosophy of Zionism – how far 'Messianic' and, if so, in what terms? A deeply secular instinct was somehow also fulfilling, or at least recruiting, a profoundly religious mission concerning a people and a land and their inter-standing. It is not surprising that Judaism should have a divided, indeed a fissiparous, state of mind concerning it – whether to salute it as laudable, to reject it as blasphemous or to wait on its 'providential' unfolding. It was this persisting abeyance of Judaic decision, this hesitancy of Zionist Judaica, which sadly inhibited Jewish religion from due 'conscience sifting' in the making and perpetuating of the Zionist state. Judaism could in no way ignore it. For, with or without the diaspora, it was carrying its future: but neither could it confirm it wholeheartedly. For it was confounding or undoing its meaning and the deep mystery of its soul.

Thus, whether teased or tormented by the postures of official Judaism in Israel, the Ben-Gurions, the Begins, the Shamirs, the Sharons of the State 'had religion in the palm of its hand', unchastened and unrestrained by any monitoring or rebuking of conscience on the part of the established custodians of the State's religion. These vital constraints would be left to the 'souls of the seculars', to the Peace Movements or to religious minds who, like Jacob, had 'not ceased to wrestle with the angel'.[38] That it should have been so is one measure of the 'forfeiture' that Zionism has brought to Zion.

VI

The seeming, and then the actual, victimization of the Palestinians already noted, has to be seen as tragically part of any verdict required to be negative about the Zion in Zionism. Thanks to the making and shaping of the State, a measure of what – though only with careful reservations – we must call 'anti-Semitism' has entered into Arab culture. It has often been stressed, even as a plea for the acceptance of Israel, that Jews had long lived unmolested and secure in Arab lands. Why, then, should it not have happened so when these same Jews came into Palestine – many of them doing so when newly menaced where they had long belonged?[39]

The 'anti-' factor stemmed from the 'Semitism' present in the new State and its form as something inevitably seen as inimical to 'an existing population' confronted by it in political (rather than merely human) form. Similarly, the new insecurity of, for example, Tunisian or Iraqi Jews, had been a result of what the emergence of the Jewish State was seen to hold for that extended Arabism in respect of confrontation. If, in whatever way the Jewish mind understood, the State was for 'Semitism', dispute of it could not escape being 'anti-Semitic' within those parameters.

Politics then being what they are, it would become impossible to unlink this predicament from the charge, or the onus, of 'anti-Semitism' in the normal sense, namely a 'hatred of Jews'. Reciprocally then, from the Jewish/Israeli side, the 'myth' of Amalek would be reborn. Hence again the inveterate 'enemy', once again 'the eternally unwanted Jew'. Given what had eventuated in both parties, how could a countering *animus*, rightly to be called 'Semitism', not arise to be responsive to that 'anti-'?

Many of the same kindling factors were present – a persecuted psyche, doubts, fears and symbols, and warranting doctrines from given Scriptures. And for Jewry – ex Europe – there was the ever burning duty never to be vulnerable again, which *in situ* could only take an anti-Palestinian dimension. In the given situation of conflict and the demands, genuine or contrived, of military exigency, endless occasions of humiliation could be devised and victimization inflicted. As the seer in the Book of Revelation was reminded, 'vines and olive groves' are highly vulnerable items whose uprooting can have prolonged effect, as bitter as the denial of wells and the bull-dozing of dwellings, the expulsion of farmers, the isolation of villages.[40]

The element of deliberate hostility in these measures and in more awesome atrocities as those of Dair Yassin and Cana and Bait Jala spoke more massively still in the 1982 invasion and near prostration of Lebanon and the tribulations of South Lebanon. There were innumerable humiliations before and during the first *Intifadah*, distinguishing between 'acceptable' Palestinians and 'non-acceptable' in negotiations to the point of scrutinizing the make-up of delegations. The total dependence of a Palestinian economy on the will of the occupying State made for endless petty victimization at checkpoints and crossings, permits to go or to come. The low point of that Oslo provision effectively making the PLO leader liable for Israel's assessment of his performance in 'policing' its 'foes' among his own people, came in 2001–2 by his confinement and 'near assassination', and the breaking up of his one airport runway and the destruction of his two civilian helicopters. There was no logic in the bombing of the police buildings and personnel seeing these were the very agencies being held to account, 'to do more' – by Israeli reckonings – to baulk and rein in the 'terrorists'. Meanwhile the factors most bitterly contributing to these were continuing apace, when any wisdom about pacification demanded their cessation.

The hidden or blatant animus of 'Semitism' in this sense reflected itself in the increasing militarization of Israeli society. Many have a sense of nakedness for lack of a weapon on hand or over the shoulder. It was recorded during the first *Intifadah* that gunshops were besieged with purchasers of 9mm guns with 100 rounds of ammunition available to every owner. Would-be owners could readily show 'good reason' at the Interior Ministry to obtain the licence, such as threat to personal security or travel in 'occupied territory'. After annual reserve duty in the Defence Forces many keep Uzi or M-16 carbines in their private hands. Israel is thus a highly militarized society both physically and emotionally, with a psyche all too liable to belligerence both against its 'enemy' or the 'peaceniks' in its own midst. The murder of its own Prime Minister at the hands of a private citizen, and the ease with which, apparently, he could succeed, sent shock waves throughout Israeli society. It boded little comfort for the Palestinians.

This desolating scenario, the darkly shadowed face of Semitism, at the opening of the 21st century, has an Ariel Sharon for its insignia. As effectively unready to clinch the definition of its borders, Israel fails to define its soul. Zionism stays in desperate suspense about its integrity. 'The land' it so devoutly prizes as the very element of its destiny it will not politically and morally designate map-wise with any assured finality. Thus it leaves the territorial 'open question' the ever delayed and vacant 'answer' of its own right mind. There is a poetic justice in the fact that 'the land' where the goal belongs is the crux where the goal is betrayed. Even when the anti-Nazi war was at its height, there was a pragmatic Zionist decision, at the 'Biltmore' meeting, that 'the land might be divisible' while its indivisibility remained the ideological truth of it. The newly fledged Israel in 1948 accepted the 1947 partition Resolution but not the frontiers in its map-drawing. Through all the subsequent events, the policy of aided settlements has been abetting a virtual indivisibility, inasmuch as (a) these will ensure a non-viable fragmentation of 'Palestine' and (b) they – being irreducible – will pragmatically veto any real alternate statehood but their own.

Is Zionism thus betraying itself in the ethics of land-love itself? Is it not the more culpably doing so in that a hapless 'official' Palestinianism is bludgeoned into 'doing more to combat terrorism', and bombed for 'too little, too late', when Israeli policy itself denies the hopes that could forsake the terror?

It will be urged that this scene of strife is totally mutual, with innocence nowhere and the passions reciprocal. That is tragically true and the conflict endlessly obfuscates its analyses by partisans. It is, however, a very unequal confrontation, not only in the incidence of victims but the means to make them. Statistics of the dead and maimed are only odiously compared but disparities have meaning. One does not read of Palestinian gunboats marauding off the coast of Ashkelon or of helicopter gunships overhead. 'How many tanks does he have?' is a query Sharon has no need to ponder about Yasser Arafat. The odds have long been utterly unequal, which explains why the 'respectabilities' of action (democracy, legitimacy, and due exercise of power) have also seemed one-sided. Tragedy is intensified, not eased, when the ways it eventuates over long decades are either confused or distorted.

'I can wait ten years,' Ben-Gurion said after the combats following the State's creation, when colleagues were worrying about delay in turning truce and armistice into treaty and peace.[41] Zionism *qua* statehood has been ready to 'wait' for four more decades, one brand of Semitism waiting – as we have traced in Chapter 7 – with dignity and integrity in genuine will to have its statehood finally in mapped definition securely agreed with an adjacent statehood also in authentic territorial expression. The other Zionism has been waiting in a calculated ambiguity, 'a time on our side' stance of fact-creation and inflicted frustration of the 'other' and thus in steady forfeiture of the vision in its own 'dream', the compatible humanities of its own ambition.

It is this forfeiture which tells itself in the adulation of the murderer, Baruch Goldstein, in the wreck of the King David Hotel, the ousting of the Arab mayors, the dying of Count Bernadotte, the 'map in the Netanyahu mind', the post-Oslo deferments, the intermittent dead-hand on Palestinian economy and the despoliation of homes and villages, the rigours of military occupancy. Must the observer conclude, appreciating Zionism as an enterprise of supreme hope, that its 'Zion' is forfeit in the terms of its success?

There is one final haunting fear. What neighbouring state, it may be asked, has reason to bless Israel's neighbouring presence? Not Egypt, an invader once repulsed, then twice invaded and, retaliating finally 'peace-treated' to recover its Sinai and re-absorb its half million refugees. Not Jordan accommodating refugees, some into citizenry and incurring the internal costs of their will to resist Israel from its soil prior to passing that dilemma to Lebanon. Not Lebanon, brutally invaded, embroiled in civil conflict and plagued with the armed accentuation of its own tensions and often enduring punitive strikes it had no capacity nationally to recipro-cate. Not Syria with Jewish forces in permanent territorial occupancy in uncomfortable proximity to its capital.

All these 'sequences' might be said to be merely the arbitrament of war and response (except for Lebanon) to their own aggressions. So much is true but these, in turn, derived from how Israeli presence was, at length, perceived as intrusive. That perception, however the fact of it is read or mitigated, has far more dire consequences, when deeply religious emotions supervene across a much wider spread of history and locale. Backed so formidably by the United States both politically and militarily, Israel emerges to the Arab and the Muslim mind as a tragic provocation, irrational doubtless but for that reason the more unlikely to admit of conciliation and that on two counts. American policy and/or its Jewish lobby is neither minded nor able to bring to pass any genuine Palestinian statehood, whatever noises may be made in that direction in the flux of global high politics.

Nor is the Muslim perception of Jerusalem and – no less – its 'securing' inside Palestinian/Islamic statehood likely to be surrendered to the arguable exigencies of world peace. Thus 'the Temple Mount, *Al-Masjid al-Sharif*, the one *Al-Quds*', engages Semitism as expressed in Israel with Islam as felt in its soul. If these stay mutually incorrigible a global, more than a local, peace is darkly at stake. According to the great Maimonides, Judaism is inherently 'messianic' which will

> entail the restoration of Jewish sovereignty in the land of Israel including the full restoration of the Temple and its cult and it will culminate in universal monotheism.[42]

The 'sovereignty' is in hand, while most of Jewry would gladly forego the return of the Temple and its cult – but not all. The secular will and mind, however, still tarry in Islam and 'may for ever tarry'.[43] What then of any 'universal monotheism' and of Islam's share it defining it?[44]

Sovereign Semitic statehood is set in this entire quandary of at once ensuring its own continual safety and resolving its own religious meaning. Neither are only a theological task. They are a desperate item in the peace of the world, the world which in Israel Semitism has so decisively, so ambiguously rejoined.

The desperate pathos in that conclusion is only the more deepened by the chronic partisanship in which the whole long story is embroiled. Honest minds can find respite from the pathos only if, on the one hand, they relinquish the visionary idealism in which Zionism was once loved, or if, on the other, they reconcile to a realism that accepts an actual Zion with neither apology nor lament. To care overmuch about how, so long as whether is not at issue, is to have no lively measure of world politics or of human nature. Even so, to care too little is to surrender the noble vision of some 'final solution', a Jewish fulfilment at Jewish hands, the possession and satisfaction of realized destiny, a Zion not forfeit to the means of Zionism.

'Whose wheel the pitcher shaped' was only saved from being a dark analogy of fatalist despair by Rabbi Ben Ezra's emphasis on Jeremiah's vision and the metaphor of clay still in shaping hands, not baked and hardened beyond return. How long in pottery can such deciding moments last, how long in world affairs? In the latter there are always pasts no future can expect to overtake. Hope has to be the will as well as the wish in 'plastic circumstance', the more so when – divine potterhood apart – it seems so far to seek. Or perhaps human will, in measure, is how the divine 'potter' moves his hands, the more so since the 'marring' has been ours in history.

In a final chapter we can best bring together the pathos and the critical present by dint of Marc Chagall's Jewish art and his deep poetic wisdom. This will allow the course of thought to take up aspects only latent in Chapters 7 and 8, in their study of Semitism in its ambiguously Zionist shape.

From Chapters 4 and 5, however, we have incurred crucial issues of Jewish/Christian relations on the contemporary stage, both for their inherent Biblical quality and for their critical bearing on the themes, political and moral, of Zionism and the hope of Zion. These are taken up in Chapter 9.

Chapter Nine

INTER-TESTAMENTAL
RELATIONS NOW

I

In academic circles 'inter-testamental' is normally applied to literature of the centuries between the strange end of prophethood and the literary completion of the Christian Canon. It referred to so-called apocryphal and pseudepigraphical writings like the Book of Jubilees and the Gospel of Thomas. Even more aptly, it fits the things at stake between the heirs of the Old and the community of the New 'Testaments'. For it was precisely the concept of 'covenants' that divided them. It did so with increasing finality, once the heirs of the former consolidated in disallowance of any Judaic validity in the latter – a validity its custodians could only more resolutely affirm as the very shape of their integrity.

Thus the burden of the tension between them lay in the inherent disqualification either had for the other simply in sustaining how they knew themselves. It was a burden set to be differently borne by the parties, the one in a superior condition as a *religio licita* under Roman law, the other for three dark centuries surviving only in powerless tribulation as both *illicita* and socially despised. After Constantine early in the 4th century a regnant Christendom darkly reversed the fortunes, in the terms studied in Chapter 6. All contemporary reckonings between them have to live with the tragic legacies in the disputatious history whence their present destinies have come.

At once there are two too easily assumed reciprocal attitudes each has differently held concerning the other. The one is that Jewry can well adopt the stance of simply ignoring the Christian faith and church – 'ignore', that is, conceptually, for physically and effectively it has for long been forced to live perpetually apprehensive with it. The other is that Christianity should instinctively deplore the abiding Judaism of Jews, with 'deploring' so long taking forms of harsh hostility.

'Ignore' and 'deplore' are a sorry impulse either way and a wise disowning of their mutual self-treachery is the first necessity in being inter-testamental now. Why rightly called 'self-treachery' is the first duty for study here.

In respect of Jewry a familiar tendency has been to say that Judaism has no problem with Christianity. It is simply an aberration which has gone its own way. There was, and is, no such thing as 'the Judeo-Christian tradition'. It never credibly existed. Christianity can conveniently be seen as an independent religion owing much to pagan factors. It is only pretentious and usurpatory in clinging to its pseudo-Hebraisms so wilfully prominent in its liturgies and memories. It has no credible right to Jewish heritage and must be read as for ever at odds with what it succeeded only in distorting totally.

There are endless factors, political and emotional, that conduce the Jewish mind to this 'ignoring' verdict but it may not hold. It cannot credibly belong with an honest Judaism fully aware of itself. For it is things precious in its own story it massively ignores – the long dream of Messianic prophets, the essentially Jewish context of the apostolic Church (as studied in Chapter 5) and the inherent liability of 'covenant' to inclusive human relevance via 'the blessing in Abraham'.

Supremely, it would impossibly include Jesus in its 'ignoring', as indeed for long years did many Jewish minds, seeing him as lost in Christian monopoly and so, for that reason, a figure of necessary exclusion from Jewish piety. Happily, and to the alerting of Christian scholarship around the New Testament, that Jewish neglect of Jesus has been reversed by Jewish experts from Joseph Klausner to Geza Vermes. The old silence or reserve could never have held, once a certain trust in the Enlightenment and a mental will to participation in Christian themes had developed. For it was always in his very Jewishness that Jesus could not be in doubt or question. Christian Christology was the very fruition of Hebraic Messiahship, as divine action reciprocal to the hope of history. What was at issue was 'What manner of Jew? In significance and experience?' – the question which returned all who cared to the honest liability of either testament to the other. Jesus at its heart could never be faithfully ignored nor – by any sane logic – could that defining 1st century Jewish/Christian reading of him.

If a Jewish impulse to ignore Jesus was impossibly disloyal, so likewise must be any Christian instinct to deplore Judaism. The deep disappointment around the post-AD 70 Jewish abeyance of participation, by and large, in the new fellowship was puzzling and grievous. For in one sense it orphaned as well as implicitly disqualified what had been experienced as a great emancipation. The sense of being disqualified will always arouse human unease in relating to disqualifiers but the ruling principle of 'Whosoever will may come' is not rescinded because of those who 'will not'. Long centuries would turn that unease into resentment and hostility. In the dark tragic retrospect we now have of them, love and sanity can have no option but to hold in an awed and genuine esteem the fidelity of Judaic faith. The Christian conviction that the theme of 'divine people-hood' was duly destined to be fulfilled in an entire human openness cannot well be surrendered. To do so would be to surrender also its first shape of original privacy. It need not, however, be to deny the ongoing heirs the privacy of their conviction – a conviction which must remain a theme of religious relationship, revered in the holding.

Furthermore, it would be part of a Christian awareness of being heir to its vision – as something needing radical sharing – to acknowledge how difficult Judaically the inner crisis was. To forego an assumed indispens-ability to divine purposes could never be 'a light thing' for any so required. There is always the fear of treasures not being safe with others, the alibi of their needing always the right custody as essentially one's own.

Such acknowledgement of the Jewish reasons for remaining Jewish would always be an aspect of the debt owed by those who first read those sources as ripening into a founding Christianity. Moreover, it is a sensi-tivity required to be for ever answerable to the harsh centuries surveyed in Chapter 6 and to the Christian guilt which remains their legacy. Honest Jewry would not ask this in the emotionally exploitative terms that make its quality as genuine and spontaneous the more problematic.

Further again, despite the burden of the implicit disavowal of things Christian that belongs in ongoing Judaism, there are rich common themes by which either can enrich the other, or around which dialogue can the better comprehend what the separate stakes are. The things that contro-versy itself requires us to share, precisely by joining them at all, potentially chastens and matures our possession of them. One does not have to accept the Jewish matrix to be arrested tellingly by Martin Buber's philosophy of the eternal Thou addressing the essential 'I' of the human soul, never to be relegated to the 'it' level of a mere thing, forfeiting the personhood of both parties. Nor is a Christian less continually so in savouring grate-fully the theme of divine pathos, eloquently discerned by Abraham Heschel in his studies, for example, of Hosea and Jeremiah. Reader and author are immediately akin around what was, and is, the defining dimen-sion of all things divine Christians discern in the Cross of Christ.

Even where the mental tensions are made most acute by the emotional demands of either side, neither can escape the positive onus of relation-ship. For to refuse it would merely let emotion rule as if the issues had no other logic, as, for example, when Jacob Neusner writes:

> For my part, if I am accepted as 'a human being' and not as a Jew, I do not accept that acceptance. I aspire to no place in an undifferentiated humanity. Take me despite my Jewishness and there is nothing to take. Overlook what is important to me and you obliterate my being.[1]

This stance, if pressed, is to go out of this world. At some point one has to accept to be 'a human being', a participant, on common terms, in the human whole. Being 'accepted as a Jew' cannot preclude this, since Jewishness is human-ness, provided that the former does not 'obliterate' the latter. Whether it does or not, is the entire issue of how it sees itself, i.e. whether its claimed exceptionality shares, in some sense, with all those not-exceptionalized in Jewish terms. That it ought so to share we have seen in Chapter 2 to be the corollary of the Biblical, Quranic doctrine of creation. Whether it does or not is the whole puzzle of the concept of 'the Gentiles'. For these could well react to Neusner's logic by:

> If I am only accepted as a 'Gentile' I do not accept that acceptance. I aspire to no place in a differentiated humanity if the differentiation is radical . . . Take me despite my 'Gentile-ness', and there is everything to share. Otherwise you locate my being in a contrast – I lack 'chosen-ness'.

What we are calling 'the inter-testamental situation' has to be intensely an inter-human one, disowning the bias whether of 'election' or of 'supersession'.

II

An immediate corollary of that necessity must no less surely be the rejection of the now popular 'two covenant' theory, of which James Parkes was a main 20th century pioneering advocate.[2] It purports to argue that Christianity, from the outset, ought to have been understood as 'God's grace towards the Gentiles', never meant for the inclusion of Jews, who were 'already there' in the inviolate election of YAHWEH from Sinai. Its attraction was that it eased the awful post-Holocaust burden on the Christian conscience, offered a total relief from the long inter-testamental theme and promised a future of irenic partnership. Its naïveté was that it 'eased' the burden all too lightly, that it betrayed the apostolic vision studied in Chapter 5 and that it forfeited all loyalty to the New Testament text and community. Further, it risked becoming, if unwittingly, a most bizarre and sinister form of anti-Semitism, by positing the Christian Church as where Jews were – by definition – unwanted. It surrendered the whole theme of a Jew-'Gentile' inclusion and presented the faith of Christ as having an 'exclusion clause' *vis-à-vis* the present heirs of those to whose forbears it was most in debt. It was the ultimate form of gross ingratitude, while relinquishing the pain and travail of an ongoing duty. It pre-empted what a longer patience has still to undertake.

Parkes' thesis was that, seeing the Sinaitic covenant was inviolate to all generations, the allegedly 'new one' must have been intended only for those whom the first did not embrace, i.e. the non-Jewish 'others', to whom at length reparation for their long exclusion was thus being made. The scantiest study of the Gospels and Letters in the New Testament could never intelligently allow that reading. The initial welcome had been from Jews to 'Gentiles', nor had the latter assumed any unilateral declaration of independence. The notion that the new faith in 'Christ crucified' ought never to have been preached to Jews is to turn a deeply Jewish impulse into a deplorable aberration, and takes no account of the calendar of later events. The eventual near 'Gentilizing' of the Church could never have been the thing it was if it had been so from the start.

Furthermore, the 'two covenant theory' of Christian validity leaves painfully unresolved the perennial theme of the 'old' covenant, namely how – if it is never consummated – it is ever blessedly fulfilled. Zionism, as we have seen in two previous chapters, remains a deeply ambivalent answer, perpetuating an identity-anxiety. It is not that tender non-Jewish conscience urgently needs, and seeks, to preclude covenantal 'supersession'. 'Supersession' was never the crucial theme, given that the gift and calling of YAHWEH are divinely pledged. The vital theme is how they are Jewishly realized in their acknowledged duty to the rest of human history. The 'two covenant theory', essentially excluding Jewry from the alleged account of how that duty was 'realized' in Christian faith and community – and 'realized' with Jewry ironically exempt from its meaning – leaves the age-long destiny unresolved, still elusively a differing humanity, with Zionism accentuating its elusiveness. How can the second be a 'covenant' at all if, by its lack of Jewish relevance, it has no status inside the first? Surely covenantal privilege either way, old or new, has duly sacred obligation to those said to be outside it no less than to those inside. Otherwise, it has nothing in trust and becomes only an exercise in self-esteem.[3]

Paul's invocation of peace upon 'the Israel of God' (Gal. 6.16) was not a language dubiously used by him as Jew, except in one respect, namely that it could now include a wider, non-ethnic, reach into a 'Gentile' people of grace. Need it then have been seen as Jewishly disloyal? Was not such a wider 'Jewry' already in being? Would it not continue so beyond his age and on into our own? By his inclusive usage, 'the Israel of God', he was both conserving a precious concept and insisting that no embrace of 'Gentiles' could lead into a Jewish unwantedness. The age-long term had, by due consent, assumed its new dimension. The Fourth Evangelist was of the same mind in writing (3.16) that 'God so loved the world . . . ' and never 'God so loved the Gentiles,' divine love being – as all the prophets said – the supreme emotion between YAHWEH and Israel.

The two covenant theory has to jettison this whole Biblical perception, in holding it to be against its grain for Jews to be involved. It is, therefore, at issue with the very capacity of divine love, thus inwardly obliged to discriminate – in Parkes' words – between 'the dual inheritance of humanity'.[4] By the same token it entails itself in a dual concept of human wrongness, one realm of which can be 'cured' by legislation, the other only by 'justifying grace'. The community of the former can be essentially corporate while that of the latter can only be 'collected' by private, personal consent to join, so lacking the coherence of an authentic people-hood. Only the first is truly societal – a view which ignores how intensely personal is Jewish piety, how fully incorporate the 'gathered-in-grace' have been.

The whole theme of a dual reading of humanity this way stands in a state of unresolved paradox. It believes in the validity of the preaching of grace in Christ. The 'Gentile' direction of the Church's mission was no aberration. It was entirely right. The Cross of Christ truly avails in redemption from sin and guilt. 'Messiah crucified' was in God and from God, indeed in New Testament terms, 'God manifest'. All the corollaries about the inadequacy of law, the radical reach of human wrong, the near despair of honest selfhood, are recognized in the very necessity, and reality, of divine grace. But their relevance belongs to the non-Judaic realm. The whole New Testament measure of what, as to God and humanity and grace and sin and hope, is taken as inclusive and universal, is acknowledged as radical and realist save among the heirs of Sinai and David. For these, the physical and metaphysical reality of that heritage suffices.

It follows that the two covenant theory has drastically re-written the New Testament literature. It has also implicitly, if not explicitly, renounced the mission inherent in those writings as not rightly to be taken into the audience round Sinai.[5] Jewish exemption from their Gospel has to be operative as well as conceptual.[6] It should certainly be accepted by a truly gentle Christianity that vulgar, aggressive, triumphalist evangelism among Jews has no place, that it needs to listen to how and why so many in Jewry must insist that, since the Shoah and long before, Christians have nothing credible to tell to Jews except a saga of compromise and shame. That Christians should know it so only deepens the honesty demanded of the trust with Christ.

It may not cancel it. In that world 'harsh and strange', it could be no part of *parrhesia* to be 'a sounding brass or a tinkling symbol', only empty in its heart and noisy in its sense.[7] Always the issue round mission was not 'whether' but 'how', and the 'how' has always to be what, in their like-ness, interprets the wounds of Jesus as the theme of the grace of God.

But the final doubtfulness around the two covenant theory of inter-testamental relation is that it forecloses the real task, does pseudo duty for what asks of each a richer, surer engagement with the other. It does not enter as the Christian must into the full measure of the reasons for the Jewish self-exemption from a Christian Christology, nor with the deeply Judaic case against such self-exemption. It is clearly suspect, on the Christian side, as deriving from a will to make reparation for a heinous history, in fee also (as is much of Christian Zionism) with a hope to ease the burden of the moral dilemmas incurred by the politics of the State of Israel.

These points have been handled elsewhere. That they have had their bearing on the will, as it were, to compensate for a bitter past by dint of a present congruence with Jewish aims and needs, is not in doubt. Jewry, however, is not well served by such emotive compliance with its mind, even were that mind not manifestly unanimous. Religious relationships can never ignore contemporary *mise-en-scène*. They deserve to delve below it to their own full liability to God and truth as being, alone, their good faith with each other. The world 'harsh and strange' is not addressed by hearts 'fond and strange', to what is asked of them. Where, then, should they be going?

III

Given that on no count of honesty or realism can we forbear to relate, that by no inner loyalty can we disown each other, we both are bound to seek an inter-testamental integrity, answerable to where we now are and to the sombre histories through which we have passed, histories where the Christian has the heavy onus of reproach and guilt, the Judaic the burden of suffering and adversity. The legacies, either way, are loaded with the emotions of controversy and the arguments of prejudice.

These are such, as all the foregoing has shown, that defy all neat analysis. Accepting the risk of seeking one, perhaps we can occupy the course of thought with two inter-locking themes. How may/should history underwrite and justify God? How does a religion suffice humankind in the form of its belonging with it? Both Jewry and Christianity stand, or fall, by their confidence in having answered both questions in their own distinctive terms. Both, as we have studied in Chapters 1 and 5, root themselves in events where they perceive 'the place of the Name', the divine summons into tribal, ultimately national, vocation as 'elect people of YAHWEH', and 'the Christ event' of 'God thereby reconciling the world' and commissioning an entrusted Church as 'the open people of God'. In neither case is the sense of defining history a matter of mere 'faith saying so', an arbitrary 'faith-in-faith' situation kept impervious from enquiry as to its credentials, though many outsiders have been minded to see them so. Others have scouted the very idea that time and place could ever sustain 'metahistories' or be, in their transitory fragility, any habitations of the divine.

The scholarly aspects of this common theme-at-issue are more tractable than the philosophical. It will be well to take them first. Intelligent folk, whether sceptical or trustful, are well aware that academic queries around the New Testament as history have been intense and sustained for generations. We need not rehearse them here.[8] It is not always recognized that the Hebrew narratives, from Abraham, via Moses and Joshua, to the Hebrew monarchies at least as far as Solomon, are no less fraught with imponderables than is the 'Jesus of history/Christ of faith' scenario of the New Testament. Nor are the stakes less loaded, the suspicions less radical. Is 'election' the 'myth' of a nomadic tribalism, the Exodus a mythopoeic fruit of ethnic genius? 'The mystery of Israel' has long been, not the last refuge of illusion, but the ultimate appeal of conviction.

But need it, should it, matter what the facts were? Should faith require more evidence than the conviction explicit in identity itself and the perpetuity that – now incontestably – sustains it through the sheer existence of the Jewish people?

It would seem that, in both cases, Christian and Jewish, the faiths, in the last reckoning, can only be intrinsic to the faithful. For, as with Islam also, that is the situation with which we have to deal – a situation responsive, we must hope, to outside query and responsible for its own due scholarship within, as crucial for its own integrity, even though with some of its believers the situation may be quite otherwise. Its archaeologists, time-sifters and text scrutineers will have their place but in the end faith will supervene as the great determinant. The Jew will truly say: 'We are a people. We are party of a covenant which binds us together . . . the reality of a people with a land.'[9] This 'divine *menage à trois*', as 'the self-perception of a society' is, like 'any faith assumption', 'an irrational act', writes Jonathan Magonet, in the sense that all religion, *per se*, must pass beyond the empiricism of the sciences. He wisely adds that the 'freedom to be critical' (which he would not exclude) 'seems to depend . . . on the depth and security of our faith in the first place'.[10]

Thus, among thoughtful Jews, the possibility that the texts' view of patriarchs and Pentateuch may well be post-exilic will not put their faith in jeopardy. Nor will thoughtful Christians revise their commitment to Christ because the usage 'Jesus said . . . ' is too naïve, for example, about the Fourth Gospel. A right faith will always have room in itself for doubt of itself and, inclusive that way, remain conclusive for discipleship. Given that religious reality is this way, that the situation is intrinsic for all and that to be faith-based is not to be faith-inventing, perhaps the Judaic and Christian versions can engage in mutual and intelligent acceptance of their being each intrinsic to themselves. Exchanging this way an honest and gentle esteem will not mean there are no exacting issues of relation: it will set these in the only context apt for their transacting.

Semitism, then, its nature and character, will be the first fact in any proper discussion of anti-Semitism, since it is there that what is adversarial has its motive. Esteem of Semitism, however, in the sense argued, will turn from sheer negativity – still more animosity – into patient attention and an honest quest which asks why Jewish mind and heart disqualified and persuaded its soul against the Christian sense of the Messiah in Jesus and its sequel in an open peoplehood. The question and answer will lead us back into how either faith 'justifies' God and suffices the human situation.

The twin reasons, it seems clear, were a disowning of Messiahship in those Jesus terms – or, on a later time-scale – *any* historical terms,[11] and, sequentially, the threat it seemed to hold for Jewish particularity, as divinely covenantal, by the 'Gentile' welcome into which it ventured. It was those two defensively Semitic positions that led to a perverse reaction slowly but darkly shaping an anti-Semitic mind. The one unbelief prompted pain and anxiety in the other. Explaining why Jews had not believed became a necessity of Christian believing and took shape in competitive possession of the same Scriptures, which in turn deepened the tensions implicit in their exegesis and the presumption either way the other claimed.

Tension could then accentuate into an idea, to which both were liable, namely that the other lacked capacity to comprehend. This could then descend into reasons like: 'It is because they are stubborn', or 'they are blind', or worse again: 'they have been blinded', and again: 'they have been blinded as a curse because they are wilful or immoral' – all in heightened contrast to the 'chosen', the sight-gifted, the wise and uncorrupted.

We can only escape this morass and its tragic narrative shape reviewed in Chapter 6 by forsaking its emotive logic and seeking how we might relate together in the one divine/human situation from which both had started, only thus to embroil into fruitless contention. If Semitism understood that the sole and sovereign Creator, purposeful Inaugurator of all human creaturehood, had willed for one tribal dimension a singular role and privilege, it would be congruent with *both* elements in that scenario that its particularity carry *some* universality and its 'electing' be more than privately fulfilled.

Such a conviction had been the stuff of Christian beginnings. Nor was the Semitic thing, in its supreme prophetic mind, ever careless of its more than private import, its human liability. The post-Christian question for it was, or should have been, if not that way, then which other? Sadly, as we have seen in Chapter 4, its self-query went the other way into urgent self-preservation, into a still tenacious coupling of folk and Torah-folk, the more steadfast as the loss of the land came home in identity-anxiety.

What then today after so many haunted centuries? Is it enough simply for Semitism to argue that divine love, like human love, has always implied a 'jealousy' about where it comes to rest?[12] For what selects will also uniquely cherish and abstain elsewhere. The sense of having a prerogative position will still have in its meaning those excluded from it. 'Thus divided from you, we (Jews) have been assigned to you for your help,' wrote Martin Buber.[13] Such 'help' is, of course, conjectural where it is offered in a Zionist form that involves displacement and distress, making it difficult to discern the spiritual in the political it employs, as we have seen in Chapter 8.

Elsewhere and state-making apart, there is a ministry that 'Gentiles' must readily recognize and greet as part of a listening, not a quarrelling, relationship. Many 20th century Jewish thinkers, Buber and Gershom Scholem and André Neher among them, have stressed that it consists most of all in the protest from Jewry to Christians that a 'realized Messiah' is not to be reconciled with the actuality of human history. To have faith about a fulfilment is to renounce future hope. This is more than the point earlier asked, as to whether history can ever under-write belief, or trust turn upon event. It is the charge that to say: 'Christ came' is always premature. Manifestly history stays unredeemed. The only true Messianism is the one that waits in hope. Expectancy is never self-fulfilling.

Here the two strands of our will to relating come together; namely sufficing human history and being apt to God as history's Lord. With a slight hint of disdain Buber writes to the Christian:

> You who live in an ecclesia triumphans need a silent servant who reminds you, every time you believe you have partaken of God in bread and wine, Sir, remember the last things.[14]

At least then we can share the faith that 'something' is to be anticipated. Were neither of us to fail to be saying with the psalmist: 'My expectation is from the Lord,' we would both be betraying our theology. For us both a historically indifferent divine sovereignty is a contradiction. So the issue between us as to hope proper to us in God is whether it is fact with prospect or prospect without fact.

The New Testament would say that the 'silent witness' is there in 'bread and wine' of Eucharist as being 'till He come' who also definitively came. It would say, as Joseph Fison wrote: 'Only those who know the Presence can hope for the Parousia.'[15] The *ecclesia* is only ever rightly *triumphans* in being consecrated to what stays future in the memorializing of what is past. The achieved/to be achieved Messiahship is its own speaking witness. The inclusive paradigm of redemption requires its ongoing resemblance in the community of the redeemed, whereby 'Messiah becomes all of us', but only in the meaning of the once for all. Those who confess themselves redeemed are to be themselves redemptive, as 'letting the mind of Christ – this Christ, this way – be theirs'.

When it proves otherwise the Church ever needs the 'silent witness' yet is truly at odds with the idea that nothing has ever already happened, by which 'last things' might be foreshadowed as well as awaited, thanks to the eternal actuality of vicarious love. On such holy ground in which to move, two faiths have no need to be in strife but only for either to perceive where the other should be heeded. With their own case for ever made out of what was past event, need Jewry wonder why Jesus called his Passion his 'exodus' (Luke 9.31) or why that 'bread and wine' was through a 'Passover'? The essence of Judaism, as seen in Chapter 1, was an abiding prospect out of sure retrospect. To share this way the inter-play of past and future, of event and hope, is a far truer vision than any 'two covenant' apartheid, excluding all that is mutual by a wanton separation.

IV

Divine sovereignty, so vigilantly vested by Jewish norms in Hebrew peoplehood, was a deeply law-centred thing. The theology of 'covenant' was with a view to obedience that 'glory might dwell in the land' through the due norms of its habitation. The reason why, in part and at length, Jewry declined the Christian venture into 'Gentiles' was a holy concern for sacred law, both liturgical and social. Doctrines of grace, as Paul expounded them, seemed risky, even 'anti-nomian' in their implications. Could it even be that the wretched impulse of a Christendom to dub Jews 'immoral' – as reason for their 'stupid' refusal of 'true faith' – was a sort of criminal *tu quoque* to such a self-consciously law-alert society?

In any event, a theological ethics is bound by sacred honour to be meticulous and to locate the inviolability of its law in the inviolate character of their society. 'The casting pearls before swine' analogy seems to have been common parlance' before the 'Gentile' mission gave it so sharp an edge.

What might have re-assured Jewry necessarily took a form that tended to dismay still further, namely the very ardour with which the apostles and their writings strove to 'educate' their erstwhile pagans out of Hebrew texts. That 'education', making plain and urgent the moral claims of new-found 'Gentile' admission into divine peoplehood, was the central feature of the New Testament Church. 'See that none render evil for evil to anyone but ever follow that which is good,' in the earliest text in 1 Thessalonians 5.15, is representative. Jewish observers could be assured that here was no dismissive scorn of ethics nor yet despair about its human reach.

But the matter went further – further far than the 'two covenant' theory let itself ponder – since that resolution of Jewish/Christian relation saw 'grace' a necessity for 'Gentiles', while 'law' was properly viable for Jewry, each in a different God-relation. The whole point, however, for the New Testament mind, was that, while law was meant for all, no less were all in need of grace. Was there not a strange circularity in the people/Torah situation? Their being 'holy people' by 'covenant' possessed them of the holy law; having the holy law made them the holy people. This unison was only sharpened by the close nexus between the moral and the ritual elements of Torah and the necessity, to both of them, of the right people in the given land, where they were 'placed' with 'the Name'.

The New Testament moved in another sort of inter-weaving, namely a law whose ethics summoned all and sundry in a folk diversity but whose moral demands found them all wanting of themselves and 'falling short'. The inclusiveness went either way, so that 'all have sinned', 'missing the mark of the glory of God', by their frailty or perversity. Thus the very law their conscience could equally acknowledge was for them all – in Paul's pointed metaphor of the pedagogue – 'the schoolmaster' to escort them to their common need of grace. The issue was not that some were inherently 'lawless' and others 'law-shaped', by a distinctive destiny, but that all alike conceded their 'law-meantness' as humans and – for that very reason – betook themselves to grace, for forgiveness, cleansing and the answer to their guilt.

This fully inter-human perception of the ethical and the redemptive in the New Testament was, it is fair to say, pointedly anticipated in the Old. How should we read that 'and' in the familiar phrase throughout – 'the law and the prophets'. It is much more than merely additional. Prophethood, as a theological conscience, accused, reproached, chastized and refused ever to exonerate the law's people. Its conjunction with law was always the moral sequence between obligation and violation, between compliance and non-compliance. 'The law and the prophets' had to be coupled, the brief of the one in need of the vigilance of the other. Thus the prophets became the clearest symbol that law, alike in its demand and its failure, pointed beyond itself to what, of itself, it could never achieve. It was in its very nobility the hard school of grace.

That being so, 'the Old' – or should we rather say 'the Inaugural' – could be seen as not in entire contrast with 'the New', but as proleptic, containing it as its own logic and thereby, not superseded but vindicated. Perhaps we should speak of 'the two-part one covenant' experience? It is well to note how the command to be inclusive of 'all nations', according to Matthew 28.19, could well be translated 'talmudizing them in the Name . . . '. *Matheteusate* is 'studying them into so that they become learners', which is precisely how the Talmud perceives itself as the practised 'learning' of Hebrew life under Torah. If so, then the 'baptizing' of the nations should not be seen as some anti-Jewish gesture but as a very Jewish *mitzvot* if only their inclusion is allowed.

If so again, the testament Christians call 'the New' is significantly loyal to 'the Old', taking as it does the twofold witness of 'the law and the prophets' to a moral humanity set under God and, in the crisis of that dignity, experiencing its own history as requiring it to anticipate in hope what it has not possessed in fact – a history for which the Messianic was the ultimate logic of the Sinaiatic. The only – if radical – development from the one testament to the other is the extension of that double experience of being divinely moral and duly schooled into hope against its proven odds, to all other haunts and societies of the human world.

But need such an extension be threatening the custodians who had so long and so strenuously in their custody meanings only they had attained to possess? Might they ever be, not parted from the watch, but somehow partnered in it, being not relieved but joined? Had there not been between YAHWEH and themselves a mutual avowal for that very end?[16] The questions take us to the heart of the emotional, as distinct from the intellectual, issues of nationhood where the passions of identity and of a retrospect 'harsh and strange', prove more vexing than the theology of law or the discipline of tradition.

V

This theme of Jewry and their nationhood is yet another consideration fit to query any 'two covenant theory'. To see why is a useful way into it. Aside from Judaic usage and other usage drawn therefrom, 'Gentile' was simply a synonym for 'human' and, as we have seen in Chapter 4, could include Jews too. For they, by their own insistence, were among *ethnoi* having ethnicity, land, rituals and culture among their defining features across all human diversity. It was, indeed, precisely to distinguish and exceptionalize these features that they came to apply the word, for discriminatory purpose, to all humans save themselves. The continuing double sense of the 'Gentile' word is frequently forgotten. When it is kept in mind, the confusion in the 'two covenant theory' is at once apparent. For, if we take the 'two' in an arithmetical way – 'this is one and that is another' – as if we were merely adding, the fact that *both* are inclusively human is ignored or denied, when in fact it is vital to both parties. The contrast in the religious Jew/'Gentile' formula takes Jewry out of this world if exempting them from being *ethnoi* in the simple meaning of the word.

Thus, either way, we are conspiring with confusion, as if the first covenant was not a human fact and the second only a partial human one. For, on the contrary, everything Judaic was profoundly human in its significance, while testamentary Christianity believed itself called to be co-extensive with all that being human meant. Hence in the latter case the steady emphasis on the 'nations bringing their glory in' and the doxologies on all their tongues. Hence in the former case the constant appeal, direct or indirect, to the nations to acknowledge their distinctive presence.

Zionism in recent and current history is only the most insistent and assertive form of that appeal, though one whose shape and thrust have enormously complicated it. However 'apart they were dwelling', Jewry always anticipated recognition of their distinctive identity, whether by acceptance or by enmity. Jacob Neusner, quoted earlier, did not want to 'be accepted as a human being' – surely an odd plea – but 'as a Jew'. Why not in both capacities together? Any Frenchman or Pakistani or Laplander would want to be accepted in that guise but surely, for us all, on the inclusive ground of being human. And the human comes in endless particulars, seeing that races, places and cultural graces are distinctive. Thus it seems odd that Chief Rabbi Jonathan Sachs should risk a contradiction in terms by writing that 'universalism is the cultural counterpart of imperialism'. For once we are in to 'culture', diversity is what we must expect – diversity, however, only out of the universal human order of a common creaturehood.[17] The task of Jewry as a people, no less than any other national or notional identity is, in John Donne's immortal phrase, to 'belong with mankind'.

'National or notional' is indeed the situation. For 'a nation' is always difficult to define. Perhaps the best attempt at a definition must be 'Any people believing themselves to be one.' That still leaves us with big questions concerning what the word 'people' connotes and of what their 'belief' consists. This is the more difficult in respect of the Jewish 'nation'. If nations are defined by 'land', the Jewish one has been absent from its terrain for long centuries and those centuries arguably among its most heroic and determinative. Yet being for and in the land has ever been its making. If language is the vital factor, as the amazing Zionist recovery of Hebrew attests, Jewry has long been multi-lingual, has much of its Talmud in Aramaic and possessed a loved Yiddish literature.

Do we, then opt for 'race' as 'nationizing' Jewry? Certainly, some would say, from Moses to Franz Rosenzweig.[18] Indeed, ethnicity is there, in the criterion of Jewish motherhood, in the anxiety of Jewish Rabbis, with Nehemiah, about mixed marriages as 'haemorrhage', and the ritual concept of 'the purity of the family'. Yet Jewry has long been multi-racial so that the biological factor alone will not suffice.

Must we then conclude, in spite of its circularity, that Judaism and Jewry are simply mutually definitive, that Judaism constitutes the Jewish nation existing by Judaism as its consciousness? Yet somehow, all the other factors of ethnicity, territory and language stay crucial inside the identity of the defining Judaism. And what when the 'yoke of Judaism's Torah' and *Mitzoth* are discarded by the secular Jew who, nevertheless, Jew remains? Can we say that what Jewry and Judaism have as their defining criterion is a criterion by intrinsic quality – absent from all other peoples so that they can truly ask their Lord: 'What one nation in the earth is like your people Israel?' (2 Samuel 7.23)? That would be true about land and language concepts, about Temple ritual and its sacrificial system. Could it be true of the sense of moral destiny hallowed by 'God-fearingness' and 'the love of mercy, doing justly and walking humbly with God'

– criteria of moral peoplehood that – thanks in part to Jewry – have been widely shared across the human world?

Perhaps we are left in the end with Judaism and Jewry as 'inter-defining' and maybe want to add that there is 'mystery' we should cease to seek to fathom? If so, the conclusion *must* follow that *'am segulah'*, 'chosen people', is no intrinsic uniqueness, no empirical phenomenon, but only 'a moral task', a task which can never be displaced by a status, a datum, as if it existed *per se*, whether by race, or land, or exodus, or prophet, or priest, or revelation or an arbitrary gift that was not a vocation, first and last.[19] If so again, this will have deeply disconcerting implications for political Zionism if deploying only a merely assertive warrant.

Even more importantly, it will mean that 'the Old', like 'the New', can only be a 'given' – whether as 'people-election' or 'Messiah known' – as also a task, only a claimed past as a present and a future obedience. Maybe, therefore, there is some point after all in the 'two covenant theory', under strict conditions, namely that Jewry is 'a being that has to become', Christianity is 'a becoming that has to be'.

Martin Buber was fond of insisting that whereas Christians had 'to become', by faith in Christ, Jews were 'already there' by Jewish birth, the one – he alleged – 'always trusting *in*', the other needing to 'believe *that* . . . ' a false dichotomy between confidence and creed.[20] If the 'being' of Jewry, as Yeshayaho Leibowitz pleads, stands only in the 'becoming' of their Judaism, then there is some kinship with the New Testament which was always telling its people 'to be' congruently what they had 'become'. 'You have Christ formed in you', 'walk as children of light'. That New Testament 'Messiahship realized' need then be no 'scandal' for Jewry, seeing that it has always to proceed into Messianic community – a profoundly Judaic task.

If God truly transcends can *any* faith be monopolist of the divine Name? Surely not in tribal way as it would seem the Deuteronomist thought. But a faith might hope to be definitive of where it believed the clues might most tellingly point. In some measure, being a religion at all, theist or other, is to think to see – and say – where the clues point, if point at all, in all circumambient conjecture.

The thought, or fear, of being potentially monopolistic about having God in trust, has thus led us back to our initial double question as to what might both suffice, as to divine glory and suffice in answer to human need, provided there was a wonder at the one and a realism for the other. Jewish 'election' has often said that the Christian Gospel is no less particularist, no less a 'peculiar' identification both of YAHWEH and His people. Is not baptism a sort of Christian 'circumcision', the mark of the true 'participant', not 'in the flesh, but 'the seal of faith?' Its 'universalism is, therefore, a pseudo thing, as Chief Rabbi Sachs implied, as earlier quoted. The Church has no ground on which to reproach Jewry as being 'chosen people'. With less reason, it makes the same claim, having the criterion of 'new birth' as its conditionality.

Yet, if truth as to divine clues is identifiable, must it not also be possessable and if possessable, must not community in and with it ensue? It will be a different community *qua* Church than *qua* Jewry, seeing that a consent rather than an accident is the constituting factor. The particularity issue, central to all inter-testamental study, has to turn on content and its bearing on universal inclusion.

Perhaps the confusion around John's words: 'No man comes to the Father but by me,' as Jesus telling his significance, best takes us into this burden round 'monopolism'. The words in no way override the inclusive 'Our Father who art . . . ' nor deny that Abraham, Jeremiah, Job or Muhammad ever 'came to God'. Indubitably in differing terms they did. John's words are about a 'predicate' to which the 'coming comes'. They are saying that in Christ there is a 'sonship' (cf. 'no man has the Father but through the Son') to which *this* 'Fatherhood' is reciprocal, so that they are mutually definitive and fulfilling. The verse is analogous to saying. 'No one arrives to Beethoven the musician except in the music of Beethoven.' For the music that derives from him alone draws you back to him. Or as one might say, after the play: 'I've seen Shakespeare tonight.'[21] The drama meant encountering the dramatist, both carrying the same name but only because they were in a fulfiller/fulfilling relationship.

There is exclusivity here but only by inherent inclusion of a divine 'whence' and a divine 'hither' such was always the import of YAHWEH 'having a Name' and how that 'Name' could never be a mere noun but a meaning dramatized in an event and imparted in experience, whether an exodus, an entry or an exile, whether a birth, a man and a crucifying. Theology would all be 'in a Name', a thoroughly inter-testamental idea.

But (whatever verb we employ) why should this 'Fatherhood' beget, send, have this manner of 'son'? The answer will have to lie in two counter-partnering concerns of any theological faith, namely 'what manner of God' and 'what adequacy in the human scene'? For, in our humanity, we humans are not corrigible by good advice, nor amenable to honest rationality, nor sustainably minded for the exacting good for which our societies yearn. Our perversities are such that only 'a man of sorrows' can measure what our retrieval costs. There must surely be in the eternal mind a drama of redemptive compassion as alone realistic for a sovereignty of creative goodness truly *vis-à-vis* the human world. The fully divine will be the humanly interventionist with credentials in the here and now.

The two testaments, Jewish and Christian, can only honestly meet, as the Rabbis would say, 'for the sake of eternity'. For not otherwise was their divergence realized.

VI

If the distinction we have made between a Judaic 'being in order to become' and a Christian 'becoming in order to be' is at core of what distinguishes either from the other, we still have large issues of substance. These only a mutual love can undertake. There will be this 'Fatherhood' in the necessary terms of this 'Sonship' in comprehending divine unity. There will remain 'Messiah crucified', only so sufficiently 'Messianic' and a humanity hopeful enough via Torah and *Mitzvoth*. Nevertheless, inter-testamental purposes can have these contained inside 'two covenants' no longer warranting any Jews-excluded idea on the one hand, or a 'Gentile' alien condition on the other. Political Zionism, as we have seen, greatly compromises this vision, tangled grievously in Jewish 'being to become' as long as it will not territorially co-exist. Christian 'becoming to be . . . ' must thoroughly undertake remorseful recognition of the long negations of original 'newness' in Christ endorsed and committed by the centuries since Constantine and Theodosius, and also discern, with the help of Jewish testimony, the true measure of its liability in the Shoah.

Other aspects of being heirs to two testaments may be taken into a following chapter on 'Marc Chagnall's Prayer-Shawl'. Still inter-testamental here, it remains to ask: 'Are not the faiths of the two testaments involved in a perpetual human quandary, namely the nexus – we might almost say the twinning – of religious faith and people-identity?' The Hebraic testament meant uninhibitedly to identify them entirely. The Christian testament meant resolutely to unlock them. Hence the long reactive Judaic rejection of, at times scorn for, the notion of being universal as a faith that needed none to be 'Gentiles'.

Inevitably, however, after Constantine a sort of 'Semitism' overtook the Christian Church in the sense that it became readily, indeed strenuously, pre-occupied with a 'folk expression', and even with a 'Davidic' sort of kinship with the Roman, the Visigoth, the Carolingian, the medieval State, assuming its role in 'establishing', sustaining and serving the faith, and that faith now quite 'Semitically' married with socio-cultural peoplehood. This steady approximation into one of faith-with-liturgy and power-in-politics was no small part of the rise of anti-Semitism. The more the New Testament faith took on Old testament shape in peoplehood sanctioning 'folk' awareness and sanctioned by statehoods held kindred, the more antipathy emerged on the one side and jeopardy on the other.

A figure, for example, like Ambrose, for all his contemplative asceticism and the intense power of his sermons, could still connive with the spoiling of synagogues that 'there might not be left a building in which Christ is denied'.[22] The Church, too, constituted 'a holy people', whose liturgy and life deserved, expected and warranted the caring protection of the State expressing the same 'folk' concern to be 'who we are'. By the time we get to Martin Luther there is no mistaking the Germanism of his Christianity and, on that ground, his anti-Jewish animus. Sacred – or better sacrilized – identities find it hard to co-exist. The whole tragic story we have surveyed in Chapter 6 turned on this 'proud-peoplizing' of Christianity with a catastrophic guilt toward the synagogue of Israel.

It is vital not to understand that tragedy as some 'left hand of the Cross' or a vicious logic of the Incarnation. Christian faith, in New Testament definition, was a deliberate inclusive humanism: in mission, then and since, it proved itself evidently transnational. It cannot loyally ride with patriotism, yet, by very Jewish norm, it succumbed to reading and wanting its 'new peoplehood' in terms of 'Christ Pantocrator', Saviour of all its Byzantiums and hallowed sovereignties, its 'Solomons' consecrating its temples, 'the place of the Name' in the shrine defined by a people.

There is a clear corollary of this Christian quandary evident in the 'faith and people' situation. It is that modern Jewry in and after the 19th century, experienced the same 'quarrel in the mind'. Two contrasting Jewish historians suffice to show it so. There was the great Simon Dubnow seeing Jewry as truly valid in diaspora, a people right in, and apt for, world dispersion, needing no dependence on territory or political statehood. If it had any 'nationalism' it was entirely of the Spirit in the obedience of Torah.[23] By contrast, his contemporary, Heinrich Graetz, insisted that Jewry are a nation and must be politically defined. David had not lived in vain. Jewish history could only be read as political and in non-theological terms. Jews were not a religious community and should be explicated, not from holy texts, but by historical action in a human praxis which was not a God-cult but a vital dynamism where land and state were crucial. Joshua had not lived in vain.[24]

Simon Dubnow almost reads as if Judaism has to resemble a New Testament Church and rejoice in diaspora, while, for example, the old Christian Salic Law crying: 'Long live Christ who loves the Franks . . .' sounds like a full-throated Judaism of the sort Hosea deplored, lest the cry be only presumptuous self-esteem.[25]

Are we then reinforced in our earlier tentative conclusion that, if not 'two covenants', there are for each of them two tasks in being 'testamental' either way. The one is entering faith-wise into the wideness of humanity, the other is rightly to subdue to faith all nation-wise expression. The New Testament faith was authentic in not letting 'Gentiles' remain excludedly such, and right in believing itself set to embrace all nations. By the same token the Old Testament was wrong in radically exclusifying its own relation with God, yet authentic in being the tutor for us all that nationhood, if 'not far from the kingdom of God', could be its instrument. The issues we have reviewed in Chapters 7 and 8 are still precariously locked in this tension Jewry has always known between the versions of itself.

It remains to add that, if neither faith can belong with absolute nationalism, this should not mean that folk-cultural shape and alert political engagement are not legitimate, so long as these are not allowed their untamed claims. Religious faith is not a mere phenomenon about which sociology may debate as to its social role, nor are politics fit to make it a facilitator. Precisely in 'requiring truth in the inward parts', faith must stand above all these. By the same token it cannot well ignore them, still less despise them. History lays a long sanction on cultural and ethnic identities and faiths are long enmeshed within them. Should we then find it strange that faiths have known dispersion in the world as either fit to their genius or threat to their soul? What did Marc Chagall mean to signify by Jesus with the prayer-shawl? Was it not out of his kinship with the Christian tradition that Robert Browning could prove himself so ardent a voice of suffering Semitism?

Chapter Ten

MARC CHAGALL'S
PRAYER SHAWL

I

The Jewish *tallit* or mantle with fringes belonging to synagogue worship figures largely in the paintings of Marc Chagall (1887–1985), the celebrated veteran of modern Jewish art.[1] Congenial also to his genius is the representation of Jesus crucified. Nowhere are they more arrestingly together than in *White Crucifixion* (1938), painted at the time of Picasso's *Guernica*, where a wide beam of light flows down like a river on which the cross floats, with the Christ draped from above the knees in the prayer-shawl, while the seven-fold candelabra burns in its own circle of light below his feet. Other ritual objects are being scattered to the winds, while houses tumble in a chaos, marauding bands advance in threatening array and anguished figures mourn above the wooden beam and others in the foreground plead to understand.

The town-scene of the painter's early youth is there, his beloved Vitebsk, but only enigmatically. The bearded face of Jesus is set against a halo that the stream of light behind the wooden beam does not absorb. With eyes closed and head bowed towards the leaning ladder that does not reach the cross, he is already dead, the teasing text of 'kingship', only in the Hebrew, legible above the brow crowned only with a cloth.

Here, as ever, Chagall is eluding reason and logic, these stays of sanity themselves somehow homeless: he takes what refuge avails in the poetry of his art, the place where 'the poetic sense is the only lantern in the darkness'.[2] Only the rash would think he is making any statement, whether about the synagogue or Christianity, still less about the quest of Zionism. We must heed his own warning:

> If a symbol should be discovered in a painting of mine, it was not my intention. It is a result I did not seek. It is something that may be found afterwards and which can be interpreted according to taste.[3]

Yet even where 'intention' is disowned, a 'pre-occupation' is every-where and 'result' follows the more it was 'unsought'. There could only be irony in a Chagall saying that 'what is found' turns merely on 'according to taste'. For he himself had written:

Will God or someone give me the power to breathe my sigh into my canvasses, the sigh of prayer and sadness, the prayer of salvation, of rebirth?[4]

He meant 'to know what he thought about Christ whose pale face had long been troubling me'. 'O God, help me to shed real tears only before my canvasses.'[5] Students, readers and admirers of his art can do no less.

We must see behind Chagall's deliberate invocation of the bizarre and the fantastic, a studied defiance of the normal and ambiguous delight in the grotesque. These are no pose, no mere craze. They mean profoundly in their very abandonment of meaning's norms of gravity, proportion and design, of congruity and the familiars of sense reckoning. He invites us to explore all sensations, yet his work is everywhere replete with Hasidic echoes and the heritage of Hebrew lore. He can give his enigmatic Jesus the Russian peasant's cap his loved father wore and blend his own parents into the figures of Madonna and disciple waiting by the cross.[6]

What, in such receptivity – if we can achieve it – of that ladder, recurrent in his *Calvary* and *The Yellow Crucifixion* as well as in *The White Crucifixion*? Figuratively it yearns but only fails to reach. It has no firm footing. In *Calvary* it is longer but the man is running with it. Is it, like the Madonna with naked breasts, half her face in dark shadow and hand raised towards her child, only a symbol of Jewish *angst*? Do the ladders tell a compassion that could not reach into fulfilment? Or do they tell a bad conscience gesturing vainly about the finished evil? The point is there in *The Roofs*, one of his latest paintings, where the crucified has the background of a Russian Church.

These 'children of sorrows' that are his art's creation bring two faiths uneasily together in the single theme of human suffering. There is no doubt that the defining Christian sense of 'God in Christ' had its source in the Biblical, Judaic perception of divine participation in the human burden as grief and tragedy measured it. There was truly a *unio sympathetica* between 'Lord' and 'people' as in the 'I know their sorrows' of the exodus liberation, and later told crucially in the life and mission of Hosea. It belongs with all the suffering prophets and Chagall translates it into all his down-to-earth portrayals of sorrowing Jewry, as in *Solitude* (1933) where a seated Rabbi, clad in *tallit* with bowed head resting on his right hand, lifts high with his left hand a large Torah scroll, and the dark sky over Vitebsk is lit with lightning flashes blazing through the brooding clouds.

When in mid-life Chagall went to Palestine/Israel to illustrate Bible texts he recalled in the same idiom the grieving figure of Jacob at tidings of Joseph's 'death'. In *The Creation of Man* YAHWEH is hastening down to earth with a sleeping Adam in His arms, giving the sort of aura to space that yawns in yellow depth as the background in *Moses Receiving the Tablets of the Law*. The patriarchal figure is reaching in awesome wonder towards a pair of arms holding the tablets as the common territory of our extended hands. Moses, at once myth and history, is depicted as if soaring, not standing, on Sinai,[7] his whole frame stretching to receive while all but the hands of God is hidden in the storm cloud. Crowding below we see a sea of faces waiting on the issue, their secret etched into a cluster by a golden calf venturing towards the crest of the summit. They have a counterpart in a group of faces on the right whom an angel with a scroll strains to reach to renew the mystery to all generations. Below a rabbi in purple robe holds the sacred candelabra, the perennial legacy of Sinai, while rays of celestial light break from the divine cloud on every side.

In this long maturing creation, Chagall has caught the divine-to-the human, the human-for-the-divine in the great moment and movement of Torah with the Moses from whom he thought all else derived, including Christ.[8] It was from this *unio ordinatio* of the Law that the *unio sympathetica* of the great prophets sprang – and sprang precisely from the Law's own grievous story as measured in the Exile. Sincerity may count each *unio* associate with the other, so for ever mediating between all things Hebraic and Christian in terms of that anxiety through sorrow toward truth, which was the vision of Chagall's creative genius.

It was one to which he could recruit all else into its telling. How recurrent, for example, is the cow in his artistry – the domestic indispensable whose ritual killing he remembered so vividly from childhood.[9] She is there accompanying the Rabbi in *Solitude* and the *Peace* window he did in 1964 for the United Nations Secretariat Building in New York. And what of *Cow with a Parasol* (1946), a most comic celebration of peasant life and humour. Asses and donkeys, fowls and roosters, served him equally well, so that his register of mortal pathos was shot through with the celebration of the simple and the serene. Thus the 'tears before his canvasses' were ever genuine and fully human. It has been noted that if his moods were often like those of Tennyson in *In Memoriam*, the explanation was the same.

> It is rather the cry of the whole human race than mine . . . private grief swells
> into thought of, and hope for, the whole world.[10]

It must surely be this sense of things trans-human because inter-human that makes Chagall's deep Semitism and Christian faith concerning Jesus a comradeship of heart. It was inevitable and communally fitting that Jewry should want to see all things anti-Semitic, and the Shoah most of all, as inexorably a Jewish 'exclusive', a lot, or fate, that somehow set

Jewry in an utterly distinctive privacy – if that word fits the most self-affirming and corporate entity 'chosen people' have ever constituted. Yet that sense of identity in the unique distinction of wrong-suffering has warrant for its grief and grieving only in the inclusive human truth of what, in entire inter-association, humanity proves to be.

It is this defining truth of an unexceptionalized human-ness that Marc Chagall's genius portrays. His devotion to his Jewish roots watered in Russian soil, his steadfast loyalty to his parental love, his synagogues and sabbaths, his violins and harps and Hasidic soul, the wistfulness of his travels and the warmth of his friendships – all were witness to a sheer human Jewishness in generous possession of identity. He read orthodox Jewry profoundly, as in his *Feast of the Tabernacles* (1916), *Feast Day* (1914) and *The Praying Jew* (1914) with once more the *tallit*, but without sharing it in orthodox terms. His *Lovers in the Lilacs* (1930), like the parables of Jesus, has a universal range.

In this ecumenism he also handled classic themes with zeal, like *The Fall of Icarus* (1975). He was open to commissions on every hand, windows for Cathedrals at Metz and Rheims and Zurich; mosaics for a bank in Chicago and a Chagall Museum in Nice; murals for opera houses or for the Knesset in Jerusalem; theatre designs for Moscow and studies in glass for the United Nations.

Thus he loved and served a cosmopolitan humanity, imposing on himself a dedicated ministry to human meaning through the long and arduous decades of his almost biographical century. When he left France under Vichy it was his painting that enabled his grant of exit-permit, thanks to the New York Museum of Modern Art. He travelled in the same ship with the canvas that had earned his liberty.

The work (1940) in immediate question had the title *Martyrdom*, where a Christ-like figure is tied to a stake, his Russian cap, peasant-style, displacing any halo. All is turmoil and devastation. The study tells of agony. A cow and a cock come tumbling down from open sky, while a mourning woman bewails – we must assume – the Nazi invasion of France coincident with Chagall's brush. The stark reality is there, houses grimed with dust or devoured by flames. The menace is personally known but inclusively portrayed. Horror is suffused with human tenderness.

In Chagall's art the Jewish does not arrogate the human, nor does the human fail to be expressly and expressively Jewish. What is unique is allowed to belong with what can never be. It was perhaps in 1945 in *The Soul in the City* that he most bravely stated this inclusive theme. He was bereaved by the death of his beloved wife Bella. Much of continental Europe was strewn with ruin. The Vitebsk he loved had been laid waste. Out of his Jewish fervour he had loved the city also for its Russian-ness. The painting belongs with lines of a poem he wrote at the same time. 'Only that land is mine that lies in my soul.'

The Soul in the City, unlike so much in Chagall, lacks all colour, save the dull red of an 'Ark of the Covenant', and a slight touch of blue on the rump of goat and sheep. All is ashen and sombre, as if painted out of ashes. To the right stands an easel – that devout ministrant to soul. Its solitary figure is a crucified, impaled on the same timbers as later in 1951 and clad in the same prayer-shawl. An unfinished picture with a table leans upon it. An arm and hand point towards the canvas. They belong to the central figure, the painter himself, depicted with two faces looking either way, to and from the picture on the easel. In his other hand he holds a pot of brushes. Below him is a woman cradling a bird. Far above their heads houses are tumbling into smoky desolation and above these a sleigh has a man with a whip persuading the goat in its shafts, while from the upper left the red curtain of the Ark floats downward to blend with the ghostly winding sheet (or wedding veil) of Chagall's Bella, the wife he mourns inseparably from the trauma of his birthplace. Her face appears below his shoulder with three of the seven candles evident beneath her gaze.

Never a crucified without the shawl. Chagall always insisted that any symbolism lay with the option of the viewer. We must respect his will to leave his meanings open. Yet there is evidence that somehow, by painting the stricken city, he would 'save its soul', 'getting it out of harm's way'.[11] Setting it on canvas would give grieving voice to its fate, yet not finally an angry one. Having the tragedy 'out of harm's way' could never have been a counsel of indifference. As all Shoah memorializing knows, wrongs can never be abandoned to oblivion. Negligence does no justice by enormity. If, as with Chagall, there can be compassionate remembrance, as a canvas with him can attain, then 'the harm that is never out of the way' may move out of 'harm's way' – the harm of the necessity to hate.

It is not, for Chagall, that painting rids of it but perpetuates it in a context that both retains and contains the wrong. That context is the compassion that moves within a common human-ness, a sense of one humanity which rules out the necessity of hate in response to evil suffered. This willingness to 'belong with mankind' as that of which one is consan-guinially a part and one whose appeal is always to its kindred quality,[12] turns wrongs suffered into wrongs absorbed. It is a sort of consecration of experience out of tragedy and into hope.

Was this the meaning of Chagall's prayer-shawl in its steady associa-tion with one crucified? For getting evil events 'out of the harm's way' that betakes them onward into hate and enmity was certainly the pattern with the Christian Jesus,[13] according to the perspective faith had of him in the birth-story of Christianity. It has been rightly said of Chagall's several 'crucifieds' that the silent Jesus there is rather an emblem of a victim world than in any sense its victor-saviour. Yet did either role exclude the other? In realism do they, did they, not belong in one? If only inwardly, the silence was breathing: 'Father, forgive them'; and 'Into Thy hands my spirit,' that would suffice. The *tallit*, as enmantling the worshiper, was always telling such God-awareness. Nowhere could it have been more silently vocal than as a girdle round the nakedness of human frame, erect – as Chagall always saw his sufferer – mutely present before God.

It was part of this artist's open heart that he left his symbols also open to his reader's mind. He comes again and again to this 'crucifixion' out of the tribulations through which he passed, the memory of pogroms in the days of his grand-father Rabbi, the drama of the rising tide of Nazi barbarity, its long aftermath of desolation across the breadth and length of Europe. But why always with that prayer-shawl, reclaiming Jesus for the synagogue perhaps, yet doing so, not as taking the Scroll (as once in Nazareth) and exhorting from the *minbar*, a Hasid of godly piety and holy discipline? Would these suffice the travail of the Europe he surveyed? They could tally with the sensuous wonder of the natural order, of the animal realm and the ever grateful benedictions of the observant soul which Chagall celebrated in his canvases at large. All these returned him by a realist compulsion, born of Jewry's, Europe's tragedy to the sufferer in the shawl.

II

The quality of invitation, rather than clear tuition, in his art leaves us free for the conclusion only such a sufferer knows and tells about our human condition and, therein, about the caring sovereignty of God. It means, and requires of us all, a participatory humanity through all that human perversions do against it, because we believe that in those perversions our common humanism is betrayed and defiled. Precisely in defying their deeds as perversely inhuman do we rescue them, as human doers, for the authentic human-ness they have denied. This hope-retaining posture redeems the future, theirs and ours, from the deadly entail of the past, but only by firmly believing in the inter-human dignity for which we all were meant. The necessity to hate obtains only for the doings and no longer for the doers. So much we may discern in a prayer-shawl and a crucified.

It soon becomes clear how such thinking bears on the fears and hopes of Semitism, on the ever urgent determination never to let remembrance of the Shoah die, and in that context to cherish at all costs the significance of the State of Israel, however embattled in the very psyche its affirmation proves to be. As the popular song has it:

> The entire world is against us.
> It is an ancient melody
> That we have learned from our forefathers,
> This song from our elders we learned . . . we sing it as well

Here in Eretz Israel.
But whoever is against us can go to hell . . . [14]

What is popular is likely to be ribald in the music of any and every vulgar patriotism. Here, however, the sense of a 'Semitic blighty' (if we may so speak) has warrant from long and bitter centuries, seemingly confirmed by present traumas in the Mid-East region.

Yet requiring or allowing one's own condition of human meaning and existence to be finally discriminatory and unilateral is to jeopardize the only ultimate ground of its viability. There is no singular human shape of culture and identity that can be self-sufficient, least of all in the total inter-exposures of the contemporary world. We can have our own humanity only in a tolerance of its inclusive range.

For reasons evident enough it is upon the Semitic mind that this truth of things weighs so cruelly, thanks to things wanton and guilt laden in the non-Semitic world. The burden Jewry faces demands the utmost recognition and all the moral aid non-Jews can bring, but bring in somehow precluding the damning suspicion of patronage or condescension.[15]

The sense of loyalty to the victims of the Shoah is where Semitism finds its deepest travail. As Chief Rabbi Jonathan Sachs has it, a determination to remember means that 'hate never dies'. We defeat it if we resolve never to forget. The burden must be undertaken through every generation ahead.[16]

Yet, if there *is* inter-humanity, if the Semitic-human is not to be for ever accusatory, hate has to die – not the hate that indicts the deeds endured but the hate that would otherwise perpetuate the right to live as if exempt from the humanity to which it had so tragically been victim.

So much in history derives from people determined to remember. The intimate, yet ever ambivalent, relation of Semitism to Zionism might be read, by the cynical or the despairing, in the way in which heavy misgiving about Israel is crudely read in the age-long terms of anti-Semitism.

> Archetypal anti-Semitism has moved from the Christian world to the Islamic. The State of Israel now plays the role of the classically persecuted Jew . . . Anti-Semitism has moved from the individual Jew to the Jews as a sovereign nation. Essentially it remains the same – the inability, or at worst refusal, to grant the Jews a space. We are seeing the vocabulary of the second millennium transferred to the third.[17]

Does remembering a paradigm discerned transfer properly to a different scene without remainder or confer exoneration? The same source states that Palestinianism is essentially engaged in a conflict of attrition. He does not realize that the very same 'attrition' must be read in reverse. Thus it runs:

> The leadership (Israeli of Palestinian) thinks: 'Let's make hell for them for fifty-three years and they will go.' The Arabs, (the Jews) don't have patience

for the long haul. Now (The Israelis are putting the Arabs) (the Arabs are putting the Israelis) through a spiritual crisis by investing daily living with uncertainty. Spiritual destabilization – that is what it's all about. Neither can acquiesce in the other's permanence. If we hold on long enough 'they' will capitulate.[18]

Thus tragically reversible are the postures either party reads in the other's actions. Zionism has certainly been putting Arabism through a prolonged crisis and what it has thereby evoked is a sustained crisis for Israel and the meaning of its political Semitism. Will the mutual crises ever resolve each other? How will they contrive to read what their own crisis is about and bring it to viable success?

III

What might Marc Chagall with his cherished prayer-shawl have us think of Zionism and its expression in the State of Israel? It seems clear that he was a Jew of diaspora. On leaving Vitebsk and Moscow finally in 1922, he lived successively in Paris, with sundry travels to exhibit or visit in, for example, Holland, Spain and Mexico, until his departure for New York. From America his travels were almost global in their reach as his fame spread and his output abounded. In 1930, having illustrated an edition of Gogol's *Dead Souls*, he agreed to illustrate the Bible, a task which took him to Palestine the following year. There he felt 'the air of the land of Israel makes one wise . . . In the East I found the bible part of my own being.'[19] The commission fulfilled in studying and depicting scenes from Syria and Egypt as well as Palestine, he returned to Europe and six years later became a French citizen. Again in 1951 he travelled to Jerusalem for the opening of an exhibition. This was the year of his *King David*, perhaps the closest of all his paintings to an arguable 'Zionist' theme. With crown and harp and embroidered robe, a bright sun shines on the walls of his Jerusalem. A green Rabbi bows in the centre while a bridal pair salute each other. We perceive a painter among the faithful who are processing towards the city.

That vision, albeit in characteristically ambivalent terms, is renewed in *Exodus* which he was painting from 1951 till 1966. Moses stands modestly in the lower corner, tablets in hand, witnessing, not leading, the mass of humans crowding the lower two-thirds of the canvass. Crowning the upper centre, as if embracing the whole yearning quest for liberty, stands the figure of a crucified with head upon a pillowing halo of sharp white, itself surrounded by a huge circle of grey. Beams underline the outstretched upper limbs but the hands are innocent of nail-prints. A little cluster of Vitebsk-like dwellings stands on a tract of water where the canvas ends. Was Marc Chagall mirroring the *aliyahs* of those years – and earlier – by which Israel had been reborn? The feet of the presiding figure are concealed behind the mass of people, replacing the absent prayer-shawl which, elsewhere this 'Jesus' never lacks. How aptly American Christian Zionism might read itself – against the grain of all his conscious elusiveness – into the 'message' of this *Exodus*.[20]

If never Israeli as an immigrant – in which he resembled Elie Wiesel – Chagall was ever ready to adorn Israeli halls and walls with his mosaics, his murals and tapestries and to lighten their interiors with his windows. These purposes found him in Jerusalem in 1962, 1966 and 1969, just as they took him to almost a score of other venues. He died in his beloved Saint-Paul-de-Vence where he had built his 'fixed abode' in 1966 at the time of completing *Exodus*. He paid to Israel his loving tributes as a man of the diaspora.

Does this leave us to conclude that the prayer-shawl pleads *for* Israel but also *with* it, concerning that instinct of its Zionism to lay on Arab-Semites the onus of an acceptance which inevitably brings a relational discrimination? How then is a humanly spontaneous, uninhibited relationship achieved, one which could readily say, in Dante's words: 'By so many the more that say "Ours," by so much the more of good is each possessed'?

Clearly, as witnessed by the Chief Rabbi's analysis just quoted, political Zionism in Israel has not accomplished such compatibility of human-ness. The necessarily political shape and context made it grimly unlikely. The non-acceptance it aroused has, indeed, been ill-served in its own counsels, erratic, ill-fated, confused, violent and strategically inept.[21] Yet these dark and tragic features have not cancelled their utter human legitimacy as soil-loving, home-making, fallibly loveable occupants of a disputed nation-making territory by ancient quality and usage.

The politics and their complexities apart, have Jewry and Judaism ever fully reckoned with what 'chosen-ness', as the constitutive pre-requisite they bring to inter-human-ness, places as a liability on human 'Gentiles'? For something definitive in the one identity tells a basic distinction from the other. Where that situation is resented, anti-Semitism is guiltily latent or aroused. Where it is ignored from the 'Gentile' side, something Judaic is tacitly and inwardly offended. Where, by warm human effort, it is welcomed or even congratulated, there is an ever-present risk that Jewishness will feel 'recognized' in some sort of condescension or gratuitous 'tolerance', hardly less unhappy than neglect. Somehow the Jewishness is not being conceded in adequately Jewish terms.[22] The heart of the matter is not having the justice which would satisfy it. Is it, perhaps, a justice which, somehow the 'Gentile' can never bring? If so, can the 'Gentile' ever be delivered from that inability, seeing that the 'Gentile' status – by Judaic necessity – will always carry it?

Was there about Marc Chagall's deeply reverent, compassionate humanism – yet a humanism so gladly and unmistakably Jewish – a clear resolution of this dire situation? It could perhaps be expressed in the ready grammatical distinction between noun and adjective. Let the noun be 'the human' and the adjective 'Jewish', and the same rule obtain likewise whatever the particular adjective may be. Then all that the adjectival may aspire to be will be contained within it in interior terms. Then culture, or society, or religion, or identity via story are all tributary to, but not discriminatory about, the human meaning in the whole. Such adjectival condition will leave all free, Jewry most notably, to pursue, express and commend its own human reach of experience, but only in interior terms. The interiority can suffice the identity as so duly 'belonging with mankind', and in quest to hold the will to diversity as reciprocal.

It has been said that 'Christianity does not really consider Judaism to have survived'.[23] Such has often been the wilfulness of rampant anti-Semitism but, as we have seen with Robert Browning, never the truth of a parallel inter-face which was at its most pregnant within the New Testament itself. The continuity of Judaism was there in the saying: 'Israel is Jesus,' so tantalizing an aphorism both could claim.[24] The perpetuity of things Sinaitic, Davidic and prophetical, while always a heart-ache for a Christian faith cherishing their ecclesial destiny in its evangel, belongs safely and sanely enough inside a humanity that says 'Ours', namely a humanity about which our faiths are distinctly adjectival and live in co-existence – a co-existence which will not inferiorize.

IV

In this relational human vocation we have differingly difficult tasks in avoiding to inferiorize. If, as we have been arguing, positive acceptance somehow means for Jewry a 'de-Gentilizing' of the non-Jewish world, the politic shape of Zionism has contrived the reverse. Yet that Zionism proceeded from the interior self-possession of Jewishness which we have safeguarded (as far as exposition may) from the menace of anti-Semitism, the anti-Semitism which made political Zionism a radical imperative. Neither way can the logic then be some disavowal of the resulting State of Israel.

In present political terms the ultimate viability of Israel, in any moral quality worthy of its Judaism, turns on a full recognition, inside the human noun, of its Palestinian adjectival expression – one responding in the same terms. Otherwise the continuing Semitism of a Zionist Israel can only be in police-state terms, disowning all ethical Jewishness and conveying its world to an impasse of human despair. The parties can only be each saying a Dante-style 'ours' by a readiness for final territorial definition. The plea duly made for 'Israel's right to exist' still ignores the geographical question: 'which Israel?' It is one that half or more of Israelis have been tactically, or permanently, happy to ignore, defer or exclude from question, while exploiting its ambiguity. David Ben-Gurion in 1947 accepted the partition vote but not the map integral to it. The ever open question of the map fits the pragmatists and the doctrinaire while bedevilling the situation of the peacemaking realists.

Given the tactics of settlements, the dismantling of Oslo, the accentuation of the *Intifadahs* and the long festering of enmities, the question 'which Israel' is now liable to embroil Israel in civil strife between those who would assassinate a leadership – if ever again elected – set to finalize it in terms remotely satisfactory to the Palestinians, and any who read Israel's authenticity in reaching just such terms.

Can it be that Israel has arrived at a point where it cannot realistically negotiate, seeing that no régime can adopt a policy that tends to civil war? The tragic irony is that Palestinianism too may have arrived where no agreeable map-writing with Israel can fail radically to engender a state of insurrection there also. Have events – and their mutual liability for guilt of them – made neither party feasible as to peace? If so there would seem to have ensued a tragedy of miscarriage on all hands which the given-ness of Israel with all its tenacity will not undo.

If time and tempers allow, the only reversal of that prospect must be a shared will by either party to identify in the other the elements of honest mutuality and of will to its territorial decision. It has an eleventh hour urgency. It returns us, for re-assurance, to Marc Chagall and to his 'sigh of prayer and sadness, the prayer of salvation', to the shawl of aspiration girding the very elements of tragedy. The parties to be mutually identified must then be assured and enlarged, on either side by genuine evidence of action and result, shaming the obdurate and draining the oxygen of fanaticism from the bigots by dependable measures of common good faith about a map of peace, about peace on the map. Only so can complexities be reduced to their essentials. Only so may time hasten to its true redemption. Chagall insisted that 'if a symbol were discerned in his painting', it was a result he did not seek, 'something that could be found afterwards'. As a supreme artist in the Jewish tradition of comprehensive piety,[25] his windows gracing both Israel's Knesset and the United Nations chamber, we may invoke him to point the way to the humanity that can shed inclusive tears and, as he said, engage them to the salvation of the world they weep for, alike in the politics that scheme and the values that belong.

NOTES

Introduction

1   Franz Rosenzweig: *The Star of Redemption*, trans. W. W. Hallo, New York, 1970, p. 341. He is squarely in line with Ezekiel's reiterated accent on 'blood', whether his own or that of his foes. Note 19.10: 'Thy mother is like a vine in thy blood, planted by the waters . . . ' where the prophet merges 'blood' with the long revered metaphor of the 'vine' in its 'vineyard'. There is a similar note in the Biblical concern for 'seed' and the perpetuity of 'generation after generation'.

2   See: James H. Charlesworth, ed.: *Jews and Christians, Exploring the Past, Present and Future*, New York, 1990, pp. 226–7. The writer is Robert T. Gordon. There would seem to be a deliberate use of the word 'Aryan', suggesting the Nazi doctrine. Gordon implies that there is a 'blasphemy' in the – alleged – 'de-Judaizing' of Jesus committed by Christianity. So doing, he disqualifies the whole Judaic loyalty of the New Testament itself. It is this which makes the more urgent the disavowal – argued here in Chapter 9 – of the so-called 'two covenant theory'. As explicated in Chapter 5 there was never any doubt of the Jewishness of Jesus. The question always was: 'What manner of Jew?'

3   Genesis 26.16–33 (selected verses) in the *Jerusalem Bible*, London, 1966. Cf. Elie Wiesel: *The Oath*, New York, 1973, where this passionate 'martyrologist' of the Shoah writes: 'Whoever opposes man-as-a-Jew to man repudiates both,' p. 76.

4   Can history ever underwrite faith? The three Semitic faiths are persuaded it can. The issues they thereby incur for scholarship differ as between, for example, Exodus, the historical Jesus and the *Tanzil* of the Qur'an. Insofar as faiths 'credit' the authority to which they submit they 'warrant' that authority as deserving their reliance on it. Surely it must be the duty of such authority to seek and await faith's acceding to it and not arbitrarily impose itself. But the situation can often be tense and testing. There is a lively instance of it in Tony Bayfield and Marcus Braybrooke, eds.: *Dialogue with a Difference*, London, 1992; see below Chapter 9.

5   Cf. Jeremiah 6.14 and 8.11. 'They dress my people's wound without concern' reads the Jerusalem Bible translation.

6   The 'questing' is necessary about Browning's 'Christianity'. On the one hand, his lines seem conclusive:

'I say, the acknowledgement of God in Christ
Accepted by thy reason solves for thee
All questions in the earth and out of it,
And has so far advanced thee to be wise.' ('Death in the Desert')

He wrote of how 'the truth from heaven slid into my soul' ('Christmas Eve'). Yet his love for interior dialogue gives us pause. He wrote: 'I know the difficulty of believing . . . I am none the less convinced that the life and death of Christ, as Christians apprehend it, supply something which their humanity requires: and that it is true for them.' Cited in A. S. Byatt, Introduction to *Dramatic Monologues* (of R. B.), London, 1991.

7   The 'particulars' concerning the *tallit* are in Number 15.38f. Care for detail instils a care for obedience. Talmud and Zohar enlarge at length about fabric (wool or silk) and on the use of *tallit* at weddings and *Bar Mitzvoth*. By donning the shawl, piety will say, 'we respond to what the heavens say'. Even 'fringes' and ribands can be part of 'for the sake of heaven'.

One   'The Place of the Name'

1   Isaiah 51.9–10 makes the close association between 'Art Thou not He that cut . . . and wounded the dragon . . . ' and 'Art Thou not He that made the depths of the sea a way for the ransomed . . . ? Cf. Psalm 74.13–15 – the 'cleaving' of the sea and the 'slaying of the dragon', and Psalm 78.13.

2   'Yielding' in the sense of 'giving throughfare' as the emigrants issued from the weeds and shallows of 'the Sea of Reeds'. Could it be the creation element that makes those waters like 'cliffs', suggesting the rearing entrails of a slain 'dragon' through whose demise, as 'old chaos', all emerged?

3   Reading it so has always in mind the double sense of 'history' as event-in-its incidence' and how event contrived to have itself told out of both reverie and consequence.

4   In context the neologism is both apt and necessary. 'Land' was no neutral factor but something for mutual belonging.

5   It is evident from persisting struggles in the Book of Judges that Judaization was only partial and, even as such, suffered constant inroads needing vigilant Gideons, Samsons and others by whom 'the land had rest'. That formula, however, is notably omitted in the case of Samson.

6   Robert Frost: *Collected Poems*, New York, 1940, 'The Gift Outright', p. 467.

7   For 'history', not least in this context, recalls the past in terms of defining the present and the future. It would be simplistic to think of Biblical narrative in the modern sense of 'impartial elucidation of facts'. As J. H. Plumb has it, told or written 'history is imagining the past and remembering the future'. See his: *The Crisis in the Humanities*, London, 1964; where he fears that 'history has lost all faith in itself as a guide to the actions of men', p. 9 (or 'historians'?).

8   How the eminent anthropologist has it in B. K. Malinowski: *Myth in Primitive Psychology*, London, 1926, p. 21. There is about the exodus narrative a mythicization of history with a historicization of myth – not one without the other, authentic as memory held it.

9   The words became for the great prophets almost a descriptive for Messianic

peace and security. Hence the cryptic comment of Jesus to Nathaniel in John 1.48 referring to v. 47.

10 A turn of phrase in W. E. Hocking: *Human Nature and Its Remaking*, New Haven, 1923, p. 20. It would seem that he has overlooked some forms of Judaism when he adds: 'No accident of birth by the major religions (with the exception of Brahmanism) is held to exclude any human being from the highest religious attainment.' For not to be born Jewish can altogether disadvantage the 'Gentile' if the true monotheism is that of Jews only.

11 Passages below. The 'now' is significant since in each case there is a sort of irony: the 'presence' is elusive, whether for a remotely distant devotee, or for a scoffing enemy, or for a puzzled assumer of idols as numerous, perhaps as on an Indian shrine, when Jewry allows none.

12 David Blumenthal in Cohn-Sherbok, ed.: *Problems in Jewish Theology*, New York, 1991, p. 80f.

13 It was close to Heliopolis. See Josephus: *Antiquities*, xiii, 62–8. The Qumran sectaries in their 'Temple Scroll' were highly critical of Sadducee Jerusalem but did not create a rival Temple of their own. They visualized and designed one that would be for 'the offering of lips' not a holocaust of beasts. Nor were Babylonian exiles minded to 'forfeit' (or forsake) Jerusalem.

14 Emil Fackenheim: *God's Presence in History*, New York, 1970, pp. 16–19, commenting on the Sinai saga. It seems odd that, when writing later of human tragedy in history, he should exonerate God by observing that everything 'grim', from 'the ultimate perspective', is 'a cosmic game', p. 24.

15 'That one may be mistaken' is always an urgent posture for religious zealotry to learn to take. It seems clear that the loss of the Temple need never have occurred had it not been for a refusal to read Roman political hegemony as compatible with Judaic spirituality. Did the mass suicide of the heroic Zealots on Masada misread its true destiny and deliberately flout 'the patience of YAHWEH' and, with it, their own proper devotion to Him?

16 'Isolate', not in the sense that 'grace' happens apart from 'means of grace' (always in play) but that it will be unrestrictive in its responsibility for all. See below.

17 All religions entail paradox though Muslim thought has often tried to escape it. Solomon's question: 'Will God indeed dwell on the earth?' is the paradox alike of Judaic 'holy land and Temple' theme and of the 'God with us' meaning of 'the Word made flesh' in Christian faith about the Incarnation.

18 Julius Guttmann: *Philosophies of Judaism: A History of Jewish Philosophy from Biblical Times to Franz Rosenzweig*, New York, 1964, pp. 5–6.

19 Martin Buber (1878–1965). See *Moses*, Oxford, 1946, p. 7. See also Maurice S. Friedman, *Martin Buber: A Life of Dialogue*, New York, 1955.

20 Cited in P. S. Schilpp and M. S. Friedman: *The Philosophy of Martin Buber*, London, 1967, p. 693. The words from Psalm 73.23: 'Nevertheless I am with you always' are inscribed on Buber's tomb in Jerusalem.

21 Martin Buber: *I and Thou*, trans. R. Gregor Smith, New York, 1958, pp. 111–12.

22 *Ibid.* For the 'I–Thou' of inter-human relation (as never rightly an 'I– It' which merely 'thingifies' 'the other' and so degrades the human in both) appertains

across all races, the 'I–Thou' we say to God seems mysteriously separate and distinctive when the 'I' is Jewish and 'God' is YAHWEH.

23   Abraham Heschel (1907–72) See John C. Merkle: *The Genesis of Faith: The Depth Theology of A. J. Heschel*, New York, 1985, esp. Chapter 5, pp. 104–49. Also Heschel's *The Prophets*, New York, 1955, pp. 307–23.

24   A. J. Heschel: *Who is Man?*, Stanford, 1965. 'Who' not 'what?', the human is constituted in relation with God.

25   See C. T. R. Hayward: *The Jewish Temple, A Non-Biblical Source Book*, London, 1996, for detailed analysis of these sources.

26   Hence the crucial 'kings and priests' theme stretching also through the New Testament to the Book of Revelation.

27   There were many such occasions of jeopardy in the time of the Seleucids. On this one see also Josephus: *Wars*, 1.13.9 and 6.5.2.

28   Though, of course, a broad 'Messianism' enters far into religious and philosophical ideologies, born of apocalyptic zeal, as in Marxism and also in Mahdi ideas in Islam. 'Apocalypse', following on the strange close of prophethood, was a striking dimension of Jewish Messianism before and after New Testament times.

29   See Jacob Neusner: *Judaisms and their Messiahs*, Cambridge, 1987, and Gershom Scholem: *The Messianic Idea in Judaism and Other Essays*, New York, 1971.

30   The phrase used in Scholem, note 29, p. 35.

Two   Our Human 'Corn and Wine and Oil'

1   There have been sundry explanations of this summons to exempt 'the oil and the wine' from the toll of dearth and destruction. For example, these were the indulgence of the rich who look after their own privileges. That heavy satire seems less credible than the simple, obvious fact that blasted vines and olive trees take far longer to replace than annual crops like corn and wheat. Thus their loss would take far longer to repair. It would be good to think that the story of the Samaritan (Luke 10) was in mind. At all costs compassion – and its means – must abide in being.

2   'Hymns in the Scrolls', No. xvii, in Geza Vermes: *The Dead Sea Scrolls*, Oxford, 2000, p. 236.

3   A. Deissmann: *Paul: A Study in Social and Religious History*, trans. W. E. Wilson, London, 1926, p. 40.

4   The Exodus 'naming' of YAHWEH and Hosea's perception of it come in Chapter 3 below. Cf. B. F. Westcott in *The Epistles of St. John*, London, 1883, p. 312 – 'The very act of Creation is a self-limitation of Omnipotence.'

5   Homer: *Iliad*, Book 8, lines 557–9, trans. A. E. Tennyson.

6   Following a marginal reading in the A.V. that replaces 'the former rain moderately', the case for doing so makes the point about 'former and latter rains' so that the A.V.'s preferred clause is superfluous, being repeated in what follows. 'The Teacher of Righteousness' was, of course, a crucial figure in and for the community of Qumran but must be understood in Joel 2.23 as the human conscience tutored – but surely not over-ridden – by sacred law.

7   See Christian discussion, passing from creation to Incarnation, in Westcott:

loc. cit., note 4, p. 296, 'teaching justice, as in a school', being the significance of both the word: 'Let there be . . . ' and 'the Word made flesh'.

8   It is this human – and inter-human – context that reproaches all particularist versions of a world de-sacrilized, however painful in their incidence. One might reflect on George Eliot and F. W. H. Myers conversing in Trinity College garden, Cambridge and visualizing 'Titus at Jerusalem, gazing on vacant seats and empty halls, on a sanctuary with no Presence to hallow it and Heaven left lonely of a God.' True enough *in situ* but not of the whole created order. See G. Haight: *George Eliot: A Life*, Oxford, 1968, p. 464.

9   Alfred N. Whitehead: *Science and the Modern World*, New York, 1948, pp. 12–13.

10   That 'ignoring', however, in no way extends (or should not) to the claims of justice and compassion across borders and peoples. See below. It is only because sciences can be indifferently ubiquitous that they must be ethically liable.

11   Even those who insist on blind, fortuitous, random evolutionary 'selection' processes can still marvel at them in those God-excluding terms and even come to a sense of surprise about existing which might ripen into some emotion about 'creation'. Do we really think of parental love as 'an adaptation' that has allowed of infant helplessness for neural purposes outside the womb? Examples of such conjecturing are many.

12   André LaCocque and Paul Ricoeur: *Thinking Biblically: Exegetical and Hermeneutical Studies*, Chicago, 1998, p. 324.

13   Where the story of the Exodus is often grafted on to a drawing forth of cosmos out of chaos and the Red Sea linked with the primeval 'deep', as in Psalm 89.10 and 136.6 and 14–15, and Isaiah 27.1 See Chapter 1.

14   Creation as 'taking nothingness away' was a theme of the celebrated Spanish poet, Antonio Machado. It is true in the sense that a work of art 'creates' what did not exist before, yet did so by canvas and paints etc., that did. 'Genesis' likewise moves from 'the vast deep' as a *fiat* that creates the -existent out of its non-being prior.

15   It is just this 'suspicion' of the 'goodness' of our being that blights all such – and so perverse – response to it. The Qur'an, too, condemns *zann* as mostly iniquitous (e.g. 49.12)

16   John Milton: *Paradise Lost*, Book ix, lines 194–6.

17   C. H. Dodd: *The Bible Today*, Cambridge, 1946, p. 113.

18   See the fine study by Sebastian Moore: *The Inner Loneliness*, London, 1982, p. 117. It is noteworthy that 'desire' in much Hindu and Buddhist tradition is seen as the 'snare' by which we are caught and deceived.

19   Leopold Senghor: *Négritude et Marxisme*, Paris, 1962, p. 17, trans. in *Africa in Prose*, ed. O. R. Dalthorne and W. Feuser, London, 1969, p. 339. He continues: 'A nothing . . . which only knew how to implore and receive, a lump of soft wax in the hands of the white God with his rosy fingers and sky-blue eyes.'

20   Happily there were versions of Christian mission well aware of the pitfalls. The life and writings of Edwin W. Smith (1876–1957) are a salient example of a perceptive 'appreciation' of the missionary experience in Africa. See his *The Shrine of a People's Soul*, 1929 and *African Ideas of God*, 1950. It is no

accident that he was a linguist. For it is translation that brings relationships into radical encounter, more than anthropology. Moreover, the missionary urge to 'write down' and translate from 'native' dialects and tongues has contributed massively to the self-awareness – and the 'nationalisms' – of their cultures. Nor was this an un-intended side of mission. See, for example, Lamin Sanneh: *Translating the Message*, New York, 1989.

Three Interrogation from Within

1   For his is the mind that, as noted earlier in Chapter 2, gave such currency to the theme of corporate 'weddedness' to the land, with the repeated imagery of 'corn and wine and oil'. He turns the tables on 'fertility-rites' by lifting the crudity into a celebration of divine 'gifting' under Hebraic norms of 'covenant'. See below.

2   As noted in 2 Kings 15.20 – a way out of slavery in high contrast to the Exodus, the more so for its being short-lived.

3   Samuel Sandmel's verdict. It is well to note, however, that textual criticism today tends to be much more cautious about the traditional Hebrew text than it was some decades ago. J. Alberto Soggin: *Introduction to the Old Testament from its Origin, to the Close of the Alexandrian Canon*, London, 1989, p. 37.

4   Such was the reciprocal concept. Cf. Psalm 76.1: 'In Jewry is God known.' 'The knowledge of God' which Hosea so strongly cherished (4.1 and 5 and 6.6) could only mean, when forfeited, that the 'I am' no longer had a 'used' Name. A true theism, this way, depended on a true Judaic 'theological people'.

5   On the one hand 'covenant' – both ways is irreversible: yet disloyalty of the human party happened – and happens. The renegade 'Jew' is, at once, within it and 'self-outed' from it. The paradox persists through Jewish history and is no small part of contemporary Zionism. See later chapters.

6   It is noteworthy that the 'datings by-reigns' in 1.1 has only Jeroboam II of the northern Israel. Could it be that the listing of the contemporary kings of Judea in the south hints at how hope still lay there despite the northern debacle through which Hosea's ministry passed? Otherwise, the listing seems odd. Y. Kaufmann, in *The Religion of Israel from the Beginnings to the Babylonion Exile*, London, 1961, holds that the real 'Hosea' begins at 4.1 – the three earlier chapters extraneous.

7   On the complexities see H. H. Rowley: 'The Marriage of Hosea,' in his: *Men of God*, London, 1963, pp. 66–97 (written in 1955). More recently see G. L. Davies: *Hosea*, Sheffield, 1998, pp. 79–92.

8   As, for example, Isaiah (7.3 and 8.3) and the namings of the sons of Jacob.

9   Most conspicuously Ezekiel with his fastings, long strange postures, symbolical bereavements and deliberately bizarre behaviour. Or was it that idiosyncrasies constituted his vocation *per se* in ecstatic ways? Hosea's situation is of a different order.

10 Not, of course, in the sense of that odd turn of phrase that speaks of 'illegitimate children', as if he had known in advance of how marriage with Gomer would eventuate, he would have reached for these names. Only in appreci-

ating how all was parabolic of the national apostasy he came to read a parallel. There was no onus on them in their innocence. Anyway, the names were not theirs (on this exegesis) for family use but only for public signifying.

11 On any other count, the whole prophethood would be less intelligible.

12 Could it be that *Ruhamah* and *Ammi* were original 'names' of the second and third child and that negating their meaning would be what the import of events required as being implicit from the beginning and so 'true' proletically, in the way we have argued? Either way, the theme of being 'God's people' must have been salient in his mind.

13 Here, surely, historically and to make an ironical point. There *is* a theme of 'second exodus' for which the first – as inaugurating the cleansing 'wilderness' – could be analogy. See below.

14 'Elohist' because Hosea stems from that tradition belonging with Ephraim.

15 To the one in search of alliance, to the other in forced migration. Even the gentle Hosea was capable of biting humour.

16 It may seem odd to use the adjective 'Israeli' – true as it is in this context of the northern kingdom – because it echoes with the current term in Zionist nationalism. It is just this fact which makes it apposite. For Israel chose to name itself such back in 1948 and all the implications of its doing so must be taken in hand.

17 Cited, without reference, by E. G. Browne in *A Year amongst the Persians*, London, 1893, p. 407.

18 'Legend' in the strict sense of 'legenda', 'that which is to be read' concerning an event of history, the repute it acquires.

19 *Tanazzuh* – 'exaltedness' or 'transcendence'. Such doxologies may be consulted, gathered into 'God and His Praise' in my *Readings in the Qur'an*, London, 1988, 2nd ed. 1999, pp. 86–108.

20 The word *tilth* – earth for ploughing – is used in the Qur'an in sexual sense (2.223) but in denoting intercourse it adds: 'but keep in mind the fear due to God'.

21 See H. Keith Beebe: *The Old Testament: An Introduction to its Literary, Historical and Religious Traditions*, Belmont, 1970, p. 236. He cites Genesis 4.1 and Judges 19.25 and 21.12 as other occasions where the term denotes sexual intercourse. In the agricultural realm and 'promised land' it is a daring analogy for 'knowledge of God'.

22 See E. G. Selwyn: *The First Epistle of St. Peter*, London, 1946, p. 169. It is sad that *paroikia*, meaning 'abode everywhere', got impoverished into the English 'parish' gathered round its 'pump'.

Four 'Gentiles'

1 'Throughout your generations' is also a steady refrain as in Exodus 12.14, 29.42, Leviticus 7.36 etc. Or 'our generations in time to come' (Joshua 22.28). See Isaiah 13.20, 34.10, 34.17, 51.8, Jeremiah 50.30, Lamentations 5.19 and Joel 3.20. The insistence on blood sequence is everywhere crucial. To be sure, the New Testament is interested in families, parenthood and heritage, but not in the sometimes desperate terms felt in the Tanakh.

2 *Goyim* is significantly inclusive, for example, in Psalms 22.27, 67.2, 72.11,

86.9 and 117.1. It would seem that the Greek *ethnoi* which the New Testament employs for 'Gentiles' remained a non-restricted usage and could well be translated everywhere 'nations' or 'peoples' without the subtle differential implied in *goyim* in its ultimate 'Gentile' restrictive sense.

3   Readers of Thomas Mann's trilogy *Joseph and His Brothers* (trans. H. T. Lowe-Porter) will remember the vehemence of the scene, the sense of rage he infuses into his prose, the explosive nature of what erupts in their hearts. 'With . . . a furiously exultant yell of rage and hate and sudden release, they all sprang upon him as one man . . . as a pack of hungry wolves fall upon their prey.' 'Young Joseph', IV, p. 373.

4   There are many issues around the logic of Psalm 2. Is it a coronation hymn, calling the nations to recognize a new Israeli sovereign? But why in such extravagant terms of threat and pomp? 'Kissing the feet' is an abject gesture. What 'iron fetters' had Israel at its disposal to fasten on Assyrians or other such?

5   John Lyly: *Euphues and his England*, London, 1580.

6   Ernst Fischer: *An Opposing Man*, trans. P. and B. Ross, London, 1974, p. 352.

7   David Polish in *Judaism*, Vol. 28, Winter, 1969, p. 10. Surely the point would be true of 'the way it confronts any people'? – unless somehow, Jewry has become uniquely representative of all humanity. Yet, if it has, what then of its uniqueness? This seems confirmed when Jacob Talmon remarks: 'He who will dare to attack the man in the Jew will bring upon himself all mankind.' *Israel among the Nations*, London, 1970, p. 26.

8   'The hand of them that hate us . . .' – the refrain in *Benedictus*, 'the Song of Zachariah' (Luke 1.68–80). This sense of 'unwantedness' sometimes deepens into a sort of quiescent 'self-hatred' as if Jewry were a 'pariah' people, or it exudes into a passion that sees everywhere among *goyim* an inveterate foe. Thus, Rabbi Ephraim Zemmel of Gush Emunim sees 'consistent and perpetual ambush against the sons of Israel', and censure of Israel by the UN Security Council as 'one with the enmity of Esau'. 'The whole world is on the one side and we are on the other.'

9   A. R. Eckardt: *Elder and Younger Brothers*, New York, 1967. He argues, further, that because of the Holocaust, the Resurrection should be dropped from the Gospel. 'That Jewish man from Galilee sleeps now, He sleeps with the other Jewish dead.'

10   *Encyclopedia Judaica*, Vol. 7, pp. 411f.

11   *Ibid.*

12   In T. T. Milik: *Discoveries of the Judean Desert*, Oxford, I, p. 129 relating to the 'Teacher of Righteousness'.

13   As a *religio licita*. Titus was not initially set on Temple destruction and, later, when urged to lay waste also to Jews in Antioch, he refused. But for its political zealotry, finding Rome intolerable, the Revolt was quite unnecessary for the survival of Judaism.

14   It is curious also how far Zionists at the outset drew on the arguments of the anti-Semites – 'It's true: you are misfits: you don't belong: you cannot be normal: you are incorrigibly 'other' and will always remain so – unless you see that you have to abstract yourselves. The nations that cannot abide you

will say: 'Good riddance.' Such Zionist/anti-Semitic case-making only made diaspora Jewish insistence on good Germanism etc. the more dubious. Hence the hard going of incipient Zionism. See Chapters 7 and 8.

15 Nathan Rotenstreich in: Ninian Smart and J. Clayton, eds.: *19th Century Religious Thought in the West*, Cambridge, 1985, p. 81 in reference to Nachman Krochmal (1785–1840).

16 What awaits Chapters 7 and 8 – Zionism the interrogation of Judaism and Judaism the interrogation of Zionism, each in a necessary mutual allowance and disavowal.

17 *Loc. cit.*, note 3, p. 30.

18 Sharp irony here, too, Shakespeare knew that 'gaberdine' was 'a frock worn by Jews – and beggars'.

19 William Shakespeare: *The Merchant of Venice*, Act 3, Scene 1, lines 54–63.

20 So, for example, Leo Abse in *The Times* (London), 7 February 1970, Cf. the famous remark of Sartre: 'The Jew needs the Anti-Semite.'

21 J. L. Talmon: *The Unique and the Universal*, New York, 1965, p. 72.

22 The plural 'Zions' because, in truth, there are several.

23 Cited from L. Hanke: *The Spanish Struggle for Justice in the Conquest of America*, Philadelphia, 1944, pp. 31 and 120.

24 Robert Frost: *Complete Poems*, New York, 1942, p. 565.

25 It was in 1861 in Trenton, New Jersey.

26 Herman Melville: *White Jacket*, 1850, London, p. 189.

27 Ludwig Feuerbach; *The Essence of Christianity*, 1841, Eng. trans. George Eliot, London, 1851. pp. 112f.

28 Wilhelm Hauer: *Germany's New Religion*, 1937, cited from T. S. Eliot: *The Idea of a Christian Society*, London 1939, p. 71.

29 Yeshayahu Leibowitz: *Judaism, Human Values and the Jewish State*, Harvard, 1992, p. 108. He holds that 'Israel' should not be understood as having a 'destiny', via land, covenant and 'election', but 'a task', the only 'holiness' being YAHWEH's alone. His logic is obscure. No one ever sanely held that God was 'a Jew' as ever the conclusion to be drawn from the assured inter-association between YAHWEH and Jewry. Equally to assert that 'the God of Christians' is 'a Jew' grossly distorts the nature of Christian faith. See further Chapter 9 and note 21.

30 It is well to remember that in the American War between the States, it was not the abolitionists who won. The war was about slavery only in also being about 'non-secession', the right of secession being what the South demanded. The one cause was won only in the context of the other. Similarly, in 1939–45 there were numerous factors of the allied situation and war-strategy making the context of what – in the terminating of the Holocaust – it was able to achieve, not 'in spite of itself', nor as its only aim, but because of the 'self' it availed to be.

31 Robert L. Wicken: *The Myth of Christian Beginnings, History's Impact on Belief*, New York, 1972, p. 197. To want to 'mythicize' is sometimes to fail to understand. Is it what 'history' does to belief or only 'historians'?

32 Emmanuel Berkowits in *Judaism*, Vol. 27, 1978, p. 325. Save Luke, the New Testament writers were all themselves Jews.

33 Solomon Schechter: *Some Aspects of Rabbinic Judaism*, New York, 1909.

Schechter coined the phrase 'Catholic Israel'. He was a notable exponent of what A. A. Cohen called, in paradox, 'that universal particularism which is Judaism' in his *The Natural and Supernatural Jew*, 2nd ed. New York, 1979, p. 102. Are 'Gentiles' really left with only the first of those two descriptives? Or has Christian faith found them 'supernatural' too?

34   In Surah 7.172f. the Qur'an has 'all the progeny of Adam' solemnly being offered, and inclusively accepting, 'the trust of existence and custodianship of the good earth'. They respond with a firm 'Yes, we so acknowledge' to the divine question: 'Am I not your Lord?' See, further, my book of that title; *Readings in the Qur'an*, London, 1988, Brighton, 2000.

Five Through Jesus to Human Inclusion

1   As did C. H. Dodd in his well-known study of that title in 1970. Perhaps he meant pointedly to counter the flow of adamant notions about a 'reductionist' reading of the elusive relation between 'Jesus', 'Christ' and 'Lord'. Dodd's deep studies in the Fourth Gospel gave weightier shape to that sequence and its 'church-ward' logic than *The Founder of Christianity*, London, 1970.

2   Ecclesiasticus 42.25–26.

3   T. S. Eliot: *Four Quartets*, London, 1944, 'Little Gidding', lines 101–102.

4   Matthew 5.44–48. 'Perfect' might be the sense of *teleioi* elsewhere, but here, in 'likeness' God to and in context, its meaning is 'inclusive,' a 'taking in of all'. The restrictive greeting was common Semitic practice, at least where the 'code' phrase was used with all its binding 'feel'.

5   John Riches in his *Jesus and the Transformation of Judaism*, London, 1980, studies what he calls 'Jesus-theism,' and here, p.166, his point is that Jesus' language about God as 'Father', though of course not unprecedented in psalm and prophethood, nevertheless – in its powerfully human terms – pointed forward to what, at length, Christian faith in Incarnation reached as a theology. That theology can be seen as capturing his personality – as orthodoxy always held.

6   See G. N. Stanton: *Jesus of Nazareth in New Testament Preaching*, Cambridge, 1974, for evidence of this intimate interplay.

7   Robert Browning: *Poetical Works*, Oxford, 1940, 'A Death in the Desert', p. 488. With his convoluted sentences, Browning is often elusive but his 'Knew first what else we should not recognise' is in line with Eliot, as in note 3 – a sort of proleptic sense of what could only be in the future, yet had its intimations in the past and present, which is precisely 'through Jesus to an inclusive peoplehood'.

8   Which the Fourth Gospel, with its editorial liberty, brings to the beginning to underline the theme of critical encounter that runs through all its sequences. See Anthony Harvey: *Jesus on Trial, A Study in the Fourth Gospel*, London, 1976. See also Etienne Trocmé: *Jesus and His Contemporaries*, trans. R. A. Wilson, London, 1973. Jesus 'kept his distance with regard to the role that people wanted him to play: Messiah but in his own way, associated with the Zealots but differing completely from them,' p. 120.

9   The bearing on the ministry of those pivotal passages was most confidently

traced and documented by C. R. North: *The Suffering Servant in Deutero-Isaiah: An Historical and Critical Study*, Oxford, 1948, and by William Manson: *Jesus the Messiah*, 1948 and T. W. Manson; *The Servant Messiah*, Oxford, 1953. Their confidence has been assailed by M. Hooker in *Jesus and the Servant*, London, 1959 and the debate persists. However it is resolved, what is not in doubt is that the Gospel-writers saw and sustained the connection. To doubt their veracity is to incur a larger problem than any involved in accepting it.

10 Things are so evidently mutual between faith in its pre-credal formulation and its liturgical expression. The ultimate example must be Philippians 2.5–11, or 'Carmen Christi', at once a great hymn and an incipient 'creed'. See also Philip Carrington: *The Primitive Christian Calendar* – and *Catechism* (two works), Cambridge, 1952 and 1940.

11 Such being the view of, e.g., Geza Vermes: *Jesus the Jew*, London, 1974 and, more recently: *The Changing Faces of Jesus*, 2000. He sees Jesus as having been squarely in the ethnic tradition of Jewishness and no threat to Jewish institutions, his 'image' having been sadly distorted by the 'Hellenizing Gentiles' who took over and misconstrued his whole significance. His crucifixion was the result of his being 'in the wrong place at the wrong time'.

12 Hebrews 13.12 – the stark difference between ritual animal sacrifice with its artificial, involuntary character and the utterly 'existential' character of the conscious situation in Gethsemane.

13 Though, of course, there are those who posit so and interpret the cry 'Why hast Thou forsaken me?' in that sense of a lost 'gamble' when what he had tried to precipitate failed to happen. Some theories about Judas surmise that he 'handed over Jesus' to compel from him some provocation of that kind of finale. Such readings have large problems with the integrity in Jesus' ministry. Further, should not the cry read: 'Why didst Thou forsake me?' marking a coming through from darkness to recovered assurance beyond the deep trauma so evidently present?

14 As does Geza Vermes (note 11, *Changing Faces*) when he remarks: 'In order to legitimise the presence of non-Jews in the church fictitious sayings were inserted into the Synoptics in which Jesus himself envisages, even orders, the universal promulgation.' Note 11, p. 157. He also asks, if Jesus had ordered their admission, why such opposition to it later? – which is to miss the point of diversity in Jewish attitudes and the tenacious sense of 'theological privacy with YAHWEH' that Jesus' whole teaching called in question, by its steady insistence on divine sensitivity to all rather than a 'Lordship of hosts', Jewish only.

15 The passage in Matthew 15.21–28 and Mark 7.24–30 is feasibly read as a test of her faith as putting to her precisely the reaction she would need to overcome as a 'Gentile' beseeching a Jew. The diminutive *kunarion* is used, i.e., 'Pets'. Jesus' reluctance in any event did not end in denial.

16 Where the Greek factor was far more evident than in Judea and Jesus' language about 'the kingdom of heaven' had more appeal to 'the poor in spirit' than in the citadel of high ritual beyond 'the court of the Gentiles'.

17 Its high significance is often missed. 'A voice from heaven' announcing 'I am Christ' would be where 'the Christ' 'riding on the clouds of power' was

presumed to be and hence arresting enough but in a familiar way. To hear that office proclaimed from within its import as that of 'Jesus' was the whole core of its meaning. 'This Jesus whom you persecute . . . ', identified from the heavenly place of power, captured that entire surrender Saul had to make – a surrender the logic of which was already present in the very zeal with which he sought to suppress it. Hence that 'pricks' analogy – so apposite when he was using them on his own steed.

18 The saying is one the Gospels themselves have not supplied. His Letters make 'the (Or: Our) Lord Jesus . . . ' a frequent note along with the recurrent 'in Christ'. There is no need to divorce them. For 'Our Lord Jesus Christ' is the beginning of credal usage.

19 Romans 15.19. It is important to remember other directions of dispersion beside the western Mediterranean which, sadly, the New Testament quite fails to document.

20 John 12.32, echoing 3.14. Jesus' words in John are those that belong with Jesus as faith came to perceive him to have been but situate – by the evangelist's conscious literary design – in the ministry setting whence that believing perception had derived. 'Greeks' (i.e. 'Gentiles') were by their presence the point of the words in 12.32.

21 'Only in the sequel' in the sense that until the Passion had clarified to them both how deep human perversity could be and how incomplete teaching without redemption would be so proven, they could not have realized the inclusion of all humans in the preaching/suffering significance of Jesus. Yet, in so realizing they were not innovative about him.

22 'Anti-Semitic' despite its ringing 'Salvation is of the Jews' (4.22) and the clear distinction it makes between Jewry at large (in no way reprehended) and 'the Jews' as a usage referring only to participants in controversy who stood for the separatism the new faith aimed to overcome.

23 The 'paganizing' idea has often been urged against Christology as drawn from notions of 'divinization' which its whole rationale is in fact calculated to exclude. 'Pagan' origins have also been attributed to the cultic celebration of the 'Eucharist' in 'bread and wine', as if the highly metaphorical language of the fourth Gospel (e.g. '. . . except you eat the flesh of the Son of Man') was of that sort of literalist, cannabalist order.

24 Hebrews 5.8. There is a play on words – *emathen epathen* – that serves to cover the entire ministry with its ultimate climax as one 'education'.

25 W. D. Davies: *The Gospel and the Land, Early Christianity and Jewish Territorial Doctrine*, London, 1974, p. 375.

26 'The Gentile offering' for Jerusalem, discussed at length in the Letters to Corinth, plays a decisive role in Paul's career. In resolving to take it in person to Jerusalem he risked – and underwent – the curtailment of his itinerating career. Do we conclude that 'a sacrament of Jew/Gentile' unity was no less important than actual preaching?

27 Not actually a 'tutor' but a 'servant-boy' to ensure that you arrived at school. Truancy is no uncommon habit in theology.

28 The point is made characteristically (and without conceding anything to Christianity) by Alfred Jospé when he writes: 'Something – an idea, a moral imperative, an ultimate truth, for whose sake it is supremely important to

stand apart, to be singled out, to stand separate . . . ' – defining being Jewish. Ed., *Tradition and Contemporary Experience*, New York, 1970, pp. 126–150, 'On the Meaning of Jewish Distinctiveness.'

29 A relevant study is Walter Brueggemann: *David's Truth in Israel's Imagination and Memory*, Philadelphia, 1985. 'Historical persons are never historical . . . We look for pure faith and are surprised to find a bandit,' p. 16.

30 In *The Prophetic Faith*, trans. C. Witton-Davies, New York, 1949, p. 217, Martin Buber notes Isaiah 45.14: 'They will come of their own will in chains of iron to show that they are passing over to YAHWEH's service and will pray in the direction of Mount Zion.'

31 The words of Hebrews 12.28 might apply either way – ' . . . receiving a kingdom which cannot be moved . . . ', i.e. a diaspora in which their being Jews was their sufficient 'homeland' or 'the kingdom' which only a landed 'Zion' could emplace.

Six 'This World Harsh and Strange'

1 The question was close to the thought of the greatest prophets. There is the word in Isaiah 43.24: 'You have made me to bear your sins,' and the pained cry of YAHWEH in Hosea over Israel as over a faithless bride. Cf. the central theme of divine 'pathos' in Abraham J. Heschel: *The Prophets*, New York, 1955.

2 Clearly the New Testament literature would not be the actuality it is unless 'Gentile' inclusion had been its mind-set and Jewishness its *fons et origo*. For it is both a travel document and a steady exegete, rightly or wrongly, of an earlier body of sacred writ.

3 So powerfully did Pharaoh become a type. So the Deuteronomist warns 'Thou shalt not harden thy heart.' Cf. 1 Samuel 6.6, Psalm 95.8, Isaiah 63.17, while Nehemiah has 'hardened necks'. It was an instinctive way of accounting for any recalcitrant world or the wilfully stubborn.

4 In spite of Tacitus and his contemptuous view of Jewry, it is surprising how relatively lenient Rome was before, and even after, the Revolt of the late sixties of the 1st century – always, of course, on the condition of political docility, just the one that Zealotry would not admit. Titus had sought to save the Temple intact and even after Bar Kokhbah's insurrection religious Judaism, Rabbinic or other, still found its ready occasions.

5 The whole Gospel seems to have been constructed as a series of representative, dramatized 'interviews' between Jesus and aspects of what Jewry symbolized, of issues for the new faith in, say, an Ephesus situation by the nineties. The bitterness of John 8.44 ('You are of your father the Devil . . . ') cites Genesis 4.9 (cf. 1 John 3.14) in the context of a play on the word 'father', which attributed bastardy to Jesus. What may explain in no way exonerates. See below.

6 Not only in the Johannine writings but throughout the Pauline. 'Christ died for the ungodly', 'for *our* sins . . . '. There was the same emphasis in the 'servant songs' on the deed not the doers. Hence those passives: 'He was wounded . . . ' etc. and the inclusive range '*we* are healed'. In the famous

Negro 'Spiritual' – 'Were you there when they crucified . . . ' or 'they laid him in the tomb . . . ' and 'you's' and 'they's' can only be one if the song is to have meaning.

7 Sadly these have been many. The burden of the Holocaust both ways has multiplied them when zeal ill serves its proper impulses.

8 John G. Grager: *The Origins of Anti-Semitism*, New York, 1985, p. 269. Cf. also p. 7. Sub-titled: 'Attitudes towards Judaism in Pagan and Christian Antiquity', the study writes of 'traditional scholarship founded on a narrow range of speakers' and of 'the voices of the losers transmitted through selective filters'.

9 Rosemarie R. Reuther: *Faith and Fratricide, Theological Roots of Anti-Semitism*, New York 1974, pp. 163 and 178.

10 R. L. Wilken: *The Myth of Christian Beginnings*, 1972, p. 197.

11 As late, it would seem, as 1873 when it was coined by Wilhelm Marr in the context of the Germanic belief in biological determinants of 'race' and so of 'racialism'. See Gavin I. Langmuir: *Toward a Definition of Anti-Semitism*, Berkeley, 1990, pp. 311f. He argues that the term would only not be empty or false if 'Jews have in fact been the object of a different kind of hostility from that which all other groups have confronted', p. 351. Indeed, they have, but this does not deserve the special name 'anti-Semitism,' which is a deplorable usage that only makes 'empirical' sense because Jews have 'chimerically' been converted into a symbol which, such fantasy apart, has no rational or scientific meaning. This seems to ignore the question how the world's most avowedly 'chosen' people should have proved the world's most maligned and reprobated.

12 Jacob Katz: *From Prejudice to Destruction*, Cambridge, Mass., 1980, p. 322

13 Diaspora Jewry from the 5th century BC well into the 2nd CE related to Greek thought as the frame of the civilized world, as Philo in his Alexandria, and developed Judaic variants of that world. Rabbinic Judaism in the much longer encounter with post-Constantinian 'Christendom' related by a studied retentiveness of its 'native' genius.

14 Hans Conzelmann: *Gentiles, Jews, Christians*, trans. M. E. Boring, Minneapolis, 1992, p. 232. Also: 'The conflict is inherent in the existence of the Church itself. It will last as long as church and synagogue exist side by side' (p. 257).

15 See Bernard Blumenkranz: *Juifs et Chretiens dans le Monde Occidental 430–1096*, Paris, 1960, pp. 169–71, 269–70.

16 For any 'covenant' theme, when competitively and contentiously held, could only elide the binding factor of fellow human creaturehood, being read in categorically different validity.

17 See below and Chapter 9. As Aaron S. Klieman remarked in *Israel and the World after Forty Years*, Washington, 1990, 'It was easier to get the Jew physically out of the ghetto than to get the ghetto psychologically out of the Jew.'

18 'The Word made flesh' never meant an untenanted heaven. 'And was made man' was no unmaking of God, only a divine 'undertaking' of the human situation in grace and doing so out of the nature of 'very God as very God', 'the son' in 'God the Son' meant to say so.

19 They are rather 'the death' of love to God in the human heart. The Lord is

only 'murdered' (pace Nietzsche) when 'ignored', and only so in terms of human will to have it so.

20 Jules Isaac: *The Teaching of Contempt*, London, 1964.

21 Cited from Blumenkranz (note 15) in Langmuir, *loc. cit.*, note 11, pp. 302–3.

22 *Ibid.*, p. 302.

23 Cf. Isaiah 6.10 and 42.18–20 'Who is blind as My servant?' – a question the more pointed in that 'blindness' and 'deafness' characterized 'pagans'. Cf. Isaiah 44.22.

24 The viability, in legal terms, of such minority status under Islam gives a necessary lie to the charge that Islam was 'spread by the sword'. What is true is that it came as a power-complex and that 'submitters' for long did not know the doctrine of what had supervened against their political order. It took at least a half-century even for coinage to be Arabicized.

25 Cited in Schlomo Eidelberg, ed.: *The Jews and the Crusades: The Hebrew Chronicles of the 1st and 2nd Crusades*, Madison, WI, 1977, p. 47.

26 Herbert of Bosham (b. 1120) was in the inner circle of Thomas Becket and visited the Abbey of St. Victor in 1169. He used Jewish sources to help clarify Biblical meanings and even in the most crucial realms was ready to think himself mistaken, e.g. on 'Messiah' in the Psalms. Five centuries later John Donne was in debt to Herbert for many of his sermonic and poetic allusions.

27 Beryl Smalley: *The Study of the Bible in the Middle Ages*, Oxford, 1977, p. 163. Rashi lived 1040–1105. His successors, Joseph Kara and Joseph Shor, were other consultants of the Christian scholars. Shor suggested 'double narrative' as a clue to Genesis.

28 A view ignorant of the molecular and atomic theories of the insubstantial nature of matter, for which there is no 'substance' to 'stand under' or 'carry' the 'accidents' of colour, taste, etc. on which 'transubstantiation' relies, whereby, in the act of priestly consecration, the elements 'become' 'flesh and blood' under the continuing appearance of the 'accidents' of 'bread and wine'. Thus no change is sensually discernible in the continuing taste and appearance. The dogma opened the door wide to popular credulity with tragic consequences for the Jewish community.

29 Edward I in England was the first in 1290, with French attempts in 1306 and 1394; from Vienna, Cologne, Augsburg, Bavaria and Moravia between 1421 and 1454; between 1490–1510 from sundry other cities and states in the western Empire; from Italian states between 1485 and 1494 with Sardinia and Sicily. On Spain and Portugal see below. These expulsions from the West of Europe pushed European Jewry eastward into an Ost Judentum.

30 See Note 28. Given the same 'accidents' the 'changed substance' still possessed after consecration, no blood could be seen 'bleeding'. People like Nicholas of Cusa stressed this reality but popular clamour paid no heed. Stranger still is that the misreading never called into popular question the sanity of the dogma itself, or saw that its meaning could only be for the mind 'at devotion'.

31 Cited in Gavin I. Langmuir: *Toward a Definition of Anti-Semitism*, Madison, WI, 1990, p. 309 from Luther: Works, ed. J. Pelikan and H. T. Lehman, St. Louis, Vol. 47, p. 267.

32 *Ibid.*, p. 178 as cited by Cecil Roth: *History of the Jews in England*, New York, 1961, p. 33.

33 One such Rabbi was Yitzhak Arama, cited in Haim Beinart: *Conversos on Trial: The Inquisition in Ciudad Real*, Jerusalem, 1981, p. 3. On Herzl's words, see: Ronald Sanders: *The High Walls of Jerusalem* (on the Balfour Declaration), New York, 1984, p. 37.

34 See: Paul Johnson: *A History of the Jews*, London, 1987, pp. 317–23 on Britain and pp. 370–33 on New York. Massive immigration to New York occurred between 1880 and 1917, some two million Jews arriving. In *Haskalah*, or 'emancipation', Jews had full civil rights but anti-Semitism did not abate.

Seven Zionism –The Realized Quest?

1 Yeshayahu Leibowitz: *Judaism, Human Values and the Jewish State*, ed. E. Goldmann, Harvard, 1992, pp. 110 and 116. Scripture commentary can be very inventive in its 'findings'. What texts 'mean' is no small part of the burden of Judeo/Christian relations.

2 The only juridical basis for the State of Israel is the United Nations partition vote of 1947. The rest results from exchanges of force which, in respect of Syria and the Palestinians, have never yet been resolved in treaties mutually agreed and determining accepted borders. Hence the proper phrase about 'occupied territories'. Behind the UNO jurisdiction lay the League of Nations 'grant' of mandate which UNO terminated. That mandate, in turn, stemmed from a Balfour Declaration which had no legal status. It was no more than a statement of 'good offices' for a much provisoed intention re 'a national home in Palestine'.

3 Jacob Neusner: *Judaism in the Secular Age*, New York, 1966, p. 27.

4 C. S. Lewis: *Collected Poems*, ed. Walter Hooper, 1964, pp. 139–40.

5 'Inner slavery' was the concept he used to argue why emancipation would always unserve the Jews because it could never be had – as he said – 'with dignity'. He feared that more generations of it would lead to a Jewish elimination.

6 The remark has a strange prescience for the whole long story, but there were inter-Zionist tensions at the time on which see: David Vital: *Zionism, the Formative Years*, Oxford, 1982, pp. 360f.

7 *Trial and Error: The Autobiography*, London, 1949. He records the salute he received from five leaders in the Provisional Government on May 15, 1948: 'You have done more than any other living man towards its (Israel's) creation' (p. 585).

8 *Ibid.*, pp. 561f. It had to do with last-minute hesitancy among Truman's advisers over the allocation of the Negev. It is intriguing that Weizmann was able to bring in the South African vote by a personal cable to General Smuts as – with himself – 'the one surviving author of the Balfour Declaration' (p. 585). The attention to detail was impeccable.

9 Abba Eban: *An Autobiography*, London, 1977. He wrote: 'Israel is no more and no less than the Jewish people's resolve to be itself . . . The Israeli policy is one of cultural autonomy' (pp. 493 and 286). There would be 'no attempt

to make the Arabs into Jews or Zionists'. But could it be, as cynics have mused, that a 'ghetto' phenomenon persisted, though in virile, resourceful national form?

10 See Abraham Avi-Hai: *Ben-Gurion: State-Builder: Principles and Pragmatism*, Jerusalem, 1974, pp. 219–48.

11 David Ben-Gurion: *Recollections*, ed. Thomas Branston, London, 1970, p. 131.

12 On Ben-Gurion's dismissive attitude to Arabs see: Michael Ben-Zohar: *The Armed Prophet. A Biography of Ben-Gurion*, tr. L. Ortzen. London, 1967, 'In his state there was no place for Arabs: He did not want to know any,' p. 172.

13 The pre-emptive action should not obscure its defensive nature. 'Abd al-Nasir was intent on his appeal for Arab hegemony and a reversal of the humiliation of 1948. There was the threat to Israel's 'back-door' at the Strait of Tiran. It was, however, the thrusting will of the military men rather than the more prudent stance of politicos that fuelled the final scenes, when Jordan and Syria blundered into the fray that 'Abd al-Nasir had clumsily contrived.

14 On the original Yael with her tent-peg and hammer, see Judges 4.18–24, and her celebration in the Song of Deborah in 5.24–27. She recorded many of her father's memories and was a member of the Knesset, becoming later a passionate peace-campaigner, attacking Rabin for his heavy hand on Palestinian activists. She once visited Arafat in his forced 'exile' in Tunis.

15 William Shakespeare: *Coriolanus*, Act iv, Scene vii, lines 49–50.

16 The vessel bringing arms to the Irgun against the agreement reached by Ben-Gurion on behalf of the Haganah for a 'ceasefire'. When the ship was fired on Begin waded ashore and survived. It had been named after the pen-name of Jabotinsky. It is noteworthy that just as the more 'respectable' Haganah could not control the more extreme Irgun and Stern gangs, so in the new millennium Arafat could not control Hamas and others when Sharon menacingly demanded that he must, as a *sine qua non* of negotiations, thus achieving his aim of ruling these out in perpetuity.

17 The word 'terrorist' he always angrily repudiated, as a matter of his honour. His activism against the British he held to be 'armed struggle' against imperial power. For the civilian victims, e.g. of the King David horror, the distinction was purely academic and also desperately so for the villagers of Dair Yassin.

18 Avi Shlaim: *The Iron Wall: Israel and the Arab World*, London, 2000, p. 419.

19 See Anton La Guardia: *Holy Land Unholy War*, London, 2001, p. 284.

20 Note 18, p. 245. How might Begin have acted at that point. He was given often to recalling how, at the time of the burning of the Temple at the destruction of Jerusalem under Titus, 'the race (of Zealots) went up heavenwards in flames . . . Few against many: the weak against the strong . . . This is the lore of revolt . . . ' Menahem Begin: *The Revolt*, rev. edn., trans. Samuel Katz, London, 1979, pp. 379–80. Perhaps he would have done what Rabbi Goren proposed.

21 See his analysis in *A Place among the Nations: Israel and the World*, London, 1993, chap. 8 on 'The Demographic Demon', pp. 294–328.

22 Notably the Palestinian-American, Edward Said in *The Question of Palestine*, New York, 1992.

23 See Chapter 8 and note 32.

24 *The Times* (of London), 7 September 2001.

25 Though there is a daily *Letste Nayes*, and surviving Yiddish terms like schmalz and kosher. Yiddish had long distinguished itself from German by using Hebrew script which doubtless greatly aided immigrants in their acquisition of Israeli Hebrew, as did also the assimilation of words necessary in the new 'reach' of Hebrew vocabulary.

26 Sander Gilman: *Jewish Self-Hatred: Anti-Semitism and the Hidden Language of the Jews*, Baltimore, 1986, p. 71. He adds that German nationalism insisted on the use of German by Jewish journalists. There was a sharp literary dimension in the impulse to anti-Semitism. The marriage between Semitism and Hebrew in Palestine was the more obviously right, though 'Semitism' included Arabic also no less than Hebrew.

27 S. Yizhar, born in 1916, wrote mainly about the years of the pre-1967 period from the late Mandate era. In 1958 he published *The Days of Ziklag*, his most notable novel. He focused throughout on the inner problems of personhood around the issues of war and cultural strife, while drawing heavily on the aura of ancient landscape. See Hannan Heyer: 'Territoriality and Otherness,' in: L. J. Silberstein and R. L. Cohn, eds.: *The Other in Jewish Thought and History*, New York, 1994, pp. 247f.

28 Both a kibbutznik and an academic, Amos Oz enjoys international fame for his essays and stories and as a leader in the Peace Movement in Israel. The irony in the quoted passage is surely unintentional. See: ed. Glenda Abranson: *The Oxford Book of Hebrew Short Stories*, Oxford, 1996, p. 295.

29 Moshe Shamir in *Modern Hebrew Literature*, Vol. 3, 1977, p. 16.

30 Ezra Pound 'The First Pisan Canto' in *The Cantos of Ezra Pound*, London, 1947, p. 7. lines 1–2: 'The enormous tragedy in the dream of the peasant's bent shoulders.'

31 See above, Chapter 3. On eroticism in Zionist thought and writing see David Biale: *Eros and the Jews: From Biblical Israel to Contemporary America*, New York, 1992, pp. 176f.

32 Cited here only as a pointed example of a far-reaching quest for historical roots which could only the better underwrite the whole Zionist intent. See Yigael Yadin: *Masada: Herod's Fortress and the Zealots' Last Stand*, London, 1966.

33 See Chapter 3 and Isaiah 62.5. The imagery well fits the implicit affection discernible in Zionist ideology and, with it, the abiding kinship that weds human nature to the natural order as a sort of mutual 'home-making'.

34 The phrase 'The Excellencies of Jerusalem' frequent in Islamic prose and poetry celebratory of Jerusalem. Perhaps some of the praises came from Jews and Christians who had become Muslims. They were numerous by the 2nd AH century. See: Muhammad ibn Ahmad al-Wasiti: *Fada'il Bait al-Maqdis*, ed. Isaac Hasson, Jerusalem, 1979 and ed. L. I. Levine: *The Jerusalem Cathedra*, No. 1, Jerusalem, 1981.

35 This sense of co-affirmation, of YAHWEH ever 'having a Name' by Jewish confession of it, could reach strange lengths as in the midrashic saying, based

on Isaiah 43.12: 'If you cease to be my witness, I am not God.' Rabbi Abraham Heschel, who loved to cite it, would add: 'If there are no witnesses, there is no God to be met . . . without the people Israel, the Bible is mere literature.' *Israel: An Echo of Eternity, New York*, 1968, p. 45.

36 Was it that the inevitability of the location of the Zionist enterprise tragically ensured an inevitability in its reaching a dire impasse where righteous security could not be had? If so, 'place' and 'name' shaped a tragic irony with no present discernible relief.

37 William Shakespeare: *Hamlet*, Act 3, Scene 2, lines 202–204.

Eight Zionism – The Great Forfeiture?

1 George Friedmann: *The End of the Jewish People?*, trans. from the French, Eric Mosbacher, 1967. A secular Jew, the author reflected on a visit to Israel, describing his pages as 'riddled with anxiety' lest 'nationalism', aiming for a Jewish 'normalcy', had forfeited the diaspora concept of 'a pilgrim people'. Little since 1967 has served to diminish his fears.

2 Cited from Mirna Cicioni: *Primo Levi: Bridges of Knowledge*, Oxford, 1995, pp. 134 and 123. Levi was not speaking out of despair for he contrasted himself with Kafka, saying: 'I have always strived to move from darkness to light.' He aligned himself with S. T. Coleridge's 'Ancient Mariner' who had the same story-telling compulsion in his soul. His disillusion with Israel, therefore, was no diaspora prejudice.

3 Borrowing the words attributed by Josephus to Eleazar on Mount Masada, prior to the corporate suicide of the defenders out of a despair that their final gamble with the Romans was doomed. There is, of course, no direct analogy, except that Zionism 'conjectured a truly Semitic purpose; out of a despair about the readiness of the 'Gentile' world to allow of a genuinely Jewish co-existence. See Yigael Yadin's *Masada*, London, 1966, p. 232, quoting *The Jewish War*.

4 Arthur A. Cohen: *The Natural and the Supernatural Jew*, New York, 1962, p. 6.

5 *Ibid.*, p. 6. 'The Exile', as he calls diaspora, is not for him a condition which mere security there can correct, nor – it would seem – is it corrected by 'national fulfilment' in a State of Israel. Somehow either would release Semitism from its full destiny, which is 'to make all history alive to its incompleteness'. At this point realists must feel lost in a vacuity, in a 'Messianism' ('the Jew is a messianic being') which denies itself any actual policy or practice of hope' (p. 7).

6 *Ibid.*, and p. 116 'the religion of ethical optimism.'

7 So deep did this concept run for the Qumran Community that – according to the Damascus Scroll (IV.2) – they were 'the converts from Israel', or 'the remnant of remnants', who virtually displaced the rest of Jewry and Jerusalem most of all. Ideas of such mandatory separatism could readily come to be attached the more to 'Gentile' othernesses. High School curricula in religious schools in Israel demonize 'Gentiles' and hold that 'the pure Abrahamic genes' passed down only through Isaac and Jacob, making that 'seed' 'worthily Jewish'. See below and C. S. Liebman and S. M. Cohen:

Two Worlds of Judaism, The Israeli and American Experiences, Yale University Press, 1990.

8   Echoing Amos' words of reproach to his 8th century well content with their idle luxury (6.1). Contrariwise, there could even be a laudable heroism in responding, e.g. to America, as authentically 'the land'. A writer like Kaufmann Kohler could sense the very call of God in the cry: 'The land, the land that resounded on Columbus' ship as opening up a new future for the martyr race' of fugitive Jewry. Such non-Zionist Jews, if authentic in their diasporas, could only deplore the claim of, for example, Abraham Isaac Kook that 'failure to return' meant *chilul ha-Shem* – 'profanation of the Name', or Ben-Gurion's telling the 25th Zionist Congress in 1961 that 'every religious Jew daily violated the precepts of Judaism and the Torah of Israel by remaining in the diaspora'.

9   See in David Vital: *Zionism, The Formative Years*, Oxford, 1982, pp. 3–105, analysis of the difficulties after the Basle Congress, 1890. There was also the Ottoman ban on Jews settling.

10   In *Witness on the Road to Statehood*, Jerusalem, 1959, p. 266.

11   *Ktavim (Works)*, Vol. 9, p. 128. See also J. B. Schechtman: *The Vladimir Jabotinsky Story*, 2 vols, New York, 1956.

12   *Ktavim*, Vol. 9, p. 154.

13   In an Address to the this Zionist Congress. See B. Netanyahu, ed.: *Max Nordau to his People*, New York, 1941, p. 68.

14   David Ben-Gurion: *My Talks with Arab Leaders*, Jerusalem, 1972, p. 80. Meanwhile Jewish numbers and power must be steadily built up.

15   David Ben-Gurion: *Letters to Paula*, Jerusalem, 1971, pp. 156–7.

16   'Occupied' became the UNO and the Palestinian term, 'administered' was the eulogism Israel preferred. It was 'not annexed' because annexation would have raised enormous problems for Israeli democracy and – at that point – was seen as seriously compromising the urgent aim of a homogeneous, preponderantly Jewish, nation. Even so the lavish enlargement of Jerusalem as an urban expression contrived a significant annexation of territory rapidly to be Judaized.

17   The peculiar vulnerability of Lebanon to disruption by dint of a large Palestinian presence lay in the tensions within its own structure. These made it quite unable to emulate King Hussein of Jordan and either expel them or subdue their presence to utter local state-control. 'Feds' were the *fida'iyin*, or freedom fighters, and 'Beds' the *badawin* core of Jordanian armed forces.

18   Sifting the antecedents of the June War is a puzzling task but the blunders involved on the part of Arab powers presented Israel with a situation its vigilant opportunism was well equipped to exploit.

19   Israeli policy never allowed him to make good that intention since Begin had never meant it should. Sadat's Egypt was excluded for ten years from the comity of Arab nations and – in effect – Sadat paid with his life for the courage with which he had broken the log-jam by his visits to the Knesset in 1977 and renewed Egyptian/Israeli relations (having first in the 1973 war somewhat restored Egypt's pride after the humiliation of 1967). His peace policy was eminently in Egypt's domestic interest, there being half a million Egyptian 'refugees' from the Canal Zone within Egypt itself, and Egypt had suffered

much on behalf of refugees from Palestine in three successive wars. See Note 20.

20 As President Carter discovered at Camp David, Begin was adept at claiming divergent meanings in the Hebrew version of bi-lingual agreed texts. Carter wrote 'His good words had multiple meanings.' Was there not a Hebrew saying: 'Respect and suspect'? Begin saw relinquishment of Sinai a *quid pro quo* for Israeli perpetuation on the West Bank. Securing the southern frontier paved the way for the risk of invading Lebanon. Even Begin's biographer observed: 'A man of honour, with whom it was wise to read the small print.' Eric Silver: *Begin: A Biography*, London, 1984, pp. 203 and 253.

Begin had agreed to the negotiations on the basis of UNO Resolution 242 'in all its parts'. It was a salient example of the duplicity by which all too often negotiations were betrayed of their 'good faith'.

21 Zeev Schiff and Ehud Yaari: *Israel's Lebanon War*, London, 1984.

22 The illusion was that the Lebanese Phalange, in their Maronite reading of a 'Christian Lebanon', might opt for a sort of protected status under a strong neighbour, emulate its rugged assertion for 'smallness in size, against a common Islamic enmity', and shed the Muslim areas, south and north, which the French had incorporated into Lebanon after accepting the Mandate. It was never a starter but even the idea of it darkly compromised the concept of a territorial Lebanon in its post-independence form.

23 Cited in Barbara Victor: *Hanan Ashrawi: A Passion for Peace*, London, 1995, pp. 174–5. Was it her drafting?

24 The loaded significance of Hebron, as patriarchal burial place and David's first capital, was intensified in early and later Zionist times by Arab atrocities there in 1923 and Baruch Goldstein's brutal retaliation in 1995.

25 So far compromised were the Likud Party by their verbal propaganda against Rabin and Peres (on the same theme of treachery that had inspired the assassin) that, had they not been given time partially to have rehabilitated themselves, after a short but decently sensitive interval, Peres might have been given the unique luxury in Israeli politics of a sixty/forty majority in the Knesset, so deep was the national sense of trauma and aversion. It was the first time that a home-grown assassin had afflicted the State.

26 Hamas, founded around the mid-eighties as an educational and social-welfare enterprise, was only drawn into violent tactics by the evident languishing of PLO hope via negotiation. The irony was that Israel had initially sought to use it as an alternative to Fatah and the PLO.

27 Maps circulating in Gush Emunim and other extremists Jewish bodies, showing a rebuilt Temple inside the Temple Mount area, alarmed Muslim minds. Less abstractedly, Netanyahu in 1997 allowed the opening of a tunnel beneath it and in the autumn of 2002 came Sharon's symbolic incursion into the Haram. Passions were all too readily kindled by suspicions of evil intent. Yeshivahs were studying Aaronic garments and rituals.

28 Abba Eban: *Heritage, Civilisation and the Jews*, London, 1985, pp. 332–3. See also his *Personal Witness: Israel through My Eyes*, London, 1993, pp. 462f, for the post-1967 years.

29 The date was 8 October 1968.

30 The classic story is told in Exodus 17.8–16, ending with the assurance that,

implacably, 'the Lord will be at war with Amalek through all generations'. 'Implacable' was the nature of the perpetual enmity (cf. Deuteronomy 25.17 and 1 Samuel 15.2 when it sealed the fate of the Amalekite King, Agag). The fame of this legendary hate all too readily passed over to the Palestinians.

31 The resonances of his 'song', the *Benedictus* in Luke's 'Gospel of the Infancy', belong squarely with Hebrew story and psalmody. As a 'Gentile', the only such author in the New Testament, his inclusion of it should be seen to give the lie to alleged latent 'anti-Semitism' in at least his part in Christian origins, though its purely 'Semitic' quality makes it strange usage in Christian liturgy, unless its hope of redemption is known as all-inclusive.

32 Echoing the phrase of Wilfred Owen's poem where deceased enemies (1914–18) encounter each other in the grave. The thoughts of a number of Israeli soldiers from the June War of 1967, musing on the tragic fate of so many Egyptians fatally trapped in Sinai and destitute of all air-cover, were printed in: *The Seventh Day: Soldiers Talk about the Six-Day War*, London, 1970. They registered in their hearts the desperate sense of a reversal of roles – the ancient victims of Jewry having victims now at their mercy. From non-'professional' religious sources, *The Seventh Day* was a strikingly religious quality of Jewishness.

33 Cited in Amnon Rubenstein: *The Zionist Dream Re-Visited*, New York, 1984, p. 160.

34 The reminder in Exodus 23.9 about 'knowing the heart of the stranger', thanks to experience in Egypt, had not provided for a situation where he would also be 'the native indigene'.

35 See the intriguing discussion in David Novak: *Jewish–Christian Dialogue: A Jewish Justification*, New York, 1989, pp. 26–42. 'Sexual immorality, idolatry and bloodshed were the items of Noahid prohibition which Jews were bound to requite (by decapitation) 'Gentile' transgressors when Jewish power obtained. Such, for example, was the opinion of Maimonides, who instanced the nemesis on 'the men of Shechem' (Genesis 34), whereas his contemporary, Nahmanides, held that Jews were not obligated for their enforcement even when they ruled. The State of Israel has sided with Nahmanides.

36 Yeshayahu Leibowitz: *Judaism, Human Values and the Jewish State*, ed. E. Goldmann, Harvard, 1992, p. 115.

37 *Ibid.*, p. 115.

38 An image used by Dan Cohn-Sherbok in *Israel: The History of an Idea*, London, 1992, alluding to the passage in Genesis 32.24–30. He fears that political Zionism in its current form has substituted the Jewish State for God Himself in 'a perilous shift from theological commitment'. Insisting that at all costs Israel must be 'ethical' he is only 'utopian' in how he addresses the problems in being so.

39 Only that their being 'menaced' stemmed directly from the creation of the State, or its reverberations – the great new factor in their situation.

40 Revelation 6.6, the warning at the 'opening of the third seal' – 'See that ye hurt not the oil and the wine'. The meaning seems to be that, unlike annual cereal crops, the vine and the olive tree take a long time to recover. For lack of them famine stalks longer. There has been massive punitive uprooting of vine and olive groves in 'occupied territories', ever since 1949, as well as

denial of water sources, or their unequal diversion to Jewish settlements. The Fourth Geneva Convention – repeatedly violated by Israel despite repeated invocation of it – had the same mind as the seer on Patmos in respect of human limits to inhumane policy, of which 'Sharonism' seems to be the ultimate expression.

41 See Avi Shlaim: *The Iron Wall: Israel and the Arab World*, London, 2000, p. 52. The public stance was that only Arab obduracy precluded the conclusion of a peace ('There was no one with whom to negotiate').

42 David Novak: *Jewish–Christian Dialogue: A Jewish Justification*, New York, 1989, p. 127. Teddy Kollek, the former Mayor of Jerusalem, when asked about the Messianic significance of the State of Israel, would side-step the question by noting that 'only the Messiah knew the time of his coming' and that meanwhile all was for ever irrelevant. Even so, is it not the essence of Semitism that 'the land is for the sake of the Temple'? Therefore, the potential of the State – albeit 'secular' – for the recovery of the ritual is one that the 'rite-lovers' will not, and do not. abandon.

43 It seems doubtful that so insistent a theism as Islam will ever consent to outright 'secularity' in reading the human situation as being under God. However, minds in contemporary Islam are moving to the Qur'an's own sense of human entrustment with the natural order as making all the more urgent the due 'consecration' of the technology that 'trust' pursues. This must qualify the old view of an all compulsive 'omnipotence' that left no place for human autonomy (a view never consistent with the doctrine of creation) and must reach for a human *Islam* to Allah that is truly free.

44 An Islamic share there must be if it is truly 'universal'. What strange riddle of 'providence' is it that history has left Islam and Muslims with so deep an emotional stake in the significance of Jerusalem? – one that has, therefore, tied the State of Israel (and its form of Semitism) quite decisively into the maelstrom of world politics and the Islamic factors within it.

Nine **Inter-Testamental Relations Now**

1 Jacob Neusner: *Stranger at Home*, Chicago, 1981, p. 105.

2 James Parkes (1896–1981) wrote on several inter-related aspects of his advocacy of Judaic thought and action, both in theology and politics. He held that since the Jews had never 'really' left 'the Holy land,' the anti-Palestinian case for the State of Israel was incontestable. See his *Voyage of Discoveries*, London, 1969; *Foundations of Judaism and Christianity*, London, 1960; *The Conflict between the Church and the Synagogue*, London, 1934. His career and significance are also discussed in my *Troubled by Truth*, Edinburgh, 1992, pp. 91–104.

3 The worldwide purposefulness of the 'Old' covenant was certainly crucial to the prophetic tradition from Amos through the Isaiahs to Jeremiah. For them it was never an endowment irresponsibly indulged. If the Christian worldwideness of its relevance is disallowed, the question 'how else' remains and is the more sharpened. See below.

4 In his *Foundations*, p. 187.

5 Mission is inherent in those writings, not merely that they enjoin and exem-

plify it, but that they are themselves inexplicable apart from it. For as Gospels and Letters, they were needed in communities moving out in place and onward in time by their own energies. The writings are the offspring of the travels.

6 In that there was to be an abeyance, if not a repudiation, of Christian expression to Jews. Thus it is disconcerting to find Marcus Braybrooke explaining to Jews that they must be patient about Christian delay in this operative 'de-missioning', because the instinct to mission, being so deep, is slow to consent to die. See: *Time to Meet: Towards a Deeper Understanding*, London, 1990, pp. 97f. He rightly notes that the Trinitarian formula in Matthew 28.19 indicates a formulating after Jesus' time. What he fails to note is that action was proceeding before the formula was shaped and that the impulse necessarily preceded the mandate to be finally phrased. The Trinity was 'learned' as how its origin transpired from perception of Jesus. It is false to suggest that the baptismal formula invalidates the writ of mission.

7 *Parrhesia* is frequent in the Greek Testament, meaning the 'liberty' with its content witness has, both as to what it takes and the rapport with where it takes it.

8 They were ventured in an earlier effort, *The Education of Christian Faith: Critical and Literary Encounters with the New Testament*, Brighton & Portland, 2000.

9 Albert Friedlander, in T. Bayfield and M. Braybrooke, eds.: *Dialogue with a Difference*, London, 1992, p. 30.

10 *Ibid.* Jonathan Magonet, p. 69.

11 'The Jesus terms', in their New Testament sense, but 'any terms' insofar as Messiah had to be always futurist, a hope never to be identified in an event.

12 'Jealousy' in no harsh sense but as of 'absolute relationships where no outsider may enter'. See note 9, p. 32.

13 Martin Buber: *Mamre: Essays in Religion*, trans. Greta Hort, London, 1946, pp. 30f.

14 *Ibid.*

15 J. E. Fison: *The Christian Hope: The Presence and the Parousia*, London, 1954, p. 18, see also p. 4.

16 Deuteronomy 26.17–18: 'You have avouched . . . the Lord has avouched . . .' – the mutual pledging of a people's fealty and YAHWEH's people 'adoption'.

17 *The Times*, 3 November 2001, p. 24.

18 The Pentateuch throughout affirms 'peoplehood' in the familiar 'children of Israel' terms. Nehemiah is no less emphatic about the purity of 'holy seed'. In Rosenzweig see: *The Star of Redemption*, trans. W. W. Hallo, London, 1970, where he writes of 'the eternal self-preservation of procreative blood, shutting the pure stream off from foreign admixture', p. 341. It is important to note that this emphasis has been repudiated elsewhere. Thus, Jacob B. Agus wrote: 'Rosenzweig's racial mystique is as un-Jewish as it is false,' rejecting Rosenzweig's thesis that 'the eternal people must maintain itself biologically untainted'. See: *Jewish Identity in an Age of Ideologies*, New York, 1976, pp. 280f.

19 Such is the view of Yeshayahu Leibowitz in *Judaism, Human Values and the*

Jewish State, Harvard, 1992, 'a nation exists insofar as there is a consciousness of its existence' and that awareness stands only in its Judaism, p. 81. There is no divine 'mystery' in peoplehood of itself, nor of a State called 'Israel'; all is in the vocation to Torah and *Mitzvoth*.

20 See his *Two Types of Faith*, trans. N. B. Goldhawk, New York, 1951, pp. 24–9 and throughout.

21 Analogies in theology are always at risk but there is real point in realizing that 'seeing Shakespeare' is 'seeing a mind in a play on a stage' and that the one 'name' covers all three. A 'who' has a 'where' via a 'how', which is what the Christian means in saying: 'God was in Christ' and 'the Father sent the Son'. 'The Word became flesh' rather as the thought 'fleshed' the plot and the plot occupied a place in time.

22 Gavin I. Langmuir: *Toward a Definition of Anti-Semitism*, Berkeley, 1990, pp. 63f. When Theodosius I ordered the local Bishop at Callinicum in 388 who had destroyed a synagogue to rebuild it at his own expense, Ambrose effectively had the order rescinded. His episcopate proceeded on the assumption that Imperial civil power should align with clerical behest. The quotation is on p. 71.

23 Simon Dubnow (1869–1941) *Nationalism and History, Essays on Old and New Judaism*, ed., K. S. Pinson, Philadelphia, 1958, p. 80. He saw Zionist passion for 'Return to the land' as both regressive and impractical. Jewry had amply demonstrated its more than mere survival power in the spiritual realities of diaspora.

24 Heinrich Graetz (1817–1891) *History of the Jews*. He opened his history with Joshua's conquest of Canaan. Published in Philadelphia in 1956, its 5 vols. were edited by Bella Lowry.

25 Cited in Langmuir, note 22, p. 76. Hosea's disavowal ('I am not the I am you take me for,' hence 'You are not my people' as studied in Chapter 3.

Ten   Marc Chagall's Prayer-Shawl

1 Details of the *tallit* are in Numbers 15.38–41, where they signify the holiness that belongs with Judaic identity and with memory of the Exodus. The colours of the fringes (*zizet*) are prescribed as part of the obedience by which Torah deserved to be fulfilled in careful letter. *Tallit* could be either in silk or wool, often with wool from 'shepherds of Israel'. They lent awe and reverence to ritual prayer and signified the dignity of the Talmudic *hakam*, and also told the aura of the Sabbath. Some have wondered whether they might be linked with the ʿabaʾah of the Bedouin, the familiar Arab head-dress.

2 As cited from his friend, Jacques Maritain, the 20th century French philosopher, in Walter Erben: *Marc Chagall*, London, 1957, p. 110, *The Falling Angel* (1923–47).

3 Quoted from the artist in Ingo F. Walther and Rainder Metzger: *Marc Chagall, Painting as Poetry*, Koln, 2000, p. 78.

4 Marc Chagall: *My Life*, trans. Dorothy Williams, London, 1957, p. 69 (the year was 1907, on going to St. Petersburg). Cf: 'All that clamorous love that I have, in general, for all humankind' (p. 26) and 'The Jews unfold their holy veils, full of tears from the whole day's prayers' (p. 34) and 'God, Thou who

hidest in the clouds behind the cobbler's house, lay bare my soul . . . the aching soul of a stammering boy, show me my way . . . I want to see a new world' (p. 95) on going to Paris.

5   *Ibid.*, pp. 126 and 144.

6   In *The Fallen Angel* and *Martyrdom*, and *Calvary*.

7   Painted in 1956–58 for the Musée Nationale Message Biblique, named by him in Nice.

8   See Gill Polonsky: *Chagall*, London, 1989, p. 114 in 'the lofty, perilous destiny of the Jews'.

9   See *My Life* (note 4) p. 26. The violin is also a recurrent item in the Chagall scenario, central as music is to the stage set that is in love with acrobats and clocks and dancers.

10 Citing *The Nineteenth Century*, Vol. 33, 1893, p. 182.

11 See note in Gill Polonsky: *Chagall* (note 8 above) p. 104.

12 The notion of 'riddance' belongs with the novel where, if so minded (as in the case of e.g. Somerset Maugham) to narrate a situation, or describe an event was somehow to 'have done with it' in moving, journalist-style, to a new sight and scene. Art feels differently and perpetuates the seeing.

13 The expression 'the Christian Jesus' purposely leaves open the fact that there are many other 'versions' of the one of whom the Gospel 'knows whom it has believed'. There is no doubt that such vicariousness in Jesus, taken Christianly, was also the clue to the nature of God as 'God in Christ,' i.e. the Christ whom Jesus, on this reading, had definitively been.

14 As sung by Yoram Tehar-Lev. See Ilan Peleg: *Begin's Foreign Policy, 1977–1983*, New York, 1987, p. 62.

15 The problem always faced by 'good Gentiles' wanting to relate but aware of a suspicion that they may only be 'making a gesture' which is not really allowing the Jew to be freely the Jew he wills to be – such suspicion being somehow incipient in the dual situation. See, for example, Jacob Neusner: 'For my part, if I am accepted as 'a human being' and not as a Jew, I do not accept that acceptance. I aspire to no place in an undifferentiated humanity . . .' quoted earlier, pp. 143–4. *Stranger at Home*, Chicago, 1981, p. 45.

16 In *The Times*, 27 January 2002.

17 As reported from an interview with *Ha'aretz*, the Tel Aviv newspaper, in *The Times*, 19 January 2002.

18 *Ibid.*

19 Erben: *Chagall*, note 2, p. 103. He wrote: 'I came to Palestine to examine certain ideas and I came without a camera and even a brush . . . I am glad to have been there . . . Nowhere else do you see so much despair and so much joy, nowhere else are you so shaken and yet so happy as at the sight of this thousand-year-old heap of stones and dust in Jerusalem, in Safad, in the hills where prophets upon prophets lie buried.' *Chagall*, note 3, p. 68.

20 Always an ironical factor in the 'Gentile' relation to Zionism. Frequently American Christian Zionists have raised vast sums to enable the establishing and the success of the Israeli State, on assumptions which Jewish Zionism can only have 'in derision', but yet are very serviceable. A recent *aliyah* of US Jews to Israel (2002) was funded to the tune of sixty million dollars spread for some seven years over a long followed 'return' project. These religious

American immigrants were dubiously seen by 'secular' fellow-citizens in the State.

As a Jew content to be 'of diaspora', Chagall's tribute to the United States was a generous one. He wrote: 'I have lived and worked in America during a period of global tragedy . . . In the atmosphere of hospitable welcome I was able to draw strength without denying the roots of my art.' Quoted in Walther and Metzger: *Chagall* (note 3), p. 68.

21 Not only in the early days of Mufti Al-Husseini but through the long and fluctuating years of Yasser Arafat. It would have needed a super-human foresight and tenacious leadership over a turbulent scenario for Palestinianism to have better controlled its fortunes. How could it have countered – or first gauged – the massive American favouritism of Israel, or the bungling of its Arab hinterland politics, or the odds against it stacked on the world-wide sinews of Zionism?

22 The sense of ever latent anti-Semitism means that even what could hopefully be read against it has to be instinctively discounted as either temporary or sinister. History is felt to have taught Jewry an unfailing vigilance in the context of incorrigible dislike. What then should the 'Gentile' do to prove that a common humanity obtains?

23 As in Arthur A. Cohen: *The Myth of the Judeo-Christian Tradition*, New York, 1970, p. 125.

24 For Christians, in the sense that all that is Messianic in the Jesus of the New Testament story and its ecclesial possession *is* Israel qua destiny and meaning. For Judaism, in the ongoing people are the corporate 'Messiah' of suffering that gathers Jesus to itself.

25 'Piety' of the most genuine order, a piety of 'consecration' in which artistry is born of loyal, humble, inwardly hallowing identity, moving nevertheless in the whole range of human curiosity and a will to relate as one undeceiving and undeceived.

INDEX OF PERSONS, PLACES AND NAMES

Aaron, 25
Abimelech, 2
Abraham, 2, 3, 8, 13, 20, 26, 47, 54,
    57, 70, 75, 76, 82, 148, 156
Achor, Valley of, 40
Adam, 20, 29, 30, 59, 162, 180
Adonai, 61
Africans, 33
Ahab, 12, 40
Ahad Ha-am, 96, 199
Aleppo, 92, 126
Algiers, 111
Altalina, 104
Amalek, 87, 110, 112, 133, 136, 191
Ambrose, 85, 157
America, 10, 34, 94, 167, 179, 190; see
    also USA
Amir, Yigael – assassin, 108
Amos, 16, 19, 34, 35, 41, 45, 193
Amsterdam, 91, 92
Andrew of St. Victor, 91
'Aqabah, Gulf of, 90
Arafat, Yassir, 128, 130, 131, 137, 197
Aragon, 90
Aramaic, 64, 74, 154
Ark of the Covenant, 164
Ashkelon, 138
Ashkenazi Jews, 89, 91, 93, 109, 110
    Chief Rabbi of, 101
Ashrawi, Hanan, 128, 191
Assyrians, 36, 37, 41, 42, 46
Auschwitz, 56, 60

Baal Shem Tov, 93
Babylon, 14, 84, 91
Baghdad, 91
Bait Jala, 136
Balfour Declaration, 122, 123, 186
Barabbas, 79
Barak, Ehud, 102, 131

Baruch, Apocalypse of, 76
Basle, 87, 121
Beersheba, 3
Beethoven, 156
Begin, Menahem, 102, 104, 126, 134,
    187, 190, 191, 196
Beirut, 126
Ben Exra, Rabbi, 5, 117, 140
Ben Gurion, David, 42, 99, 100, 101,
    104, 111, 114, 123, 125, 134, 137,
    170, 187, 190
Ben Sira, 20
Ben Yehuda, Eliezer, 110, 111, 113
Ben Yokai, Shimon Rabbi, 18
Bentwich, Norman, 105
Bernadotte, Count, 124
    Murder of, 129, 138
Besht, the, 93
Bialik, H. N., 113
Biltmore compact, 1940, 137
Black Death, the, 88
Boers, the, 57
British Mandate, the, 99, 100, 104, 111,
    114, 122, 123
Brooklyn, 98
Browning, Robert, 4, 5, 65, 117, 159,
    169, 171, 172, 180
Buber, Martin, 18, 134, 143, 150,f 155,
    173, 183, 194
Byzantium, 158

Cain, 31
Camp David, 131, 132
Cana, 130, 136
Canaan, 3, 10, 11, 27, 38, 43, 44, 45,
    47, 57, 58, 69, 195
'Canaanites', Jewish, 112
Canon Law, Christian, 89
Carolingian State, the, 89
Carlyle, Thomas, 58

Carter, Jimmy, 104, 190
Castile, 90
Chagall, Mark, 5, 6, 117, 140, 157,
    159, 160f., 170, 195, 196
  Bella, his wife, 163, 164
  Bible in, 167
  Calvary, 161, 195
  Cow with a Parasol, 162
  Creation of Man, 162
  Exodus, 167, 168
  Fallen Angel, 195
  Fall of Icarus, 163
  Feast Day, 163
  Feast of the Tabernacles, 163
  King David, 167
  Lovers in the Lilac, 163
  Martyrdom, 163, 195
  Meanings in?, 160, 161
  Moses Receiving the Tables, 162
  Peace, 162
  Prayer in, 161
  Praying Jew, the, 163
  Roofs, the, 161
  Russia in, 151, 163
  Solitude, 161, 162
  Soul in the City, 163, 164
  White Crucifixion, 160, 161
  Yellow Crucifixion, 161
  universality of, 168f.
Chemosh, 9
Chester, 115
Chicago, 163
Clinton, Bill, 131
Constantine, Emperor, 62, 141, 157
Constantinople, Fall of, 90, 91
Conversos, 89, 90, 91
Corpus Christi, 88
Crimea, 110
Crusades, the, 84, 85, 86, 87, 185
Cyprus, 68, 74
Cyrene, 68, 74
Cyrus, 57

Dachau, 56, 60
Dair Yassin, 136, 187
Damascus, 71, 126
Dan, 3, 13
Daniel, 14
Dante, 168, 170
David, King, 10, 12, 13, 20, 21, 26, 41,
    42, 51, 54, 77, 114, 146, 158
Davies, W. D., 75, 182
Dayan, Moshe, 103, 104, 105
Dayan, Yael, 103
Deborah, Song of, 112, 114

Decalogue, the, 18
Declaration of Independence, Israel's,
    100
Defence Forces, Israeli, 105, 108, 114,
    137
Defoe, Daniel, 110
Degania, 103
Deissmann, Adolf, 26, 174
Descartes, Rene, 29
Deuteronomy, 36, 51, 53, 155, 180, 183
Dodd, C. H., 32, 62, 175, 180
Dome of the Rock, 105, 139; see also
    Temple Mount
Dominicans, 90
Donne, John, 154
Dothan, 51
Dostoevsky, 7
Dubnow, Simon, 158, 195

Eban, Abba, 100, 106, 132, 133, 186,
    191
Eden, 30
Egypt, 8, 9, 14, 21, 24, 32, 37, 41, 42,
    56, 81, 91, 103, 126, 137, 190
Elkins, Michael, 102
Encisco, 57
Encyclopedia Judaica, 53, 178
Endor, 40
England, 10, 52, 57
Ephesus, 71
Ephraim, 37, 40, 44, 45
Eretz Israel, 112; see also the land
Eretz Keden, 112
Esau, 50, 178
Eshcol, 27, 38, 101, 103
Ethiopia, 68
Europe, 29, 85, 88, 89, 94, 95, 98, 110,
    116, 136, 165, 167
Ezekiel, 30, 171

Fada'il al-Quds, 115
Ferrara, 92
Fez, 91
Fichte, Johann, 58
First Zionist Congress, 96, 121
Fischer, Ernst, 53
Fison, Joseph, 150
Fourth Lateran Council, 86, 87
France, 89, 162
Franks, the, 158
Frost, Robert, 10, 57, 172, 179

Galilee, 37, 64, 70
Galileo, 29
Gamaliel, 71

Gaon of Vilna, 93
Gath, 56
Gaza, 2, 63, 92, 108, 129, 131
Geneva Conventions, the, 107, 192
Gerar, 2
German language, 110, 111
Germany, 88, 89, 95, 116, 158, 179
Gethsemane, 25, 26, 66, 68, 78, 181
Gilead, 11
Gogol, *Dead Souls*, 167
Golan Heights, the, 91, 103,
    annexation of, 104
Goldman, Nathan, 100
Goldstein, Baruch, 138, 191
Gomer, 38, 39, 40, 43
Gordon, R. T., 2, 171
Goren, Chief Rabbi, 105
Graetz, Heinrich, 158, 195
Grager, John, 10, 81, 184
Granada, 90
Gregory the Great, 84, 85, 86
Greek, 1, 116, 181
Greeks, the, 12, 50, 68, 74, 182

Haganah, 104, 187
Hagar, 76
Haggai, 14
Hamas, 130, 191
Hasmoneans, the, 16, 41, 120
Hauer, Wilhelm, 58, 179
Hebrews, Letter to, 19, 67, 75, 81
Hebron, 13, 129, 191
Heliodorous, 21
Herbert of Bosham, 88
Hermon, 13, 129, 191
Herod, 14, 15
Herzl, Theodor, 41, 79, 90, 96, 97, 98,
    99, 100, 104, 106, 109, 111, 113,
    116, 119, 121
    Altneuland, 121
Heschel, Abraham, 18, 19, 143, 174,
    193, 188
    Who is Man?, 19
Hess, Moshe, 97, 98, 116, 119
Hezekiah, 84
Hiram, king of Tyre, 56
Hitler, 116
    Mein Kampf, 60
Hizballah, 130
'Holy Land', 92
Homer, 26, 28, 174
Hosea, 4, 9, 24f., 34, 35, 36f., 42f., 50,
    57, 64, 97, 113, 115, 121, 143, 158,
    161, 176, 183, 195
Hoshea, King, 37, 41

Hugh of Lincoln, 88
Hugh of St. Victor, 87
Hussein, King, 103, 190

Idumea, 14
Illyricum, 73
Isaac, 2, 3, 5, 20
Isaac, Jules, 84, 185
    Teaching of Contempt, 84
Isaiah, 9, 16, 19, 22, 42, 47, 180, 181
Israel, land of, 4, 10, 20, 22, 31, 32, 37,
    42, 51, 118, 119
Israel, State of, 42, 56, 95, 97, 100f.,
    165, 169; *see also* Zionism
Israel, Ben Eliezer, 93
Istanbul, 92
Italy, 91

Jabotinsky, Vladimir, 98, 103, 112, 116,
    121, 122, 123, 181, 187, 190
Jacob, 20, 29, 40, 50, 51, 108, 135, 162
Jebusites, 13
Jehu, 140
Jeremiah, 15, 16, 19, 35, 42, 85, 140,
    143, 156, 171, 193
Jericho, 25, 57, 114, 129
Jerusalem, 7, 12, 13, 14, 25, 26, 57, 64,
    68, 73, 75, 76, 84, 111, 115, 125,
    131, 139, 163, 167, 181, 182, 188
    Council in, 72
    Fall of, 4, 69, 73
    Next Year in, 45
    Old city of, 102, 105
Jesus, 15, 62f., 80, 81, 87, 160, 162,
    171; *see also* Christology
Jewish Agency, the, 99, 123
Jewish National Fund, 97
Jezebel, 12, 40
Jezreel, 40
Job, 12, 25, 26, 37, 156
Joel, 25, 29
John, King, 89
Jordan, the river, 57, 106, 124, 125,
    132
Jordan, State of, 121, 125, 137, 138
Joseph, 34, 51, 55, 56, 162, 178
Josephus, 20, 173, 179, 189
Joshua, 3, 9, 10, 51, 57, 114, 148, 158,
    195
    redivivus, 134
Jubilees, Book of, 20, 141
Judah, 41
Judea, 11, 70
Judenstaat, Der, 79, 98f., 109, 119
Judges, Book of, 51, 172

Katz, Jacob, 82, 184
Keren Kayemit le-Israel, 97
King David Hotel massacre, 104, 138, 187
King, Martin Luther, 128
Klausner, Joseph, 142
Knesset, the, 102, 112, 132, 133, 163, 170, 187
Kollek, Teddy, 115, 193

Labour Party, Israeli, 100, 103, 130
League of Nations Mandate, 99, 123, 186
Lebanon and invasion of, 105, 125, 130, 136, 139, 190, 191
Leghorn, 91
Leibowitz, Yeshayahu, 59, 96, 134, 155, 179, 186, 192, 194
Leontopolis, 14
Levi, Primo, 109, 118, 119, 189
Lewis, C. S., 98, 186
Likud party, 104, 121, 129, 130, 191
Lincoln, Abraham, 58, 128
Lithuania, 93, 110
Lo Ammi, 36, 47, 177
Lo Ruhammah, 40, 47, 177
London, 91
Low Countries, the, 89, 91, 167
Luke, 76, 133, 179
Luria, Isaac, 91, 92
Luther, Martin, 88, 158
Lyly, John, 52, 178

Maccabees, the, 14, 54, 68, 75, 122
Madonna, 161
Madrid Conference, the, 107, 128, 129
Maghrib, 91
Magna Carta, 89
Magnes, Judeh, 105
Magonet, Jonathan, 148, 194
Maimonides, 58, 97, 139
Malta, the Jew of, 79
Mann, Thomas, 55, 178
Mantua, 92
Marlowe, Christopher, 79
Marr, Wilhelm, 1, 184
Marranos, 90, 93
Masada, 114, 173, 188, 189
Matthew, 64
Mazzini, 97
Mediterranean Sea, the, 24, 26, 91, 182
Megiddo, 114
Meir, Golda, 101, 125
Melville, Herman, 58, 179
Menahem, King, 37

Merchant of Venice, the, 55, 56
Mexico, 167
Micah, 107
Miletus, 71
Milton, John, 32, 175
Moab, 3, 9
Moriah, 13
Moscow, 163, 167
Moses, 3, 8, 11, 13, 16, 21, 29, 36, 37, 41, 50, 57, 92, 148, 162
Muhammad, 156

Naaman, 70
Naboth, 40
Nachman of Bratislava, 110
Narkis, Uzi, 105
Nathan of Gaza, 92
Nathaniel, 173
Nazareth, 15, 70, 165, 180
Nehemiah, 15, 27, 53, 154, 183, 194
Neher, André, 150
Netanyahu, Benjamin, 107, 129, 130, 138, 187, 191
Neusner, Jacob, 143, 144, 154, 174, 186, 193, 196
New Jersey, 58
New York City, 94, 162, 163, 167
Nice, 163, 196
Nicodemus, 73
Noah, 20
Nobel Prize, 94
Nordau, Max, 98, 122
Normandy beaches, 56
Norwich, 88
Norway, 129
Novak, David, 53

Odessa, 94, 98
Origins of anti-Semitism, The, 81
Oslo, 107, 128, 129, 130, 131, 137, 170
Ottomans, the, 91
Ottoman Caliphate, the, 96, 99
Oz, Amos, 112, 187

Pale, the, 94
Palestine, 4, 11, 84, 90, 91, 94, 98, 99, 114, 125, 128, 136
Palestinians, 58, 99, 107, 110, 112, 114, 121, 125, 128, 166, 167
Palestinian Exploration Society, 114
Palestinian Liberation Organisation, 129, 130
Panthera, 81
Paris, 98, 167
Parkes, James, 144f., 193

Patmos, 13, 192
Paul, 26, 64, 67, 70, 71, 72, 74, 76, 77, 84, 145,f 151, 152, 174, 182
Pekah, King, 37
Peles, Haim, 133
Peniel, 108
Pentateuch, 32, 50, 84, 148
Peres, Shimon, 130
Perlman, 111
Persians, the, 12, 177
Peter, 64, 67, 69
Pharaoh, 8
Philip, 68
Philistia, 75
Philistines, the, 2, 56, 125
Philo, 20, 184
Picasso, *Guernica*, 160
Pilate, 75
Pinsker, Leo, 99, 116, 119
Poland, 89, 91, 93, 94, 109
Pompey, 15
Portugal, 89
Pound, Ezra, 113
Prague, 92
Prometheus, 30

Qumran, 26, 26, 54, 174, 180, 189
Qur'an, the, 35, 44, 109, 177, 193

Ra, 30
Rabin, Yitzhak, 102, 103, 129. 187, 191
    murder of, 108
Rachel, 51
Rashkalnikov, 7
Ratosh, Yonatan, 112
Rebecca, 50
Rechabites, the, 26
Rehoboth, 2, 3, 5
Reubeni, David, 92
Revelation, the Book of, 136, 174
Rheims, 163
Rhodes, 91
Rishon-le-Zion, 114
Robinson Crusoe, 110
Romans Letter to, 71, 76, 77, 81
Rome, 14, 26, 54, 68, 73, 75, 89
Rome and Jerusalem, 97
Rosenzweig, Franz, 1, 154, 171, 173, 194
Rubicon, the, 73
Russians, the, 34, 94, 111
    Tsars of, 85, 94

Sachs, Chief Rabbi Jonathan, 154, 155, 166, 168
Sadat, Anwar, 104, 126, 190
Safad, 92
Salonika, 91
Samaria, 14, 37, 40
Samson, 114, 172
Samuel, 51
Sanhedrin, renewal of?, 102
Sarah, 47
Saul, 40, 70, 76, 120, 182
Savonarola, 134
Schechter, Solomon, 61, 179
Scholem, Gershom, 150, 174
Sephardim, the, 90, 91, 109, 110
Shabbatai Zvi, 92, 93
Shabistari, Mahmud, 43
Shakespeare, William, 55, 56, 104, 116, 133, 179, 187, 189, 195
Shamir, Moshe, 112
    Tahat Hashamash, 112
Shamir, Yitzhak, 102, 124, 128, 135
Sharm al-Shaikh, 126
Sharon, Ariel, 96, 101, 105, 108, 126, 127, 131, 135, 137, 187
Shechem, 13, 14, 192
Shiloh, 14
Schlomsky, Abraham, 113
Shylock, 55, 56, 91
Sinai, 10, 20, 64, 76, 102, 137, 144, 152, 162, 191
Singer, Isaac Bashevis, 94
Six Day War, the, 102, 103, 108, 126, 133, 146
Smyrna, 91
Solomon Bar Simon, 86
Solomon, King, vi, 13, 14, 15, 20, 26, 57, 148, 158, 173
    'Song of Songs' of, 61
Solomon Molcho, 92
Sophocles, 26
Spain, 89, 90, 91, 167
Spanish Jewry, 90; *see also Conversos*
Stalingrad, 56
Stephen, 71
Suez Campaign, 102, 126
Sussex, 88
Syria, 37, 91, 139, 167, 186

Tacitus, 54
Talmon, Jacob, 50, 178
Tanach, 109
Tehiya Party, 112
Temple, William, 134

Tennyson, Alfred Lord, 162
In Memoriam, 162
Theodosius, 85, 137
Thirty Years War, the, 93
Thomas, Gospel of, 144
Timnath, 114
Tunis, 91, 92, 127
Turks, 90
Tyre, 26, 30

Ukraine, 92, 110
United Nations, 100, 123, 130, 133,
162, 163, 170, 186, 190
Agencies, 126
Resolutions, 107, 124, 125, 137
United States, 58, 99, 123, 128,
139

Vaal River, 57
Vale of Elah, 114
Vatican, the, 97
Venice, 91, 92
Venetians, 91
Vermes, Gaza, 142, 174, 181
Vilna, Gaon of, 93
Vitebsk, 160, 161, 163, 167, 168

Washington, D. C., 98

Weizmann, Chaim, 99, 100, 113, 122,
125, 186
Trial and Error, 100
West Bank, the, 108, 125, 131, 191
Western Wall, the, 105, 135
Wiesel, Elie, 168, 171

Yad va Shem, 7, 23, 115, 116
Yadin, Yigael, 114, 183
YAHWEH, 2, 3, 8, 9, 10, 11, 12, 13, 14,
15, 17, 22, 23, 30, 34, 36, 37, 38,
43, 46, 48, 51, 55, 59, 76, 78, 96,
107, 113, 144, 145, 147, 153, 155,
162, 173, 174, 181, 183
Yavneh, 73, 75
Yeshivah students, 108, 111, 135, 191
Yitzar, Smilanski, 112, 188
Yom Kippur War, the, 39, 126

Zachariah, Song of, 133, 178
Zaccheus, 64
Zaddik, Simon the, 20
Zealots, 15, 64, 66, 114, 173, 180, 182
Zechariah, 120
Zedekiah, 14
Zeus, 30
Zipporah, 8
Zurich, 163

INDEX OF THEMES AND TERMS

acceptance as human, 143, 144, 154; *see also* 'Gentiles'
adam/adamah, 32
Africa, neglect of, 33
   corrected, 175, 176
agency, divine, 74; *see also* creature-hood, prophethood
aliyah, 97, 109, 168
'all our fathers', 12; *see also* mystique of blood
'am, 50, 51
ambiguity of 'Israel', 97, 170
   in Chagall, 161
ambivalence in 'election', 15, 99, 102, 121, 123, 145
anthropology, 33
antipathy, Jew/'Gentile', 1, 90; *see also* covenant
antinomianism, charge of, 77, 151
anti-Semitism, *see* tragedy of
apartheid, Judaic, 1, 3, 80, 100, 101, 151
Arabism, 103, 127, 135, 136, 167, 187
architecture, poverty of, in Israel, 115
art, of Chagall, 160f.
arrogance, 33
assassination
   of Count Bernadotte, 124, 129, 138
   of Yitzhak Rabin, 108, 129
   of Anwars Sadat, 104
assimilation, menace of, 55
attrition, mutual in Zionism, 166, 167
autonomy, human, 30, 31, 33; *see also* dominion/*khilafah*

baalim, 36, 43, 44, 45, 57
Beatitudes, the, 63, 64, 71, 80
'becoming/being', in Buber, 155, 157
Beulah, 44, 113

Bible, the common factor of, 84, 84 *see also* Scriptures
Bifederalism, 105, 122
birth, Jewish, 59, 173; *see also* seed
Black Death, the, 88
blood, mystique of, 1, 87, 88, 89, 154, 171, 177, 194
borders, unresolved issue of 97f., 121f., 186
   and 'right to exist', 124, 128
'bread and wine', 65, 66, 67, 150, 151, 185
'bride' of YAHWEH, analogy, 61; *see also* Hosea
Buddhism, 173
burning bush, the, 8, 19

Caliphate, the Ottoman, 96, 98, 111
calumny, 87, 88, 89
Canon, the Christian, 141
Carmen Christi, 181
child murder, charge of, 87, 88
child naming, 39, 40; *see also* Hosea
'chosenness', when borrowed, 57f.
Christ, death of, 66; *see also* Cross of Christ
Christ in Chagall, 160f.
Christ-event, the, 48, 62f., 67, 74, 76, 145, 147
'Christ Pantocrator', 158
Christendom, 85, 86,f 141, 151, 184, 194
'the Christ in God', 65, 145
Christian community, 65, 70, 71
Christian inclusion, 62f., 146, 147; *see also* de-Gentilizing
Christianity, 52, 59, 75, 144f.
   birth years of, 62f., 164
   Jewish issues for, 4, 83, 84, 143, 169
   Jewish issues with, 4, 60–1, 83, 144f.

not 'anti-Semitic', 59, 60, 61, 150
transcending exclusivism, 62f., 144f.
Christology, 65, 67, 73, 74, 83, 142,
146, 182
Christian Zionism, 147, 196
Church, the Christian from Christ, 62f.,
65, 67, 70, 141f., 144, 147, 157
Gentile expansion of, 63f.
Jewish initiative in, 65, 73f; see also
diaspora, Christian
and Jewish disclaimer, 73, 74, 144,
157
circumcision, 55, 69, 155
co-existence, corollary of grace, 15, 47,
169
comedy, tragic, 131
conscience, 2, 23, 31, 41, 57, 104, 106,
107, 108, 130, 132, 135
contempt, concept of, 81, 82, 84
contempt, teaching of, 84, 108, 129,
195
contradiction, in Zion, 120
'contradiction of sinners', 46
controversy, 143, 147
self-blinkered, 83, 84
'corn, wine and oil', 26f.
cosmology, 28
cosmos, our human, 11, 32, 33; see also
creation and nature
'court of the Gentiles', 16
covenant, concept of, 4, 10, 16, 17, 33,
36, 41, 50, 58, 61, 64, 76, 120, 145,
148, 157, 176, 184
everywhere Noahid in nature, 24f.,
33
Judaic conditionality, 38
creation, 11, 19, 24, 27, 30, 31, 35, 36,
144, 175
As kenosis, 27, 30
'new', 67, 77
creaturehood, human, 11, 24f., 30, 31,
35, 44
credulity, Messianic, 92, 93
Cross of Christ, the, 6, 66, 67, 68, 75,
77, 88, 172
as anti-Jewish factor, 88
in Chagall, 166f.
preaching of, 81
realism and, 77, 80
'the cup my Father gives', 66
culture/diversity, 153, 154

dabar, 74
Davidism, 77, 183
deicide, charge of, 83, 84

de-Gentilizing in the Church, 50, 62f.,
68, 71, 72, 145, 146, 152, 157, 169
despair, about Israel, 169, 170
dhimmi system, the – in Islam, 84, 85,
91, 185
dialogue, role of, 5, 106, 143, 171
and negatives, 60, 61
diaspora, Christian, 65, 73, 76, 78, 80,
81, 158
diaspora, Jewish, 4, 17, 53, 57, 69, 73,
79f., 87, 90, 91, 96, 97, 101, 118,
120, 158, 183, 184, 189
seen as retribution, 84
discrimination, Judaic, 2f.
divine pathos, in prophethood, 19; see
also Heschel, Abraham
dominion, human, 26, 27, 28; see also
nature as cosmos
doubling dealing, 122; see also Begin;
Ben-Gurion; Oslo
dream, the Zionist, 96f., 106, 121; see
also Herzl, Theodor

ecology, 25f., see also nature as
covenant
ehyeh, 27
ehyeh ash ehyeh, 18, 36, 37, 38, 40, 41,
47, 48; see also Buber, Martin
election, sense, 3, 4, 10, 16, 17, 50, 55,
61, 76
made good in Christ, 77, 146, 154
and the ghetto, 55
emulated, 57f.
Satan's, 53
emancipation, failure of, 94
auto, 98
enigma, in Chagall's art, 161
enlightenment, human, 30, 31
eschatology in Jewish relation, 85, 86
ethics, on universal ground, 32f.
and land-love, 138
ethnicity, Jewish, 49f., 53, 64, 68, 82,
154
ethnoi, 50, 177; see also 'Gentiles'
exceptionality, reach of, 49, 50, 51, 55,
56
broken open, 68
despite one creation, 11, 31, 32, 144
ever dubious, 53, 54, 61
exclusivism, 44, 158, 159
exile, 11, 15, 74
'existing population,' the, 98, 99; see
also Balfour Declaration
Exodus, the, 31, 41, 42, 45,k 57, 172
analogy of creation, 31

Exodus, the *(continued)*
   ritual memory of, 4; *see also* history,
      Passover
   theology and, 9f.
exploitation, 34
expulsion from Spain, 90f.

faith and story intertwined, 73, 74, 148
   of the Church, 64, 65; *see also*
      Christology
   de-exclusified, 164
   self-validated?, 148
Fatherhood, reciprocal to Sonship, 156,
   157, 180
'Father, forgive', 164
fatalism, 95
fertility, a human art, 25f., 36
fertility cults, 37, 43, 44, 45, 46, 176;
   see also Hosea
flaw fatal, in Zionism?, 119, 120
'folk' and power, 157, 158
forced conversion, 85
forfeiture, the great, 118f., 135
futurism, perpetual, 97, 150; *see also*
   Messianism
   betrays hope, 23

generational faith, 12
gentes, 50
'Gentiles', 49f., 59, 60, 61, 63, 65, 76,
   134, 144, 153, 168, 177, 178, 196
   and Jewish privilege, 19, 23
   as mutually prejudicial, 4, 49, 50, 82,
      83
   as pagans, 54, 61
   second covenant recipients, 5, 144f.;
      see also 'two covenant' theory
Gentilizing the world, 50f., 72, 143
Germanism, 38, 179
ghetto, the, 4, 55f., 86, 91, 93, 94, 184
   mental, 83
God, 17, 29, 30, 33, 64, 65, 156, 165;
   see also YAHWEH
   'of the armies of Israel', 10
   'of our fathers', 9
   'justifying God', 148, 149, 156
   self-invested in human delegacy 30;
      see also dominion
   whereabouts of, 47; *see also* 'The
      place of the Name'
God as uniquely 'Jewish', 2, 3, 54, 58
'God in Christ', 47, 59, 65, 74, 77, 83,
   161, 172, 196
goi and *goyim*, 50, 51, 52, 94, 96,
   177

Gospel – Jewish initiative in, 62, 63, 68,
   69, 70; *see also* New Testament
Gospels, the, 63, 64, 70, 145, 148,
   182
   issues in, 70f.
   parallel content in Letters, 71f.
grace, 18, 48, 70, 76, 144, 146
   and law, 151f.
   'means of', 173
Great Schism, the, 84
grief, 161, 162
guilt, 152, 158, 163, 170
   in anti-Semitism, 143f.; *see also* Shoah

Halakhah, 17, 59, 94, 102
Ha Maqam, 8, 20, 21
Hasidism, 92, 93, 161, 165
hatred, 87, 88
   necessity of?, 164, 165, 166
Hebrew Bible, the, 50; *see also*
   Scriptures
Hebrew language, 94, 108, 154f.
Hebrews, Letter to, 75, 81
Hibbet Zion, 41, 44
Hinduism, 44, 175
history, sense of, 40, 46, 54, 128, 148,
   150, 166, 171, 172
   in Jewish psyche, 86, 87; *see also*
      Exodus, Passover
   momentum in, 83, 84
   and nature, 27, 30, 31, 34
   perspective in, 133, 141f., 151; *see
      also* 'place of the Name'
Hitlerism, 98
Hizballah, 130
'Holy One of Israel', the, 2
'Holy of Holies', the, 15
Holy Spirit, the, 72, 76
homogeneity, in Israel, issue of, 106f.;
   see also Eban, Abba
homo homini lupus, 122
homo sapiens, 30, 31; *see also* creaturehood
hope, 42, 106, 150, 152, 165; *see also*
   futurism
   apocalyptic, 86
   realized, 41, 65, 73, 150
   test in circumstance, 140
   travesties of, 92, 93
Host, the – adoration of, 87, 88
host-nation – illusion of, 105; *see also*
   Herzl, Theodor
'house of Israel', the, 47
humanism, 74, 165, 169
   and ultimate, 2, 156

husband/husbandry, 42, 42, 44, 45; *see also* Hosea
hymnology, Christian, 13, 14
I and Thou, 18; *see also* Buber, Martin
identity, 2, 28, 30, 51, 90, 158, 194
  and anxiety, 145
  interiorized, 3, 169
  and single creaturehood, 28, 29, 33
  in social relation, 33; *see also* Semitism
idol-making, 32, 43, 173
imagery, 43, 58, 75, 146
Incarnation, the, 27, 62f., 67, 83, 173, 180
inclusion, human in Jesus, 62f., 74, 75, 80
  in the parables, 63
innocence, myth of, 121, 138; *see also* Zionism
inter-humanity, 50, 52, 54, 80, 83, 153, 155, 164, 165, 166, 175
  in Chagall, 161f.
  in Shylock, 55, 56
inter-marriage, 53, 55, 58, 86
Inquisition, the, 90
insecurity, psychic, 94
intertestamental situation, the, 141f., 147, 155, 156
'into Thy hands', 164, 165
irony – in chosenness borrowed, 57, 58, 59, 73, 89
irony in Hosea, 36f.
  in Jew/'Gentile' distinction, 53, 56, 58, 59, 73, 89
  in Zion, 15, 96, 97, 134
Islam, 43, 85, 148, 193
'Israel of God', 72, 145
Israel *naturaliter*, 42
  and the non-Jew, 81, 82, 83, 97
  as political, 42, 96f.; *see also* Zionism

Jewish Revolt, the, 54, 72, 73, 75, 178, 183
Jewish National Fund, the, 97
Jewishness of Jesus, the, 72f.
Jewry, 12, 78, 79f., 143f., 147, 151, 153
  debt from 'Gentiles', 143
  debt to 'Gentiles', 56, 57, 69, 70
  ill-will towards, 84f.
  issue for non-Jews in, 49f., 82f., 153
  in John's Gospel, 73, 74, 80, 81
  liable for Mosaic Law, 84; *see also* anti-Semitism
  reciprocal phobias, 55, 82, 84
John's Gospel, perspective of, 73, 74, 80

Judeo-Christian tradition, 142f.
  ill-served by 'two covenant' theory, 143
Judaism, 2, 44, 55, 120, 143, 154, 169
  and egoism?, 58
  as Israelo-centric, 101
  and nationalism, in Dubow, 158
  and nationalism in Graetz, 158
  Orthodox, in Israel, 138f.
  as politicized in Zionism, 50, 121, 160f.
Judensau, 90
justice, 34, 53, 106

Kabbalah, 92, 93
kalfas, 91
kenosis, divine, in creation, 27
kenosis, divine in Incarnation; *see also* Carmen Christi
khilafah in creaturehood, 26, 27, 28
'Kingdom of Heaven', the open, 68
'knowledge' in Hosea, 46f.

land, the, 4, 10, 35, 50, 101, 106, 108, 148, 172, 176, 190
  according to Jesus, 64, 182
  and marriage with, 43; *see also* husbandry, Hosea
  traded for peace?, 106, 107
Last Judgement, 85
Last Supper, the, 68
law, 18, 76, 150, 151
  cultic and moral, 76
  'and the prophets', 151, 152
  and Paul, 75, 76, 77, 147
  and 'two covenant theory', 146f.
law and ethnicity, 61, 76
law, inadequacy of, 18, 146; *see also*, grace
liberation, 42
Logos, concept, the, 74
'Lord of hosts', 10
'Lord, land and lineage' triad, 10

'man of sorrows', 156
marranos, 90, 93
marriage, Hosea's, 39, 45, 176, 183
mass Jewish conversion, illusion of, 85, 86
mathuteusate, 152
memory, 7, 50, 166
  in the New Testament, 69
  and the Shoah, 164
Messiah, 4, 21, 22, 23, 72, 73, 96, 154, 194

Messiah *(continued)*
pseudo, 91, 92, 135
Messiah Jesus, 68, 70, 73, 77, 149, 152, 154, 181, 197
crucified, 26, 62f., 67, 77
Messianic futurism, 23, 150, 174; *see also* Scholem, Gershom
Messianic servanthood, 4, 22, 62, 64f., 70, 150, 181, 197
metaphors, use of, 40, 41, 46, 47
'mind of Christ', the, 67, 71
ministry of Jesus, 22, 46, 63, 64, 65, 69
apostolic care for, 70, 71
mob violence, 85, 86, 90, 93
monarchy, in Israel, 41, 42, 77, 85
mutual hospitality, lack of, 86, 89
myopia, one-culture, 33
myth, 172

nakbah, 106
nationalism, European, 95, 97; *see also* Hess, Pinsker
nationalism, Jewish, 96f., 105, 120f., 152, 154, 158, 159, 189, 195
nationalism, Palestinian, 125, 126; *see also* PLO
nature – in human nurture, 25f.
nature and a theology of, 19, 30, 64, 74; *see also* dominion
Nazism, 1, 58, 79, 95, 165, 171
and genocide, 85
New Testament, the, 34, 47, 48, 50, 59, 61, 63, 68, 72, 74, 80f., 141, 144, 169, 171, 174, 192
letters in, 63, 70, 72, 182
moral education of 'Gentiles' in, 151f.
New Testament Scriptures, 5, 32, 33, 63, 81
Jewishness within, 75f.
and scholarship, 69, 70, 71, 148
two covenant theory betrays, 5, 80, 144f.
nothingness taken away, 30, 175; *see also* creation

obedience, Christ's, 75; *see also* Messianic servanthood
obedience, Jewish, 68, 69, 109, 151, 158
olive, significance of, 26
omnipotence, concepts of, 30; *see also* kenosis
one-sided equation in Palestine/Israel, 138
opportunism, 102; *see also* Ben-Gurion

parables, of Jesus, 63, 64, 65
paradox, 14, 15, 19, 22, 24, 39, 52, 78, 95, 96, 118, 128, 133, 146, 173, 186
paroikoi, 47
parousia, 150
Papacy, 80, 90
parrhesia, 146, 194
Partition vote, the, 100, 125, 137
particularism, Jewish, 11, 118, 175
as divine prerogative, 17
Passion, the, 62, 66, 69, 70, 73, 80
narratives, 65, 66, 67, 69, 71
Passover, the, 67, 151, 182
pastoral nurture in New Testament, 70, 71
pathos in the prophets, 45, 46, 48, 139, 183
as divine, 143
patriarchs, the, 8, 9, 11, 25, 148
peace, as a 'means', 123
peace, the quest for, 105, 106, 108, 121, 127, 132, 135, 170
Peel Commission, the, 123
'people dwelling alone', 50, 58, 80, 100, 143
people, as self-chosen, 101; *see also* Ben-Gurion
peoplehood, new, 4, 34, 47, 48, 62, 69, 157
peoplehood, old, 3, 17, 39, 40, 62, 143, 144, 154, 155, 157, 194
as chosen, 32, 33, 34, 62, 69, 151
perpetua servitus, 89
persecution, and hope of conversion, at odds, 84f., 90
personalisms, in prophets, 45f.; *see also* Jeremiah
perversity, human, 52, 66, 156, 165
Christian, 85
Jewish, 121
Pirke Avot, 59
place and name, 6, 7f., 29, 39, 50, 59, 75, 147, 152, 172, 189
and nature, 33, 45, 50
and the Temple, 18, 19, 20, 21, 75
poetry, Zionist, 114
Poetry and Chagall, 160f.
pogroms, 85; *see also* mob violence
potter's wheel analogy, 8, 22, 140
pragmatism in Zion, 100, 101, 102, 104
prayer shawl, 160f; *see also* tallit
preaching, early Church and, 65, 70, 71, 81
inclusive, 68, 69, 71

priesthood, 75
  Temple, 20
privilege, Jewish, 19, 51, 52, 72, 83
  forfeit or fulfilled?, 72
  and the human, 28, 29, 32, 33, 83
proleptic things, 39, 177
'promised land', the 24f., 64, 121
  and ecology, 26
prophethood, 16, 17, 19, 31, 67, 152
  and tragedy, 66, 67
proselytes, 62, 69
prostitution, 43, 46

questions – the 'how' sort, 28
questions – the 'why' sort, 28; see also
  creation

racialism, 1, 94, 122, 194
  and 'Gentiles' within, 49f.
  mythology in, 82; see also anti-
  Semitism
radical realism, and Zion, 80f.
ransom, 67
realism, 102, 166, 121
  about sin, 146
'real presence', the, 87
reconciliation, 2, 3, 1 49
redemptiveness, 66, 67, 93, 150, 156,
  170, 182
Reform Judaism, 120, 135
refugees – a permanent exile?, 131, 132
relevance, the human factor, 28, 64; see
  also humanism
religio licita, Judaism as, 141, 178
Resurrection, the, 65
ritual purity, 154

Sabbath, the, 26, 39, 53, 55, 58, 85, 135
sacrifice, 75
Sanctus, the triple, 16
Sanhedrin 4.5 text, 55, 59
seclusion of mind, 12; see also ghetto,
  the
secularity, Israeli, 134
seed, as holy, 12
sefirot, 92
segregation, 86; see also ghetto, the
self-exemption from humanity, Judaic,
  50, 53
self-hatred, Jewish, 86, 87, 188
self-treachery, of faiths, 142
Semitism, 96f., 108, 118f., 131, 132,
  136, 148, 165, 166, 193, 197
  burden of, 50f., 85, 184
  in Chagall, 160f.

confusion in, 1, 96f., 102
dark face of, 124, 153
definition, elusive, 1, 59
logic in its Zionism, 79f., 102
and the New Testament, 51, 60, 61,
  62f., 153
requiring recognition, 57, 143, 153,
  154
Shylock and 55, 56
test case of humanity, 53; see also
  Neusner, Jacob
'tribe, territory and time' – a universal
  triad?, 35
in fulfillment or despair in Zion, 79f.,
  102, 118f., 169
separatism, 11, 70, 134; see also
  apartheid
serfdom, Jewish, 89
sexuality, 30, 34, 44
settlements, as obstacle to peace, 124,
  130, 131, 170
Shekinah, 93
Shoah, the, 4, 6, 7, 56, 59, 60, 81, 87,
  94, 95, 104, 144, 146, 157, 162,
  164, 165, 166, 171, 184
  and Christian relation, 60, 61, 146
  and post-theology, 62
  and Primo Levi, 119
'sin of the world,' the, 68, 80f.
  and Zionist logic, 80
'songs of Zion,' the, 14
sovereignty, divine, 33, 151, 156, 165
sovereignty, Israeli, 138, 139
sparks, divine, 92
statehood, Israeli, 5, 116, 120f.
'stranger, loving the', 134, 192
sufferance, Jewish under law, 85, 91
'suffering servant,' the, 66, 81, 179
  hymns of, 67
  and the prophetic word, 161, 162
  a theme in Chagall?, 164, 165
suspicion of God, 31, 32, 45

Tacitus on Jewry, 54
tallit, 6, 172, 195
Talmud, the, 53, 80, 81, 84, 92, 97,
  109, 152, 154
tanazzuh, 44; see also transcendence
tears on canvases, 161, 170, 195
technology in Israel, 104, 105
Temple Mount, 14; see also Dome of
  the Rock
Temple, the, 12, 13, 20, 26, 29, 74, 75,
  138, 173, 174, 183, 193
  cleansing of, 66

Temple, the *(continued)*
    as inviolate, 16
    loss, and the rabbis, 75, 76
    and Jeremiah, 16
    restoration of, 139
    universality of, 14, 20, 21
territorial indecision, the – in Zionism,
    97f., 137, 169, 170
theology, born of a story, 10, 11; *see
    also* Exodus
theophanies, 14
toleration, 119, 166
    strange logic of, 84, 85
Torah, 53, 58, 72, 73, 76, 85, 92, 152,
    154, 157, 158
tragedy of anti-Semitism, the, 1, 51, 52,
    53, 60, 61, 82, 94, 136, 144, 157,
    166, 184, 188, 192, 195, 197
    and Christianity and John's Gospel,
    74, 80, 82, 83
    and the 'Gentile' concept, 49f.
    enormity of guilt in, 51, 52, 82
    hatred and enmities in, 51, 82, 164f.
    history of, 79f.
    medieval factors in, 84, 85, 87, 89
    and Nazism, 58f.; *see also* Shoah, the
    origin, 1, 50f., 80, 81
    and psalmody via Amalek, 51, 52,
    175
    and 'two covenants' formula, 5, 157f.
tragedy 'out of harm's way' in Chagall,
    164
transcendence, 9, 30, 31, 119
    and deicide, 83
    and grief, 48
    and Jewish history, 54, 55
    as relational, 30, 31; *see also kenosis*
transubstantiation, dogma of, 87, 88,
    185
tribalism, 148
two covenant theory, the, 78, 151, 153,
    171, 193
    posits a Jewish unwantedness, 144f.
    untenable in New Testament faith, 4,
    144, 151
    untenable in New Testament practice,
    144f.

unbelief, mutual charge of, 82, 83, 84,
    85
unio sympathetica, 19, 161; *see also*
    Hosea, Heschel
unity of God, 18, 157; *see also* YAHWEH
universality, a will to, 2, 71, 154, 157,
    166

world experience and, 24, 28, 29, 31,
    33, 48, 61, 70, 71, 149, 156
uprising of 1648, the, 83
usury, Jewish, 86, 93

viability, of Israel, 169
victimization, Palestinian, 118f., 136,
    137
vineyard, the Lord's – analogy of, 27,
    171
vulnerability, Jewish, 90, 93; *see also*
    mob violence

wall, the dividing – physical and voli-
    tional, vi., 121
war between Jews?, 121; *see also* settle-
    ments
wilderness, the – concept of, 16, 46
    Jesus' temptations in, 66
willfulness, mutually alleged, 149, 150
wine analogy, the, 34
Wisdom, concept of sacred, 20, 22
woman of Canaan, a, 69, 70
'the Word made flesh', 4, 19, 65, 74, 83,
    173, 175, 184
worship, 46, 75
'world without Jews,' a, 60; *see also* two
    covenant view
wrongness of the world, 80, 81, 164
    dual notion of, 145, 146, 147
    and Zionism, 80

Yiddish, 1, 94, 95, 109, 110, 188
Yisra'el, 40
Yizra'e'l, 40
vocabulary, Hebrew, 109; *see also* Ben
    Yehuda
vocation, supernatural, 120, 156
'your heavenly Father', 64, 65

Zaddik, the, 93
Zion, how privatized?, 29
Zionism, 1, 4, 5, 22, 54, 96f., 138f.,
    153, 154, 157, 168, 176, 186
    an agricultural, 98; *see also* Hibbet
    Zion
    anti-Semitic case-making, its, 178
    despair of humankind, its, 79f., 90,
    94
    disquiet in, 118f.
    early dissent from, 79, 80, 190
    Hebrew language and, 108f.
    and Judaism, 5, 54, 56, 101, 102,
    116, 118f., 179, 189
    and the Messianic, 22, 23, 75f.

Zionism *(continued)*
   personalities in, 97f.
   secular feasibility, 54, 101, 189
   and the Shoah, 95, 116
   superseded for Ben-Gurion in success, 101f.
   tragedy of 2, 96f., 116
   yearning in, 2, 96f.
   verdict on, 115, 116, 118f.

INDEX OF BIBLICAL AND NEW TESTAMENT PASSAGES

Genesis

4.9	31
8.20	20
25.28	50
27.38	25
35.11	51

Exodus

3.14	8f., 18, 36, 37, 41
12.9	36
13.4–5	36
20.24	14
33.9	192
33.13	50

Leviticus

24.2	26

Numbers

4.9	25
13.32	27
21.17	3

Deuteronomy

4.6	16
4.38	51
7.3–4	53
7.7	16
12.5–7	14
25.17	87
33.29	16

Joshua

7.26	40
23.46	51

1 Samuel

8.20	51

2 Samuel

7.23	154

1 Kings

5.11	26
8.29	13.14

2 Kings

10.1	40

1 Chronicles

17.21	51

Nehemiah

13.32	27

Job

24.6	25
29.2–3	26

Psalm

2	52, 130
8.2	28
11.4	13
33.6	74
39.13	47
42.2	12
47.3	52
67 all	52
72 all	22
78.1	50, 51
79.16	12, 17
83.12	86
87.1–2	78
99.2–5	52
103.20	96
115.2	12, 43
132.2	25
135 all	51
139 all	12

148.11–13	21
148 all	52

Proverbs

5.15	3

Isaiah

1.21	47
40–60	22
44	43
62.4	44, 113

Jeremiah

18.2–6	5

Ezekiel

28.13–15	30

Hosea

1.2	38
1.3	39
1.9	36, 37, 40, 41
2.4	40
2.8	45
2.16	42
2.20–22	40
3.4–5	42
4.6	40
4.12	39
5.6	40
5.12	46
6.1–4	40, 45
7.2	40
7.4–7	37, 46
7.9	37
7.10–11	40, 46
8.4	42
8.14	42
9.1	39
9.3–6	40, 42
11.1	41
11.3–4	45
11.9	44, 46
11.12	41
13.5	40, 46
13.8	46
13.11	42

Joel

2.19	25
2.23	29

Amos

2.8	34
4.1	34

5.13	35
6.6	54
8.6	34
9.11	35

Matthew

5.44	71
5.39	71
5.44	71
5.48	63
15.24	69
26.13	69
28.19	152

Luke

3.8	70
4.21	151
9.31	151
15 all	64, 65
15.30	47

John

1.14	76
3.16	145
9.22	81
14.6	156

Acts

11.19–20	68
15.11	69

Romans

7 all	76, 77
14.14	71

1 Corinthians

13 all	71

2 Corinthians

5.16	70, 71

Galatians

3.24	76
6.16	145

Philippians

2.5–9	181

1 Thessalonians

5.14	71

Hebrews

1.3	19
5.8	182
12.28	183

13.12   67, 181

                                Revelation
1 Peter   6.6   25, 192
2.10   47